LESLIE ABRAMSON

with Richard Flaste

Simon & Schuster

THE DEFENSE IS READY

Life in the Trenches of Criminal Law

SIMON & SCHUSTER
Rockefeller Center
1230 Avenue of the Americas
New York, NY 10020

SIMON & SCHUSTER and colophon are registered trademarks
of Simon & Schuster Inc.

Designed by Levavi & Levavi

Manufactured in the United States of America

10 9 8 7 6 5 4 3 2 1

Library of Congress Cataloging-in-Publication Data
Abramson, Leslie.
    The defense is ready : life in the trenches of criminal law /
Leslie Abramson with Richard Flaste.
        p.   cm.
    Includes index.
    1. Abramson, Leslie.   2. Women lawyers—United States—Biography.
3. Defense (Criminal procedure)—United States.   I. Flaste, Richard.   II. Title.
KF373.A275A3   1997
345.73'05044'092—dc21
[B]   96-37512
                                                                          CIP

ISBN 0-684-81403-X

A Dedication

The dearest person in my life—in the years before I had children and met my husband, Tim—was a girl named Thalia Comninos, but always called Jijeey, after the jujubes her mother craved during her pregnancy. Jijeey, short like me but very beautiful (she looked like Sophia Loren), shared my social awkwardness and she shared my drive. In her family, she bore the emotional burden of a brother who died at the age of two (sibling rivalry had led Jijeey to wish him dead, and she never got over the guilt). She became, in effect, the oldest son in a Greek family where all three surviving children were girls. She was the one who had to achieve.

We met in high school, but it was at Queens College that our friendship became intense; we were as close to each other and as protective of each other as any two people can be. She taught me by example, taught me to do the academic grunt work. We were both history majors, so even our minds were alike. She taught me the memory tricks that are crucial for success on tests. Always, she encouraged me. Together, we got our A's.

I did not realize it at the time, of course, but she was preparing me for the brutal workload of law school in the years ahead, inoculating me against the trauma of an academic onslaught unlike anything either of us had ever known before. When I went off to California and law school, Jijeey stayed behind in New York to become a teacher.

Later, I often urged her to try law school. "You can do it, Jijeey." And I knew she could. By the time she finally followed my advice, she had contracted breast cancer (at one point she took her finals in a hospital isolation bubble because her immune system had been so compromised by the cancer therapy). Jijeey did become a lawyer. But a few years later, the cancer spread and she became increasingly ill. Whenever I thought of her and her illness—which was almost every day—I burst into tears. From across the continent, I kept willing her to live. I believed the power of my love would save her. I always felt if I wished for something hard enough, the wish would come true.

But she died, at the age of thirty-four. I flew back to New York and arrived at the funeral early. It was held in a huge Greek Orthodox church (Jijeey's Thracian family traces its lineage to Macedonian kings). No one else had arrived yet. Alone with her, I held her hand, which was very cold, and I kissed her on the lips.

Ever after, even now, I talk to her when things are going well, when I've just won some exhausting victory. I say, "See Jijeey, see what we've done."

Contents

1

Roman's Candle

Between the first and second trials of the Menendez brothers, I represented a twenty-four-year-old man named Roman Luisi, a quiet, darkly handsome, bodybuilding hulk of a nightclub bouncer. He was charged with two counts of first-degree murder and faced life without possibility of parole if convicted. As my cases go, this was an easy one. From my first five-hour marathon interview with this distraught kid to the eve of the trial, I believed it could turn out no worse than a man-slaughter. A client who is capable of testifying is a gift; Roman was the Neiman Marcus Christmas catalogue. He described the events that led up to the shooting in a straightforward way, no embellishments, no hyper-bole. And, best of all, he did it the exact same way, every time he was asked, without prodding or coaching. A simple, honest guy. But much as I liked him and found him easy to work with, his case turned out to be yet another scary and infuriating excursion into homicide land.

Roman had been working at a club named the Blak and Bloo on an unglamorous strip of Sunset Boulevard in Hollywood. The place had gone downhill from its star-studded opening three years earlier. Now its clientele was L.A.'s club-crawling youth, gang bangers, wannabes and druggies.

On an otherwise ordinary night, Roman is hassled and threatened by three loaded deadbeats who try to get in without paying the cover. He throws them out and as they leave, one of them shouts, "I'm going to come back and settle this shit. I'm going to smoke you. I'm going to cap you."

Once outside the Blak and Bloo, these three hang around at the corner staring down Roman and the other bouncers and refusing to leave even after the cops feebly try to chase them off. The cops disappear. The creeps continue to hang out, smoking dope and nursing their wounded pride. Just before closing time two of their friends join them, commiserating in their outrage at having been tossed out "for no reason." Now there are five. When three of the five roll around the corner and come striding down the boulevard toward the Blak and Bloo, the stage is set for disaster. One of them is holding a gun—the other two walk in front, screening him partially from Roman's view. When Roman spots the gun, he pulls his 9mm from his waistband and starts firing, two warning shots at first and then for real.

Three o'clock in the morning on Sunset Boulevard: the Old West and the new West collide. It isn't a fair fight either way. Three against one, but the one, Roman, is an experienced marksman with superior firepower. He gets off all fifteen rounds in his clip, killing two. There's no evidence that the other side gets off a single shot.

Was this premeditated murder? Did he act with malice? Was he simply waiting to vent his rage when they returned? That was the prosecution's theory, and if they could get a jury to buy it, Roman Luisi would be as good as dead, too, locked up in some grim and dangerous place for the rest of his life.

Or was he terrified and fighting for his own life? True, he was a professional bouncer. But even bouncers get scared sometimes. The only problem was there were two bodies and neither of them had a gun near him when, within three minutes, the police arrived on the scene. In fact, the only evidence of a shooting at that crime scene was the fifteen casings and eight bullet fragments from Roman's gun.

To win this case I'd have to make the jurors understand the law of self-defense, which I knew was very different from the popular notions that were floating in their heads. Most laymen think you can only shoot to kill someone if you're cornered and the other guy shoots at you first. In fact, the rules are less stringent than that. Also, whether the jury agreed with the law or not, I had to make them want to apply it to Roman. In my experience, jurors are generally good, decent people who want to do the job right. We—the attorneys and the judge—have to make sure they know what that job is. Killing in self-defense is legally allowed. To some people it may not be moral and it certainly isn't pretty. But it is the one area of the criminal law that most directly acknowledges a basic human reality—the instinct to survive. And, properly explained, most jurors get it. But the jury also had to be willing to apply the rule that where there is evidence of an earlier threat, the person threatened can respond sooner than otherwise and with greater force. And that, in California, there is no duty to retreat or run from a fight before you can defend yourself.

But jurors want to know why a killing happened. So, even though they are instructed by the judge at the end of a case that motive is not an element of an offense and needn't be proven, my experience tells me that people only like murder mysteries that they can solve. I knew I'd have no problem explaining the "why" of it in this case, assuming Roman was believed in his claim that the victim had a gun. If the jury didn't believe him, didn't understand the "who" along with the "why," there was still a chance that I could lose this winnable case.

The "who" was Roman. I really liked this guy. He was miserable in jail. His family lived in Boston and his new wife, Denise, could barely function without him. Big and strong as he was, every meeting we had saw him in tears, worrying about his parents, his wife and his young stepson, Joey. Everyone in his family was feuding with everyone else. And even though Roman was locked up they all turned to him, as they had for years, to solve their problems. His father, in particular, was an odious creature who had spent most of his life hanging onto the frayed edges of organized crime. He raised money back in Boston on the pretext of helping Roman's defense and then pocketed the proceeds. I tried to get Roman to see his father for the crook he was but the kid was pathetically loyal.

Roman also had that quality I most appreciate in clients: patience. He knew from the time I took his case that he would have to wait more than a year for me to get it to trial since Menendez was up next. In fact, during that year and a half I saw Roman rarely and he had no other visitors. (Denise had returned to Boston.) He'd call me at home three or four times a month, seeking reassurance that he would get out someday. But he never complained, and I became increasingly fond of him.

But then I often become attached to my clients. I've learned that good people can do bad things. When representing people accused of the most serious charges, I become immersed in their lives, their families and the circumstances that led them to a tragic moment. By the time I've prepared a case for trial I know their lives better than they do. The closeness that develops between me and my client under these circumstances may last long after the trial is over. Often, the existence of those feelings is the thing that keeps me from losing my edge as weariness and frustration set in. I don't try to hide the affection I feel for my clients from the jury, either. I want them to understand that my advocacy isn't an act or a pose. They should know that I'm not faking this; this is not just a job. I really, really believe in this guy and you should, too.

This personalizing of the client becomes such a central part of the defense because, despite whatever you may have heard about the presumption of innocence, everyone accused of a crime is immediately diminished, transmogrified into something less than human, merely by being charged. Prosecutors rarely refer to criminal clients by name; it's always "the defendant."

Although, to be honest, I don't love all my clients—and I have little in common with most of them—we inevitably share a wrenching experience. Bonds are formed in battle that would not exist otherwise.

To get Roman off, I had to show at trial that he was a decent, worthwhile young man with a loving wife and child and that this burst of violence was an aberration brought on by the fear of death. His associates at the Blak and Bloo testified in court that they found him honest and basically gentle (a "bashful bouncer" is how the prosecutor would sarcastically characterize Roman later).

After three months in trial, I was nervously optimistic about the outcome. All the breaks had cut our way, and I had done what I set out to do with their witnesses and with ours. But I was outraged by the avalanche of lying I'd had to wade through in final argument. This trial, the easy one, the one I told the judge before jury selection I could not lose (forget I said that, God), turned out to be every defense lawyer's nightmare. What happens to your own credibility when you have to call everyone in the prosecution's case a liar? I had expected lying from the dope dealers and alcoholics who had been at the club—but the cabdriver and other ordinary citizens? It was as if a mendacity microbe had gotten into the court's ventilation system. As the trial drew to a close, my head was swimming, and I had to keep reminding myself about the facts as I knew them and try not to fixate on all the lowlife lying and the laxity of the police who failed to pursue the truth. It was a crucial fact, for example, that one of the dead men, Eric Pierce, had been armed at the time he was shot by my client even though a gun was never found. I desperately needed to corroborate Roman's testimony that Pierce had a gun in his hand as he came down the street toward the club. Gunshot-residue sampling of his hands had been done by the coroner's investigator at the scene before the bodies were taken to the morgue. Apart from its well-deserved reputation for shoddiness in handling physical evidence, the LAPD homicide cops live by their unstated credo, "Ask no question the answer to which could screw up your case." So it was no surprise that the investigating officers never directed the coroner to test those samples to see if they contained the residue that could establish that Pierce handled or fired a gun.

Believing in my client (an often dangerous proposition), I demanded that the coroner's office run the tests. When I told Roman that I was going to do this, he said, "With my luck the tests will be negative even though I know he had a gun." Wrong, Roman—the tests were spectacularly positive and not just on Pierce. The other victim, Adrian Thames, the "innocent victim," also had gunshot residue on his hands. There may have been two guns in the creeps' camp. Lucky, lucky us. With the help of the acclaimed forensic pathologist Cyril Wecht, I was also able to show that someone had turned Pierce's body over after he was shot. I had no doubt—and ultimately neither did the jury—that Pierce's confederates had taken the gun away from his body.

On the day of final argument, the prosecutor gets to go first, as always. Then me. Then the prosecutor again. The happy fiction behind this is the presumption of innocence and the obstacle this is supposed to present to conviction. So the law helps out the side with the heavy burden of proof beyond a reasonable doubt. Of course we all know that unless you're O. J. Simpson you're not presumed to be innocent but believed to be guilty the minute people start calling you "the defendant." Anyway, the DA gets the last say while the defense attorney sits there, gnashing his or her teeth, unable to argue back no matter how wrong or devious or distorted the prosecution's comments on the evidence might be.

With one ear alert for statements amounting to prosecutorial misconduct (such as calling my client a monster, a typical DA dirty trick), I usually spend these excruciating hours playing hangman with my client, the rule of the game being that all the words are comments on the prosecutor's argument: "pompous," "fallacious," "moronic" show up often. I have on occasion been admonished by judges for smirking or rolling my eyes as the prosecutor gives his summation. I don't do it intentionally. But I don't try to stop myself either. I'm only doing what the jurors would like to do, except they're afraid of the judge.

I rarely sleep before a final argument; my mind is too alive. So I work through the night or lie awake thinking. But on these nights, I don't need sleep really—adrenaline will serve me well when my argument begins.

Just before the prosecutor's initial presentation, the judge will instruct the jury that the lawyers' statements are not to be considered as evidence. But we all know how important they really are. And final arguments happen to be what I do best. In some cases (I'm thinking of Menendez particularly) I've worked out that argument in my head years before I need it, silently rehearsing bits of it so that the presentation is almost automatic.

In Luisi I don't feel that degree of control. Because just about every witness had lied on the stand, I find myself wondering if my mind can possibly keep things straight, if I can possibly remain coherent in the face of such a dizzying barrage of falsehoods. God, I hate these cases, I tell myself, the ones I'm supposed to win. It's almost okay to lose a loser but to lose a winner is to fall into the abyss.

On the morning of the final argument, I put on an outfit I wear often just because I don't want to worry about what to wear if I can help it: a short black wool crepe dress and heels, but no jewelry (I don't want the jury to think that Roman is rich) and no lipstick (nothing glamorous about this business).

I drive from my office on Wilshire Boulevard, not far from Hollywood, hardly seeing the road, rehearsing my argument, testing its logic in my mind. I don't have to rehearse the drama, the modulation, the physical movements to punctuate words—that all comes automatically. In about twenty minutes, I arrive at the garage across from the Criminal Courts Building in downtown L.A., pull three months' worth of transcripts out of the trunk on my luggage cart and walk through the barely lighted, grim garage, past the boxes of garbage and up into the early sunlight where the media zoo has already gathered, although not for my case.

On this day, there's some preliminary hearing about blood spots in the Simpson trial going on in one of the courtrooms, and in another a grand jury is deciding what to do about O. J.'s buddy Al Cowlings. It's a relief to have the spotlight elsewhere, no suffocating crush of reporters and cameras now, and I can make it to my courtroom without much trouble, schmoozing a bit with lawyers, judges, the press.

"How ya doin', Leslie?" calls out one of the journalists.

"Fine, and you?"

I pass by a couple of lawyers having at each other. "Granted my guy's a scumbucket but so is yours," one of them is saying. And then I'm past, my heels clacking on the hard floor until I reach the Luisi courtroom, big and light and mostly empty. It's a reasonably important case, Luisi— every double homicide is—but, refreshingly, it is conducted in a normal, quiet atmosphere: Just the families of the men who were killed are here, sitting in a cluster in the center section of benches, and the family of Roman Luisi off to one side, their tension practically visible. I see Roman's mother and hug her hello, but that's for the sake of appearances. I have no affection for her; she hasn't visited Roman once in the twenty-one months he's been in jail and has only now attended the trial. Even so, why not be friendly, she's not the enemy of the moment. We're all trying to look confident. (Roman's father is there, too, wary around me, knowing what I think of him for stealing from his son and being a gangsta wannabe his whole life.)

Alan Carter, a generally amiable and honest prosecutor whose droopy eyes belie his alertness, starts off in spectacular fashion—for me. He concedes that his main witnesses (the other three of the original five) turned out to be liars and that the jury might as well disregard them. "Fortunately," he says with as much conviction as he can muster, "we have in this case independent witnesses and physical evidence and our logical abilities."

He argues that even if the jury allows for the fact that the loudest of the drunks, Eric Pierce, had been acting like a "real jerk" at the Blak and Bloo and even if the jury can understand why Roman killed Pierce, that doesn't explain why he killed the second man, Adrian Thames, who kept one hand in his coat pocket as the three men marched toward Luisi, and never actually showed a gun. "Do you know why Mr. Luisi thought they were coming toward him to do him in?" Mr. Carter asks. "Because Adrian Thames had his hand in his pocket on a very cold night."

The fact that Roman Luisi shot fifteen times, firing away even after he had begun his retreat back to the club, the prosecutor hopes will somehow make his point about cold calculation. But what about the warning shots Roman fired first? How is he going to deal with those? He doesn't.

I begin my argument at a lectern off to the side, and pace away from it often, using my hands for punctuation. At one point, in an effort to show that Roman could have fired all of those shots so rapidly that there would have been little time for calm deliberation, I pretend to be shooting. There I am, not quite five feet tall, but standing erect. My two hands are clasped together and I'm going bang, bang, bang . . . fifteen times to demonstrate how quickly it all happened in real time.

No one laughs at my little bit of acting, so it must have worked. Like most of the "dramatic" things I do during argument, the idea just came to me as I was talking. People think lawyers take acting lessons and rehearse dramatic bits. If some do they've never admitted it to me and I've never had either the time or the inclination to learn tricks.

I also never read an argument as I deliver it. I make a rough outline and some notes, then remember what I have to say and embellish along the way. In this argument, for instance, there comes a time when I'm carrying on about the self-righteousness of some of the liars among the witnesses and, suddenly, I have no idea where I mean to go. I stop, shake my head, laugh and confess to the jury, "When I get self-righteous myself, I forget the point." But I go on.

To hold the jurors' attention, I present my argument with spontaneity and passion and focus. I like to pick out the jurors who are really paying attention and look directly at them. I need to persuade these people and no one else on earth that Roman Luisi killed in self-defense. The judge, the prosecutor, the audience all disappear.

Looking directly at the attentive blonde in front, I say: "You don't have to wait for Adrian Thames to take his hand out of his pocket when he is in the company of someone who has been threatening to kill you, who has hung around for forty, forty-five minutes with no visible purpose except to continue threatening you. You are justified in acting quickly and you are justified in acting harshly.

"The human species will try to survive. And that instinct makes you fight. That is the same instinct that leads to flight, but it is not calm, calculated, rational thought. Even if it had been, what else could Roman Luisi have thought was up when these guys were coming toward him and one of them had a gun and another had his hand in his pocket?

"Adrian Thames was no innocent bystander. Mr. Carter wants you to separate these three people out as if there are three completely separate incidents here. But just back up and look at it. This is three against one. Don't tell me that one person doesn't have a right to shoot to clear that street. This is three against one."

My confidence is pretty high now. The adrenaline is surging. But before it's over I need to make the same point the prosecutor made about the parade of disreputable witnesses we endured:

"Really the only major problem that this judicial system has in delivering the product we expect from it, which is justice, is not things like racism and sexism, although they exist to some extent. The biggest problem is this." And here I do what I always try to do—use visuals for effect any way I can. In the first Menendez trial (the one that ended in a hung jury), I intentionally left the prosecutor's gruesome photos of the murder scene on display as I spoke so that the jury would become inured to them. And now I walk over to the big artist's pad set up on a stand directly in front of the jury, and, with all the emotional heat I can bring to the task, I begin to spell out one word. In huge wobbly letters—I'm no artist—I slowly write, L . . . Y . . . I . . . N . . . G.

I scan their faces. They are with me; maybe all of them, thank God. This point about lying is so important because my guy, Roman, was in the end one of the few witnesses in this whole deadly mess who seemed credible—the prosecutor didn't lay a glove on him and nobody ever testified that *he* ever lied.

And then I wrap myself in the flag. It's corny and overdone, I know, but I do believe in what I'm saying and I believe that heartfelt conviction is every bit as effective as an array of other powerful emotions. I say to the jury, my voice rising, that my client "has faith in this system of justice, and that translates into faith in you. And I ask you to endorse the faith that he has—and that I have—in the law and in the duty and in the conscience and in the hearts of the jury system."

It was fine, I know it was. But as often happens, when you've got prosecutors on the ropes, they come roaring back. And Carter does his best, at one point wheeling around toward Roman Luisi—who is sitting there next to me with his usual tight little smile on his lips—wheeling around toward him and bellowing, "And you, don't be so smug."

For Carter, that is uncharacteristically nasty. It is also completely improper and surprises the hell out of me. Moreover, it could have an impact on the jury. If they think Roman is smug (he was in fact a nervous wreck), that could mean to them that Roman knows he did something wrong but thinks he's going to get away with it. I can't let this incident pass. At the least I have to object to make a record for appellate review. "Excuse me, Your Honor, but I would cite Mr. Carter for misconduct." It is completely improper for him to talk to my client at all during argument, let alone to characterize his state of mind during trial. The judge does not, however, act on my citation. He just tells Carter to proceed.

But I can't let it drop. Just as the case is about to go to the jury, I approach the bench—with Carter alongside me—and plead with the judge to do something. Even Carter is contrite. "I'm sorry, Judge, but I'm human, and I reacted," he says.

The judge, finally, is won over. In his instructions to the jury, he says, in his low, studiously modulated voice, "The evidence in this case comes from the witness stand. As for the comment by Mr. Carter as to Mr. Luisi being smug, there is no evidence of that, and you are to disregard that comment and to be reminded that statements by the attorneys during this trial are not evidence."

The jury is sent off to deliberate. I reassure the family as I leave the courtroom. Then I head for home and yank a steak from the freezer, despite the damned liquid diet I've been trying. And that night I sleep poorly. I want to win badly, of course, but mostly I do not want to see Roman Luisi's life ruined. The system is just so ready to throw lives away, a few years here, a few years there, and then the guy is old.

I keep thinking about Thames, the one who never actually showed a gun. One of my supposed friends had planted it in my head that maybe the jury would side with the prosecutor on Thames, finding Luisi guilty on that count alone, and now I can't get Thames out of my mind. Maybe I should have called an expert to testify to the significance of Roman having fired all fifteen rounds. Emptying your gun is a panic reaction. Cold, calculated killers are efficient; they never shoot more than they have to. I had a psychiatrist working on the case. I could have called him.

Moreover, I've played guts ball with the jury instructions and cited cases to the court that blocked the judge from instructing on manslaughter, a lesser charge. Early in the trial the judge ruled that the prosecution had shown no evidence of first-degree murder, and now I've put the jury in the position of voting for either second-degree murder or acquittal. I'm kicking myself all night and none of my little tricks for falling asleep are working.

I live through another day of guilt and recrimination and the following morning at 11:30, the court clerk calls.

"They have verdicts," he says.

"I'll be there in half an hour." I grab my bag, rush down to the basement of my office building on Wilshire, jump in the Jag and wind my way over to the Santa Monica Freeway.

As I drive downtown, I'm repeating a mantra to save my sanity: it can't be a guilty, it's too soon. All twelve of those jurors couldn't have voted to convict him. The tall guy in the back row hated the prosecution witnesses, no way would he have voted guilty. This time, at least, the mantra works.

Not guilty on all counts. Roman, grinning broadly, turns to me and says, "Thanks, Mom." The families of the "victims," almost immediately, start making thinly veiled death threats to Roman. The judge has the bailiff escort us (the defense supporters) downstairs on the freight elevator. Roman has to go back to the county jail to be mustered out.

I return to my office and the congratulatory phone calls start coming in. Flowers arrive. And the *Los Angeles Times* calls—not for some quote about the victory or some clarification about the trial. The *Times* wants to know about charges of racism. Racism! The angry Thames family claims that bigotry led to the exculpation of my client.

So here it is: the reflexive inflammatory cry so familiar in Los Angeles, and the *Times* reporter just goes for it because it is the easy, formulaic angle. I am so furious I can barely talk to him. I tell him that there were three blacks on the jury and another was an alternate. I tell him the *Times* didn't even cover the trial and now this—this!—is the story they're going to write. I am seething. I call the city editor, Leo Wolinsky.

"Leo," I say, "there was not a scintilla of racism in this trial. . . . Ask the judge. . . . Ask the prosecutor." He says he'll check into it, but I am definitely not optimistic.

The next day the *Times* does run a brief item: "Nightclub Bouncer Cleared in Shooting Deaths of 2." It quotes Carter first. Luisi, he says, was a "Rambo." It says about me that I felt my client was "reacting to fears." It reports that the family feels it was "let down by the system." And that's it. Balance, for a change. Thanks, Leo.

Two days after the verdict Cynthia Erdelyi, my private investigator on Luisi and many other cases, calls with a request. She wants to celebrate and get a chance to say good-bye to the witnesses on the defense side, a lot of whom are Roman's buddies.

"Leslie, let's have a victory party for Roman," she says happily. "We've won a lot of cases together over the last eighteen years and we've never had a celebration. They're really a great bunch of guys."

So I cook Italian for the Boston bouncers, thirteen guys, each of whom looks like a small apartment building. Roman and Denise are the last to arrive. He's burned his skin brick-red in his haste to rid himself of jailhouse pallor and he's also done something really weird and disturbing. On his left arm he sports a huge new tattoo, a death's head covering the entire forearm. It scares me. What does it mean? I beat death? Or I am death, or death walks with me? Cindy tells me I'm overreacting. She says Roman's just a kid and he's been locked up for two years and maybe it's made him a little crazy. But I have a real bad feeling.

A week later, Roman and his family leave L.A. and move back to Boston. I implore Roman to keep some distance from his father—the old man is knee-deep in petty thuggery and I'm afraid he'll drag Roman down. Sure enough, within weeks of his return to Boston Roman is in business with his dad. At first it's a bar, then an illegal gambling club. My main informant is Denise, whose hatred for her father-in-law, Bob Luisi, goes back to his efforts to break up her relationship with Roman. She's afraid, she tells me, that Bob will get Roman mixed up in something really dangerous.

As the months go by the only other news I hear from Boston is the happy report of Denise's pregnancy.

I tell Roman and Denise I can't wait to see a picture of the baby. I also warn Roman to watch his back. "Don't worry," he tells me. "I got my father under control. Everything is fine."

Soon I go to work again in the Van Nuys Superior Court—the second Menendez trial—and thoughts of Roman and Denise and the baby are shoved aside as I resume the fight for the life and future of Erik Menendez.

During a morning session one day in early November 1995, I go to the pay phone in the hallway outside the courtroom to call my office for messages. Terry, my secretary, tells me that she has Roman's mother-in-law on the other line, hysterical. Terry cross-connects me to her and the woman is sobbing.

"They've killed him, they've killed Roman!"

"Where? Who? What happened?"

"In Boston, in a restaurant, they shot them like dogs. They killed four of them, Roman, Bob, Bob's brother and a cousin. It was a hit, dope dealers, I don't know why. Denise is on television, screaming, my poor Denise."

The story is on the TV news and, the next day, in the Boston papers. The news reports say that Roman and his father, uncle and two cousins were sitting in a booth in a crowded and noisy restaurant in the tough Charlestown section of the city. An unknown number of gunmen opened fire on them. One of them survived, a cousin who's hospitalized. Nobody in their party was armed. The papers describe it as a suspected mob hit. The implication: the mob hitting the mob.

I don't want to know what Roman was into—how exactly Bob Luisi took his son's life.

The baby's a girl, Isabella. I've seen her. She looks just like Roman; she's gorgeous.

Denise returned to Los Angeles to live with her mother in April 1996. Her older child, Joey, is in shock. He lost his daddy Roman twice, once to jail for two years and then, just thirteen months later, forever. Denise is disconsolate. I'm just sad and disgusted. This is what I saved him for?

You fear sometimes that if you get a client off on a violent crime that he'll go out and hurt people again (although, luckily for my conscience, that's never happened with any of my clients). You just don't figure he'll get murdered. Better I should have lost.

Twenty-seven years into this work and I'm wondering what it amounts to. Sometimes, it all feels like so much sand through my fingers.

2

Childhood

It's the middle of a particularly long and stressful trial and I find myself thinking about my father, of all people. I've just talked to my brother and he's reminded me for the umpteenth time that it's been thirty-four years now since I've seen or spoken to Dad, an absurdly long time to carry a grudge. "He's an old man, Sis, and he keeps asking me for your phone number. Can't I give it to him?"

"What am I, a recluse?" I ask. "My face is all over television, I'm listed. How come he needs you to get my number?" "He doesn't know your last name," Ira says. "He doesn't know you're you."

I search inside myself, looking for that familiar barrier I'd erected to keep my father away, and for no reason I can identify, it's not there. Well, I tell myself, I guess you're just not pissed off anymore. How odd. "Okay, give him my number." Ten minutes later Dad calls.

When I was fourteen, Sol Newberger—my handsome, funny, loving father—decided to skip town without so much as a word to his kids.

He sneaks out, really, in a slippery expression of his anger and his misery over the way my mother had treated him. It galls him that she rejected him for a friend of the family, good ol' "Uncle Dave," and it irritates him even more that since the divorce, even though Dave has plenty of money, she still demands child support from Sol the dresscutter, Sol the cuckold, Sol the schnook. Not just demanding, either, mind you, but having him jailed when he refuses to come across—and then this warrior mother threatens to jail him again if he drags his feet.

So Sol takes flight. Drops us a postcard from Florida. Says he's gone for good. But he's faking it. He sneaks back to New York after a year to continue his new life with the woman he married a few years before, a widow "with a few dollars to her name" and two troublesome children from her first marriage. We—my older brother, Ira, and I—cease to exist for him.

I'm not sure Ira or I would ever have known the truth except for the fact that Ira, in one of those startling coincidences that always seem to happen among the millions of people rushing around Manhattan every day, bumps into Sol five years after his disappearance while they're both crossing Seventh Avenue. It's the fall of 1963. Ira has just gotten married and I'm engaged.

"Dad?" And sure enough it is, Sol Newberger, star of his own little vanishing act. I hear about this accidental reunion the next day. Ira is all excited about seeing Dad. He's going to introduce him to his wife, they're going to stay in touch. I'm outraged. A few days later my brother phones me. He starts to talk about our father and I figure out that this is actually a three-way call with Dad secretly on the line. I hang up the phone. It's going to take more than the coincidence of two garment center mavens crossing paths to win this daughter back.

In fact, I was never too thrilled with the way my mother handled her marriage either. I could never figure out why she divorced my father in the first place for a loan shark and construction boss who wasn't as educated, wasn't as funny or cultured and, in my opinion, wasn't as good looking.

"Mom, why did you do it?" I ask her years later.

"It was like jumping off a cliff, and I just jumped," she says. And I say to myself, fine, but did you have to take your kids with you?

But kids, of course, usually have a hard time figuring out a rupture in the family. Most kids believe families are forever, even if the life inside those insular groups is a little crazy.

And we weren't very well buffered against the breakup. Today, more parents are taught to respect their kids, to try to see things from their perspective. (My mother was not big on respect for children, in any case —demands and orders, yes, protectiveness, yes, but not respect.)

At the breakup, nobody ever sits Ira and me down, the way contemporary parents do, and tells us what's going on to the tune of all those benign pronouncements: "Your daddy and I can't stay married anymore; and, of course, it isn't your fault," and so on. Instead, the two of them separate abruptly and my mother picks up her kids and plops us all down in Queens, a long way from home in the Bronx. There, life begins with Dave. And Sol shows up when he can.

I never do warm to Dave, a loud, overweight, flamboyant man who impresses the hell out of Ira with all his posturing but mostly just intimidates me. I can't stand that voice, low in timbre and dictatorial in tone. (To this day, I am amazed at the terrifying power some adults can wield over children simply with a potent voice.)

On top of all the rest, Dave is also a heavy drinker (Jack Daniel's, a fifth at a time), which in part explains the chauffeur-driven Cadillac, by far the most opulent aspect of our life. In the 1950s, in Elmhurst, Queens, ours is a family that needs a designated driver on call.

Meanwhile, Sol and I are still having good times. He picks me up on Sundays and we go to ballgames—to the Dodgers, whom I adore, and the Yankees, whom I hate, and the Giants (Dad's team) and it is always a thrill no matter who's playing. The hot dogs, the crystalline sunshine in the great stadiums, the commotion.

There are quietly affectionate times, too. Sol is an indulgent father, and when we're alone in his black Chevy he hoists me into his lap and allows me to steer. Or as we are traveling somewhere together he tells me how much he loves me and how I am his little princess and I am the most important thing in the world to him. He is wonderful that way, and I would have been pleased enough if this relationship, strained though it may have been, continued for a long time.

But, of course, two weeks shy of my fourteenth birthday he skips out, without a word.

Although the loss of my father was painful, the two dominant women in my life—my strong-willed mother and my adoring grandmother—influenced me more profoundly than he ever did. Ours was a stolidly middle-class (except for the Cadillac) New York life, dominated by politics and intense relationships that too often turned harsh and rejecting.

You'd probably recognize our Queens neighborhood, I think, even if you've never been there. Some of the blocks have that Archie Bunker look to them: tightly packed single-family houses, usually two stories, some with a bay window, a little fenced yard at the front, sometimes a green plastic awning. But we lived in the brick apartment buildings that are also common in that part of Queens, each of them six or seven stories high; sometimes they boast a courtyard. The apartments themselves tend to be functional more than anything else, but some of the buildings could be impressive nonetheless, with airy, terrazzo-floored, columned entry halls.

For many of those years we lived on Elmhurst Avenue, two fire escapes up. It was just across from the Long Island Railroad tracks—although the train was an insignificant feature in our lives, just part of the general buzz. Elmhurst was a convenient neighborhood, a good place to live. You could buy wonderful food from German grocers and Polish butchers, and we always ate well. From our corner, you could see a greenish steeple rising atop an imposing castle of a structure. That was Newtown High, my school in the later years.

For anyone whose point of reference is Los Angeles or Houston or somewhere in the suburbs, it must be hard to imagine a life where the whole world is just around the corner or maybe a little beyond.

Our apartment was tight. I don't think the floor space totaled nine hundred square feet, and for much of the day, after school, we were at least four people: my mother; Ira; my baby sister, Robin; and me.

And when Dave gets home for dinner and my grandmother is around, as she so often is, that makes six. We actually eat dinner in two shifts, although I think the main reason isn't efficiency so much as a ridiculous deference to Dave. My mother always feeds the kids early, with paper napkins, and then when Dave finally strolls in the two adults sit down together for a more civilized repast, with—the tipoff on status—cloth napkins.

The apartment this nobleman manages to provide us has just two bedrooms, one bath. I share a bedroom with Robin. Ira sleeps on a bed in the surprisingly commodious entry foyer. And it's a very noisy household; commotion is constant. Forget the political arguments that erupt from time to time. My mother is just naturally a very loud person and the rest of us aren't exactly soft-spoken. (Even today I can't do soft-spoken very well.)

In this apartment, uproar is chronic. Like when Ira foolishly decides to transfer some of his guppies into one of Mother's favorite crystal bowls —one miscalculation he talks about to this day—because he wants them to give birth in peace and he wants to watch the babies being born. Now you just don't do things like that around our house, where this authoritarian woman stakes out her territory as if each little thing is a lode of gold in the Yukon. Of course Mother notices there are guppies in that bowl. Oh, my God, pet fish! She grabs the closest weapon, the hose from her douche bag, and goes tearing after Ira to whack him with it. Ira is running wherever he can in the little apartment, running and ducking, and covering every part of his body that he can with his hands. My grandmother is on the sidelines yelling, "Don't kill him, don't kill him!" Chaos.

When my mother isn't on a rampage, she's yelling for the sake of yelling or playing classical music full blast or watching television and, spontaneously, she launches into cheerful jingles:

> Oh, Katarina, unless you're leaner
> You'll have to build a big arena.
> There's so much of you,
> Two could love you.
> Go to gym, learn to swim,
> Eat farina, oh, Katarina.

She also sings "Good Night, Irene," a little too often, amused by it each time—because she has a friend named Irene. She is proud of her clear but minor talent, and takes part in amateur theatricals with the Hadassah.

Despite everything, during all these years, I do admire her immensely. For me, she is the most beautiful person on earth, a magical woman. She goes out for the night in a purple suit, a muted classy color, with wide lapels accented with a beautiful pin, amethyst on gold; it looks like a flower. She has matching earrings.

I believe she is the best smelling, the best looking, the most important and interesting person in the whole world. (Someone else might look at that huge nose or that emphatically full figure and come to a different conclusion, but so what?) I am in awe.

I can see now how children come to love their mothers automatically. It must take an almost unimaginable degree of pain to ever make a child not love a mother.

My grandmother lived in her own apartment a block down the street for many of those Queens years. I slept over every Friday night. I'd come bursting into her apartment and she'd cry out, "Mamala, are you hungry?" Always. But she could remedy that, maybe with my favorite chicken dish—stewed with tomatoes and onions—or some homemade pastry.

Her kitchen had a comfortable, well-used feeling to it, with enameled pots on the stove. Grandma had a comfortable look to her, too, always in a housedress. And always ready to smile at me, her cheeks round and radiant, as if my very presence was the gift that made her day. As tough and critical as she might be of my mother, she was just that loving and accepting of me, praising and cooing. When I look back on it, it always seems to me that in the lifelong competition between those two women, Grandmother was somehow getting even with Mother by loving me more.

My grandmother was a terrific baker—cookies, rugelach, challah. She used to bake a fabulous zwieback, a kind of sweet version of Melba toast that was spectacular dunked in coffee (biscotti is the Italian version). We'd mold the dough into a loaf about half the height of ordinary bread and bake it. Then we'd slice it, brush the slices with milk and sprinkle them with cinnamon and bake the zwieback again. (Another name for zwieback is "twice-baked bread.") It's supposed to be dry and brittle so that it shatters in your mouth, but I liked the zwieback slices best when they were still soft. There was only a single chance for that. I had to grab one before it went in for the second baking.

The baking experiences almost all come back to me fondly, but a couple of the episodes left a bitter taste, the damned strudel incident particularly. I'm referring to the pineapple strudel, meant to be the crowning touch of Ira's bar mitzvah. My grandmother had made strudel before, but not often.

It was a big deal, time-consuming and delicate. At the reception in our apartment, somehow, although mountains of strudel were consumed by the adults, none ever made it back into the sweltering room where the kids were exiled. This was horribly unfair: I had helped Grandma make that strudel; it took us two days.

Grandmother knew all about justice. She revered fairness. And she blamed my mother for the negligence.

"Why didn't you save any strudel for the kids?"

I don't know that there was a good answer, a fair answer. How could there be?

The intensity of the politics in our family came mostly via the experiences and propensities of my grandmother, a Communist, a former labor organizer, the kind of woman who had made a name for herself with fiery street-corner crusades. She had organized for the ILGWU and lost friends in the burning of the Triangle shirtwaist factory. Her friends now were other Russian immigrants, union members and union agitators of one kind or another.

When it came to the type, she was the whole enchilada.

After Stalin died, she kept a little shrine to him, photographs of Stalin in his glass coffin, along with pictures of the Soviet Union and mementos written in Russian. Idolizing Stalin was not necessarily popular even among American Communists in these days. At this point in the 1950s there must have been many fully dedicated leftists who were nevertheless completely ready to concede that Stalin had been a repugnant despot. But not Grandmother. She held onto the party line as if it were the lifeline that kept her afloat.

The themes of our family talks were the struggles of the laboring class, the importance of unions, the evils of Wall Street. I heard the horror stories about how workers had been exploited and killed, a mantra of misery. Much of this, by the way, was reinforced in public school where I was taught about the child labor laws, about the investigations in England in the eighteenth century, about the children in the mills, the children in the mines, the crippled little seven-year-olds. It was both a shocking and an inspiring history of the struggle of the common man for a humane work environment and for dignity and respect. So I was indoctrinated very early at home and in school.

When I look back on it, I realize how much of what I really learned was essentially about fairness—and that is not necessarily a political or an ideological point of view at all. It means, among other things, that when you see some powerful system—any system, political, institutional, religious, educational—distorting basic concepts of right, then somebody ought to stand up against it, if that's possible. Grandmother was great at that and there was a time, very early on, when she won my heart forever doing it.

The family was vacationing at a bungalow colony called Newman's Villa in the Catskills.

Newman's Villa was the kind of place, popular then, that's like a hotel but you do your own cooking in a communal kitchen. I'm no more than three years old at the time of this incident, and I come walking into the kitchen with a face still wet from a dip in the lake. By accident—by accident, I swear!—I pick up a kitchen towel belonging to one of the other families sharing the kitchen. Suddenly this woman, huge, enraged, fists clenched and face beet-red, is screaming that I blew my nose in her dish towel. My grandmother is there. She understands how easily I feel shame. I am not only embarrassed but feeling fantastically wronged (I did not blow my nose—I was drying my face). Grandmother lights into that woman with the fury that comes easily in my family.

I don't remember what she said, of course, but this I know: the defense was vigorous and noble. Good people were fair people and bad people weren't.

At home the explicit worldview instruction takes place around the kitchen table or sometimes while Grandmother and I are baking together. It's about equality and the virtue of the masses. Also, Grandmother likes to take me and my brother to the movies on Saturdays and sometimes we see Soviet films, on Second Avenue on the Lower East Side. There's this one movie—my memory is so vague here but I remember the fear I felt quite well—about a troika in the woods with the wolf eating everybody.

So, yes, we got the whole spiel. Existence under the czars was torture, and the Revolution saved the lives of the Russian people, the Jews especially. It became "a country for the proletariat, for the working class, everybody's equal, no one exploits anybody." But the paradoxical thing is that her pro-Soviet indoctrination is laced with intense patriotism for America. As a little girl, I sit in her lap and she tells me why people came here to the Land of Franklin Roosevelt, the Land of Equality where everybody can be somebody, no matter rich or poor. The whole immigrant song is being sung while I sit there in her lap, sung fiercely and with great conviction.

But as the years go by, in school I'm learning the truth about Stalin and the purges. And totalitarianism. So now I'm challenging her, my ardent grandmother, creator of that mortifying shrine to Evil Joe.

I come home from school ranting. "Grandma, how can you admire, worship Joseph Stalin? He's a butcher. He killed millions of people, including Jews. He's despotic, vicious and cruel. He stabbed us in the back during the war, stole half of Europe, dropped the Iron Curtain." I mean the whole nine yards. And she gets very worked up in response. "But we don't know that any of that is true," she says. "The doctrines . . ."

After she gets excited, she calms down. She isn't angry with me. "There's nothing wrong with Communism," she says. "Maybe it's not perfect yet, maybe they haven't worked out all the problems. Collective farming may have created a hardship. It's only temporary."

And I'm saying, "It's the other side of fascism. It's just like the fascists." I am frustrated.

And I don't want her to associate with her Communist Party buddies, either, because they are doctrinaire and ignorant. All of this is not to say that the history I'm studying in school about Stalin changes my opinions about basic ideals, that the wealth should be spread around, that no one should suffer unnecessarily, that hardworking people should be able to achieve a decent life. To many idealistic teenagers that stuff sounds pretty fine even now: the whole manifesto of equality. It's just Communist Russia I'm having trouble with.

As for Grandmother's paradox—the idolization of Russia and the deep love of America—eventually, I come to understand that it isn't Stalin, it's the homeland that she loves. It is her past, full of tumult and hardship, and she insists on feeling nostalgic about it.

As for my own left-leaning views during those days in Queens, they are not at all in conflict with the society and culture around me outside the family. I'm growing up in the New York City school system of the fifties where everybody is what today people call liberal. I don't feel like an outsider. My political views are the commonly shared political views in much of Queens. We all deplore Stalinism. But the American labor movement is glorified. Franklin Roosevelt is a god. The New Deal is swell.

We don't personally know any Republicans.

The only thing that is happening outside that's really in conflict with what I learn at home about equality in America is I'm running into anti-Semitism, mostly in subtle, mostly unspoken ways where you know somebody doesn't like you because of your religion. My brother has less subtle experiences during this period; he is actually called a kike from time to time, particularly when he crosses paths with some of the local Irish. A tough school, St. Bart's, is spitting distance from the apartment, and Ira does what he can to avoid it when the school day is ending. St. Bart's is a hotbed of bad-news Queens Irish.

It's so bizarre to think of it now (especially for me with an Irish-American husband and an acquired deep love for the land of Ireland and a beautiful little son whom we named Aidan), but then the neighborhood enemy was the Irish and our allies were the blacks. In high school, we all knew that if the Irish ever picked on any blacks or any Jews, one would come to the aid of the other.

The blacks were the good guys even though they were goyim, too. They were a poor, oppressed people, much maligned, as we saw it. Paul Robeson was a hero. The stain of slavery was an ineradicable abomination. Later on when I learned there were Jews who were antiblack, and that many blacks detested Jews, the realization was a bitter one for me because I always thought there was such a clear commonality of interest.

But my family was not pure in its benevolent view of others; it preached a brand of tolerance and equality that was very specific. My mother, who was short, even called tall people names just for being tall, "giant radishes," she'd say, spitting the words out as if big radishes were indistinguishable from offal. Sometimes she'd call them "cows." And we had an enemies list. Give me a name that was prominent in the fifties and I'll know which side he or she was on. Roy Cohn? Monster, of course. I didn't even know who the hell he was but he was a monster. Clare Boothe Luce? Monster. Henry Luce was real bad, too. These people were anti-Semitic or they were Republicans, or right wing, or they were Wall Street rich. And we sure didn't love Ike. Monster. But only because of Nixon, I think, in my family's schema: Nixon, the red-baiter.

In 1950 and 1951, the arrest and trial of the Rosenbergs for treason was a personal tragedy in our family. These people, Ethel and Julius Rosenberg, were part of us, Jews in America, and they were being persecuted. Everyone we knew was in mourning when they were executed two years later. It was a frame-up, my grandmother said. They didn't have anything on them really. The only real evidence of espionage came from a confessed spy, for God's sake. Relatives and friends came by the apartment when the Rosenbergs died, almost as if they wanted to sit shiva. There was crying.

The Rosenbergs were killed against a backdrop of the Holocaust, so recent and still so vivid that it seemed somehow to be an extension of it.

My own awareness of the eradication of Europe's Jews was one of the first things I ever comprehended, ever actually thought about. I was three years old, and it was just after the war:

I hear grown-ups talking, wailing. No one sits me down and tells me what happened in Europe. But I can hear. The truth is out in 1946 and 1947. The complete, unspeakable horror of it. The picturebooks are out by 1948 and I see them. By then, I'm five. I know it all, I hear it all. I understand that the dead and the tortured are our relatives, some of them my grandmother's brothers and sisters. The stories unfold over a considerable period of time in our house, and always there is screaming and crying and carrying on. As horrific as it is, my family believes the devastation is worse for our family than it actually turns out to be. They think that everybody over there is gone. But in the 1950s, thanks to the investigations of a group of our American relatives, we do find some of our kin still alive in Russia.

But many others did die in the gas chambers, or of illness or starvation in concentration camps, or they were shot in places like Babi Yar or, with more dignity, as soldiers of the Red Army, the normal casualties of the war.

The Holocaust permeates our familial ether. I, as a child, cannot escape it. I am a little girl who, as it happens, slightly resembles Anne Frank (except with curly hair) and thinks about the torment and death of relatives all the time. Perhaps that's why, when I'm a few years older, I become a fan of horror comics. For a while, the fad is to tell Nazi stories in these comics. They always seize on the most graphic topics like the rendering of Jews into lampshades, gloves and soap, and as I read these things, nothing surprises me. I know all about it. In their perversely reassuring way, these horror comics are comforting to my young mind; they have a morality about them. They exude justice. Characteristically, the victims come back and haunt the tormentors to death.

Sometimes, I think maybe I became a lawyer so I wouldn't feel powerless when the SS knocked on the door. (But, of course, the lawyers got gassed like everybody else.)

Or maybe I grew up to be a lawyer so that I could be in charge and strong against any enemy. Forget the Nazis for a second; my mother's rejecting nature, in my little universe, was harsh enough. She was especially difficult during my teen years. She was a major-league taunter, my mother. She'd tell me, for instance, that I had book knowledge—but no common sense. So in one short sentence she managed to inform me that I was in fact stupid, even if I was "smart," undermining the meaning and satisfaction of success in school.

But it wasn't just me. She'd put other people down all the time, too. She was not happy with Gentiles in general. "The goyim," she would say, "have no taste—besides being our murderers." But that was somewhat hypocritical. She was envious of the families who could celebrate Christmas.

She was one of these parents who project their own insecurities about themselves onto their children. So it was a source of irritation to her that while I had plenty of girlfriends I couldn't locate anybody of the other sex who found me especially alluring, as if it meant she was somehow unappealing, too, for having raised such a repellent child. She harped on it. Why didn't I have a date? Why couldn't I attract boys? What was wrong with me?

What she wanted me to do, I realize now, is reorganize my personality so I wouldn't be as threatening to guys as I may have been: "You're never going to get a boyfriend because you come on too strong. . . . You should hide that you're smart. . . . You'll get more flies with honey than vinegar." Anyway, I was terrified of boys, to tell you the truth. And lack of experience was self-perpetuating. I could barely get my courage up for spin the bottle.

I was more comfortable thinking of myself as an outsider, a renegade. And there was enough anger and sarcasm in my house that I could strike that rebel pose with some confidence and familiarity. So much of being a teenager is pose, anyway. In the later years of high school, I diverged from the renegade posture for another route; I felt I could be the sort-of-popular type by using my dancing skills to become a cheerleader for the Newtown basketball team—who can say which was the actual me, probably both: the renegade/cheerleader from Elmhurst.

Sort of popular or not, I never did find a boy in all the years of junior and senior high. No romance at all, nothing, nada.

But solitude never bothered me much. (You make it work for you.) The trick, sometimes, was to achieve it. When I was fourteen or fifteen and needed to study, there was just no getting away anywhere in my apartment, except for one place, the bathroom. And I turned that little place into a welcoming warm cave. I was normally so physically cold even when other people weren't, but I could fix that just fine in the bathroom. I'd put my soft flannel gown on and sit on the edge of the tub, with the warm water running over my feet. I could do this for quite a while, reading, daydreaming. (It's a tendency that stays with me—even these days in my rather big new house in Hancock Park, where it is possible to find comfort in many nooks, I still go into the bathroom and sit on the edge of the tub and dangle my feet in the warm water.)

Ira always thought the bathtub bit was weird, that I was some kind of scholarly hermit, while he, au contraire, was off being a playboy. He remembers me as the kind of person who never expressed feelings, who "never let anyone in." Actually, I just didn't want to let Ira in. He was a relentless tease, a taunter like my mother. Not exactly the person I'd reveal those ugly-duckling insecurities to. (I, in turn, taunted little Robin; it is a continual source of dismay to me when I see how easily the worst in us can be passed along.)

But Ira could dance. And he was handsome, too—dark-complected with smallish eyes but a strong, well-proportioned face and a trim body —and it felt good for someone like me, without any boyfriends since grammar school, to be whooping it up with good-looking Ira. Although it didn't earn me too many points among the onlookers, of course, because the dancing was usually in the summer in the Catskills and everybody knew us, knew that the hunk was my brother. But we could Lindy better than anybody in the mountains. There we would be at some bungalow colony in Monticello and my mother—who thought we were good, too—was prodding us: Go, Ira, go dance with your sister. Chairs were arranged around the dance floor, the record player blasting away. (It could have been the Diamonds doo-wopping "Little Darlin'.")

Ira was seventeen and I was fourteen the night we won a bottle of champagne after wowing the good tourists of Monticello. In the light of such success, I wanted to rehearse more and get even better. But we never did. We probably could have gone on and done something with the dancing. We didn't. I never could get my brother to consider anything seriously for more than three minutes.

Our family was inept at ritual. We were especially bad at birthdays. (I never got a present from my mother that I didn't buy myself.) The low point—shared with Ira—occurred the same year we won that dance contest in the Catskills, just before Ira went off to the Army. We got it in our heads to bake a cake for our mother's birthday. But Ira and I, at that point, were very foggy on when her birthday was. Even now I can't remember with confidence, maybe December 15.

It's a winter night in New York and it suddenly hits me: It's Mom's birthday! I run to Ira and deliver the news. "My God," he says, "you're right. Let's bake her a cake as a surprise." We don't have much time. Ira runs out to the A&P, a block and a half away, to buy a chocolate cake mix and white icing with sprinkles while she's taking a nap. We bake her that cake and we ice it and write on it "Happy Birthday, Mom." The whole bit. She wakes up. We hurry to put a couple of candles on the thing and present it to her. But it's the wrong day, and even worse, as she explains.

"You idiots, it's the wrong *month*," and she's offended. I believe she ascribes the baking of the cake to selfish motives—that we wanted chocolate cake that night and were looking for an excuse. But I destroy that birthday cake, mash it with my hands and throw it into the garbage.

That cake was a goner. Nobody, she especially, was going to eat that godforsaken cake now. Another example, my mother would have said, of me cutting off my nose to spite my face. I loved chocolate cake.

•

Years later, when I finally made my way to California—after graduation from Queens College and a first marriage that would not survive long in California—people there always thought of me as this tough New Yorker, some kind of archetype. Part of that was exactly right, at least according to the macho-romantic image the culture puts out about us. When I was thirteen and fourteen—a time when I had a group of friends at school and another group from the hood—I was in fact part of a band of girls that hung out with a boys' gang. The girls were almost never violent (from time to time, the boys did get into a violent situation). Nor were we sexually active. We tried to look tough, talk tough; we cursed a lot. We were influenced by *West Side Story.* Every now and then one of us might leap at a lamppost in a moment of balletic joy and swing completely around it in a graceful arc. We called it "Hanging a Maria," and we were singing, of course, "Mareeeuh, I just met a girl named Mareeeuh." (Years later when I was in New York researching a case with one of my investigators, Casey Cohen, the exuberant moment came back in a thrust of energy and I leaped toward a lamppost, hanging a Maria on Broadway!)

The assertion of female toughness was in smoking cigarettes—but not using drugs or alcohol—and wearing very tight jeans and leather jackets and scarves, kerchiefs on the hair. If you were tough, the scarf was always black. The key to the scarf was to wear it as far back on your head as you could without it falling off. This was not an Iranian woman's scarf meant to hide your painstakingly prepared head, of course. You did the scarf across the crown and then tucked it under to show as much hair as possible. It always took me about a half hour to get the right look: put on the makeup, tease the hair. It was important to have big teased hair, but my hair was the curse of my life because it was too curly. What you wanted was straight hair that you could bouffant out.

I wasn't much of a smoker until I was sixteen. But when I started at fourteen I smoked tough, Chesterfields. Like most everybody else, I didn't enjoy it at first. In fact, I don't think I started inhaling until I switched to filters, at about fifteen. We'd hang out in the next neighborhood over, Jackson Heights, which was where the big stores were, on Eighty-second Street. I do remember seeing a couple of girls fight with other girls, but I managed to avoid that. I was as big as a minute, after all, tiny and skinny and very young looking. Violence scared me.

We did steal from stores and occasionally vandalized property. The big thing was to steal trinkets from Woolworth's in our spare time. We were drawn to the garrison belts, these big thick leather belts with huge buckles. If we wore voluminous, thick leather jackets we could wrap three or four of these belts around our waists. Mainly we stole really cheap things, like plastic beads, costume jewelry, makeup. I was nervous during these outlaw excursions but not frightened. And afterward we were all very excited, comparing the loot. We kept it all in shoe boxes under our beds and never did anything else with it.

We got caught when my girlfriend Claire told her cousin and showed her the loot and her cousin told her mother and her mother told my mother. A fair amount of screaming ensued. The jig was up and we never did it again.

Another completely wrong, antisocial thing Claire and I did was to cover most of the wallpaper in a hallway of my apartment house with lipstick. Why, I can't begin to say. We got started and couldn't stop. It took about an hour and I said to Claire, "We're going to get killed." When I told my mother what we'd done, for some reason, she resisted killing me. She paid for new wallpaper, though.

It was all a matter of thrill-seeking, a craving for stimulation. Today, in middle age, I recall these impulses vividly and it helps me understand why juveniles should never be punished like adults. You're talking about a lack of impulse control so complete that there isn't even a thought process involved. There is just a tremendous drive toward excitement, rebellion, defiance. We weren't shooting people then, of course. Kids today are similar from a developmental point of view, but the lamentable thing is that in our vicious culture, the game—for far too many of them —has escalated. We lipsticked the walls; they're killing people in drive-bys. And yet to treat them as if they were adults, making grown-up sorts of decisions, weighing consequences—as most adults do all the time—is ridiculous.

I see where some pompous judge, sitting in Florida, not too long ago went outside the sentencing guidelines to put a fourteen-year-old in prison for the rest of his life. Life without parole for *attempted* murder. You just want to take judges like that and knock them right off the bench. What's wrong with you, pal? Get a kick out of throwing a fourteen-year-old life away? Think it's righteous to hand him over to the state so the rest of us can pay for his upkeep until the day he dies after a brutalized, worthless sixty or seventy years of incarceration? The developmental psychologists who tell us about the differences between adults and children are correct. But in the virulent politics of the day, the truth has gotten lost. Completely lost.

Another of today's scourges, child abuse, did not spring full-blown into the present time. We had some pretty serious stuff then, too. In my building when I was about eight, I had a friend named Connie who was seven. She had olive skin and brown hair in a pageboy cut. We weren't great friends. I think she went to Catholic school. I'd played ball with her, skipped rope with her, played potsy on the sidewalk, but I'd never been in her apartment. Connie had a baby sister, who was maybe two and a half. I'd see the baby outside in her carriage. She was a cute little thing, unusually long hair for someone so tiny. One day when I came home from school in the afternoon there was a crowd of people in front of the apartment house and an ambulance. Connie's mother had killed the baby, drowned her in the bathtub. What we heard was that the mother was "mental." She was divorced or divorcing and she was depressed. If I got the story right, the mother was set off by some behavior, became angry at the baby and started to strangle her, and the baby passed out. To revive her, she put her in the bathtub with some water and—as the story goes—the mother got distracted, maybe the phone rang. The child drowned in a few inches of water.

One part of the sad story that's hard to forget is that she took off the baby's brand-new white patent leather shoes before she put her in the tub so the shoes wouldn't get ruined. It doesn't sound like she ever knew she would kill the baby or ever intended it. But she drowned her baby in an effort to revive her from strangulation.

I never saw Connie again. They took the mother away. For me, at eight, this was the scariest sort of death—death caused by a mother. And also there was the additional horrifying element of death by drowning with no one to notice your distress. I was the kind of kid who took baths every night, and each time for a long time I thought about that poor little baby. The sorrow and worry were compounded by the realization that my sister, Robin, was about the same age. I always wanted to be sure that she wasn't left in the bathtub alone. (This was unlikely because, as emotionally difficult as my mother may have been, when it came to our physical well-being she was on the ball.)

These days, I don't think about that drowning very often. It's just one of those stories that survive from childhood. But whenever I do think about it I usually get it wrong when the image first forces itself into my mind: the baby is in the tub—but her white patent leather shoes are on.

This family, Connie's, had more than its share of terrible times. One night, Friday or Sunday—a good TV night—my whole family is in the living room, which is on the side of the building facing the Long Island Railroad tracks, watching the RCA, when there's a flash of light, as if lightning had struck something. Screaming follows. Someone is in terrible pain. Another flash of light. It is coming from the direction of the tracks. And the screaming goes on and on and it's terrifying. The thought that keeps rushing through my mind is "Why is he still yelling? People must be there by now, helping." It's blood-curdling. We're in the living room, our own breathing practically stifled by the screaming.

I believed, as a little kid, that when things go real wrong some adult— my grandmother, my parents, the police—some adult always comes along and fixes it. But not this time. It seems like forever. It turns out that a fourteen-year-old boy had climbed up one of the power towers above the tracks on a dare from a bunch of other kids. "I dare you. I double-dare you." He went up there, the story goes, and touched one of the high-tension wires. The screaming we heard was his slow electrocution. Those rescuer-adults did try to help (although, for my part, I never fully believed in adults as saviors again). After a considerable period, they shut off the power to the railroad and eventually got him down, still alive. I heard that his whole body had turned red. I don't know if that's true, if the body really does turn totally red during an electrocution. Next, I heard that his arms and legs had to be amputated. Then I heard that he had died.

The boy—I don't know his name—was Connie's cousin.

Sometimes when I think about childhood it seems to me there are only so many memories—just a finite number of good times and a finite number of bad times—a handful, in light of all the years it took to collect them. Not long ago, when my husband, Tim, and I were babysitting for a little girl named Katie, the daughter of friends, I noticed that she was hiding a food ball in her mouth. I was feeding her chicken rice soup and she didn't want to swallow any more of it. It struck me that I had done that, too, when I was little. My mother always tried to bully me into eating too much, finishing everything. So I hid the food in my cheeks until I got a chance to spit it out. The memory made me laugh.

The recollection felt good, adding a memory. And by the same token, it's a relief when you can finally let go of some of the old resentments.

By the time I speak to my father on the phone in 1991, he is eighty-one years old and living in a trailer on the property of his stepson in Pennsylvania. The widow with the few dollars left all of them plus the house and furniture to her son. I'm about to travel to the East Coast to interview relatives and friends of Erik and Lyle Menendez in preparation for what was to be the first of their two trials, the one that ended with hung juries.

I began talking to Sol in February but now it's summer. It's the start of a very long trip, ten days or so during a horrible, hot, thunderstorming June on the East Coast. I fly in to Philadelphia. We're about to have a three-day weekend, Daddy and I, and I am armed with these wonderful driving instructions. "You take 76 to 222, 222 to 283 to . . ."

"Dad, do these roads have any names?"

"No, just numbers."

"All right, I'll do my best."

There's construction going on along most of these roads, particularly right outside Philadelphia. So I'm running real late. I'm hot and exasperated. I'm sure Sol is anxious. I finally get to the Lancaster Hotel, a down-at-the-heels, shabby place with an outdoor pool on the main road. My father chose Amish country because it was near where he lived and he figured that being there would give us stuff to do, like when we were both much younger and lovey-dovey.

I schlepp out my bags and walk in through the entrance of the hotel and this tiny guy is sitting on a sofa with a cane in front of him. He says, in his low, slightly gravelly voice, "Is that you?" And I say, "I think it's me, is that you, too?" So that's all there was after thirty-four years: "Is that you?" (No, Pop, I'm still standing on the corner of Broadway and Elmhurst Avenue, waiting for you to come get me . . . but never mind.)

We hug. He starts crying. He's evidently been sitting in the lobby for a while, I am so late. A hotel employee walks by and says, "Your father's been waiting for you for a long time." I guess I knew that.

We link arms and walk to the room to put my stuff down and talk a little—just chitchat, nothing much—and we go to eat at a Chinese restaurant, of all things, there in Amish country. Might as well have been in Queens. It's not bad actually. Then my dad unveils a fabulous plan. "Would you like to go to see Gettysburg?" he says. Damn straight I would. I never had been there before. But for my whole life, history has been my primary intellectual interest. History is what I've always been clever in. (Forget fields like cosmology: I can't conceive of the edge of the universe to save my life.) As a kid I spent an incredible amount of time trying to find out who did what, and history could answer it (and so can criminal law, for that matter). And sometimes I turned to history for comfort, too.

And now my father has the insight to take me to Gettysburg. This is better than Ebbets Field. We're at Gettysburg! I call my husband, Tim, a newspaperman who knows so much about so much that he knows even more than he believes he knows, and I say, "You are going to be envious. You're never going to guess where I am."

"Well, give me a hint."

"It has to do with the Civil War."

"You're in Gettysburg," he says with that half whisper he uses when he's really impressed.

It is a gorgeous day, although too hot for Sol to walk through the heartbreaking Civil War cemetery section of the park. Still, we arrange for a guided tour of the rest. A woman gets in our car with us, answering questions, pointing out the sites of battle and carnage. And on every grassy hillside it becomes possible to truly imagine, almost hear the rifles fire, see the gunsmoke cling to the slopes and sink into the ravines, dirty brown, like smog in the valleys of L.A., and at one point I believe I can hear the clamor of the boys falling and dying in droves. It's time-traveling. God, how great.

But as for Sol and me, nobody's kidding anybody just now. This re-union with my father isn't going to be like something in the movies, a kind of transcendent experience that heals all. First, I had already resolved a whole lot in my mind: Despite everything, I felt I had achieved a worthy life no matter where it might go from here. That was a comfort. And despite everything, I knew I didn't have to hate Sol anymore or resent my mother anymore. I didn't have to go on nourishing this well-spring of anger. It was over. Not healed in the glow of love. But just over. I wasn't going to eat myself up about these people from now on, if I could help it.

Later, before the visit ends, I do ventilate a bit. I tell Sol that it was a horrendous thing he did to me. He agrees. "You're right," of course, "you're right," he says.

"You were selfish," I say.

"Yes, I was," he says. "I wanted my own comforts and I worried about myself and I was so angry at your mother I didn't think about you. I'm not saying I did right." Actually, for the crimes of abandonment and betrayal there is no defense.

He tells me that in the later years he never made any aggressive effort to track me down because Ira said I didn't want to hear from him, which was true. But that bugs me a little anyhow, even in my relatively mellow state of mind. If my daughter, Laine, said that she never wanted to speak to me again, I'd still hire a bloodhound to find her. Anyway, I didn't mean this to turn into a recrimination session. I was just hoping for a nice weekend where we would go out together and do something. And it was. It was a very nice weekend.

3

Law School

"Oh, my God, I'll never get this." I'm reading these forbidding law texts at the UCLA law school and I'm thinking I'm barely going to scrape by, if I do at all. How can I compete with these other people? Look at that guy over there. He was in the ninety-ninth percentile on the LSAT, had an incredible grade-point average and went to Berkeley. All the other kids are like that, too, they're showing up with astronomical grades, great LSATs, and they've been to much better schools than I attended. There are kids here from Stanford and Harvard, for God's sake.

I'm thinking "Schmuck," with my high white go-go boots, my long fake hair and my insecurities about myself. To make things worse, I had just spent a year as little Mrs. Housewife, taking care of my baby. I don't regret a minute spent with little Laine, but at the time, I felt I was treading water. The high point of my days was the trip to the supermarket following the thrill of two-hour coffee klatches with the other new mothers in the neighborhood, pleasant women who thought I was crazy—and a lousy mother—because I planned to go to law school.

So I'm thinking, "I'm going to flunk out of this place."

Still, anxiety aside, I wasn't going to be beaten by law school if I could help it.

The classrooms, after all, were familiar enough—we had big lecture rooms at Queens College, too, with rows of seats in arcs reaching up from the podium just like these. Here at UCLA I decided to sit in the fourth row every time. I wasn't going to hide. Anyway, the questions came flying at you, front or back, whether you raised your hand or not.

So much reading: torts, contracts, civil procedure, property, criminal law. I'd go home at night with fifty-page reading assignments for each class, minimum. Read the next three cases, the instructor says, like that's nothing. And you have to spot the issues in the case. You have to predict what the debate's going to be about the next day. You're going to get called on to answer a whole series of questions. You've got to be prepared. You don't dare walk into class unprepared. Especially in the beginning.

"Well, Mrs. Abramson, do you have an answer?"

"Well, Mrs. Abramson, what did the court really mean? . . . So that's what you think?"

"Okay, then, you in the back, Mr. Cowell, are you with us today? You, give it a try."

It's Criminal Law, I'm recalling now, and Professor Herb Morris is sitting on the corner of his desk, one leg dangling, very casual. I may have been apprehensive in those early days but it wasn't Herb Morris's fault. He was not a frightening person; he was very sweet. It was the material that was daunting.

And my heart was in my mouth the first month or so. After that I got used to it and even began to enjoy it. I soon realized that I was good at this business: I got it. I'd found a kind of home.

The material was just so fascinating that it was hard not to think about it, once you got going. As it happens, I was mostly drawn to death and destruction: the murders and other violations of criminal law, the relationship between moral and legal responsibility.

All of us were learning to think like lawyers—but not to be lawyers. (I never saw a whole trial until I did one.) At UCLA, in the fall of 1966 when I arrived and for many years after, nobody learned anything about the actual practice of law. What we learned was the foundation on which the edifice of rules and rights and sanctions was built. The notion was that if you understood the reasons for the rules, you could analyze problems and fashion solutions that reflected society's values even if you didn't know the actual rules (the letter of the law). For the kind of insecure student who needed to know "the answer," law school was a nerve-racking three years.

In Criminal Law, one of the first cases we studied was about cannibalism. It dealt with the true story of a shipwreck and its survivors facing
starvation in a lifeboat. The issue: whether necessity is an excuse for
crime. The question: Did starving people have a right to eat each other?
And if so, could they hasten the inevitable death of the weakest among
them? Survival is the most powerful animal instinct, right? Our sailors
were like the members of the infamous Donner Party in 1846, a group
trapped in the Sierra Nevada during a brutal winter and—with some
turning to corpses and murder for sustenance—they had to survive,
didn't they? Shouldn't the law recognize so basic a fact of nature? Well,
maybe not. Survival in the absence of a lethal threat from someone else,
we learned, is not a justification for killing. The criminal law answer is
you starve to death before you kill somebody else for sustenance.

We took positions on these issues as avidly as we could without even
understanding how it all fit into the grand scheme. In law school—as it
was taught then and now—you never quite get the picture until you're
toward the end of the course. They want you to work up from the first
principle. And so you sit there and talk about murder and cannibalism
and desperation. And from these discussions you begin to understand
the moral underpinnings of the law. Even if you can't exactly articulate
those underpinnings, it's the feeling of rightness and the thinking associated with that feeling that are beginning to be part of who you are.

In the classroom discussions, I came down on the same side as the
law: I believed it was not justifiable to kill somebody else for food, thank
you very much. The taboo on eating human flesh is a pretty big taboo,
anyway. But that wasn't why I felt as I did. It seemed to me that you just
don't kill people for yourself. Selfishness is a repugnant motive.

The rejoinder to my position: But what if the prospective nourishment
was going to die anyway?

That's how the law professors played with our minds. They were
forcing us to learn moral thinking. And the way Herb Morris taught the
class, there were no right or wrong answers to a lot of it. There were
simply moral lines to be drawn. A society decides how to draw them.

The training was a license to challenge the conclusions and the thinking of others: Given how a case was decided, what were the principles?
Why did the Court come out in a particular way? What could the Court
have been weighing in the mix? And was it right?

A significant amount of time early on was devoted to the concept of
mens rea, the state of mind that made an act criminal. For any crime
there have to be two things: a combination of *actus rea,* which is the

prohibited act, and mens rea, which is the state of mind at the time of the act.

Mens rea is a powerful concept of English common law, hundreds of years old. It has to do with the fundamental notion that you do not punish people for the result of what they do, taken alone, but for their intentions.

The sad truth is that people die easily. They fall down and die; something lands on top of them and they die. Let's say that in thirteenth-century England your ox balks and your cart rolls off the road into a ditch and there's a baby playing in the ditch and you kill the baby. . . .

Although not demeaning the value of the life of an infant, the law then and now would probably not punish you for the death of the baby. You might get sued, but not arrested. In our legal tradition there is and has always been a difference between accident and murder—and many points in between. The law reflects a moral decision: to punish people only for the harm they intended to cause or for their indifference to the life-threatening consequences of their acts. (Say our ox-cart driver saw the cart straying toward the ditch, saw the baby, didn't bother to rein in the oxen, didn't care if the baby was crushed or not. That's reckless indifference to life—not an accident, a crime.)

Of course, many people would be happier with a simpleminded justice. There is right and there is wrong. How wonderful, how exhilarating it is when you know for sure something is right or wrong. But in criminal law, as we learned in law school, there is necessarily a spectrum of morality, a spectrum of right and wrong that must be confronted by intelligent, fair-minded people. Mens rea, the state of mind, is a fundamental yardstick.

The days at UCLA were invariably overwhelming in the amount of work required at school and home, both before my divorce from my first husband—Lewis, the pharmacist I married in Queens and with whom I moved to L.A.—and after it. I had to be certain either I or someone else was around to take care of my baby daughter, Laine, and I could not evade the usual homemaker chores.

As exhausting as all this was, the law was fun. Often, a few of us would carry legal arguments with us to lunch or into the hallway. We'd leave the sprawling new law building on the east end of campus and maybe walk a few steps over to the parklike lawn of Dickson Plaza and sit there on the low branch of a strangely distorted tree, one of whose branches (as if in

deference to the student population the tree served) extended low to the
ground almost horizontally, like God's bench. We'd sit on that limb in
the dappled southern California light and discuss class or argue or, more
likely, just joke around.

Sometimes we'd sing. We knew the whole Beatles catalogue and sang
the songs over and over. ("I once had a girl, or should I say, she once had
me. We sat by the fire, isn't it good, Norwegian wood . . ." What *is*
Norwegian wood anyway? No one asked.) Or we would talk about personal stuff. We called little breaks like that, just half an hour away from
the books, playing hooky. After all, it wasn't midnight yet.

Given my values, this was a great time to be in law school. I had come
here because I wanted to be a professional. I wanted accomplishment, to
make something of my life. Medicine looked good, too, and, like the law,
it involved helping people. But law had a political aspect: not letting
governments run over people, helping the underdog. By the time I entered law school, the Johnsonian escalation of the Vietnam War was at
its peak—some kids were sticking to their studies purely to evade the
conscription vacuum hose—and J. William Fulbright was describing the
government's behavior as the "arrogance of power." The antigovernment
position, of course, was the one held by the defense side of the law school
equation, not the prosecutorial. On the other side, at the top of the heap
of the prosecutors during the latter part of my time in law school, was
John Mitchell as attorney general, a criminal as it turned out, answering
to his boss, Richard Nixon, the historic nemesis of my family.

So politically this felt like a good time to head for the defense bar, to
stand up for the oppressed and the weak against the often irrational,
callous forces of the law-enforcement bureaucracy.

But in fact we were much closer in taste, if not in spirit, to our future
prosecutor adversaries than those of our classmates who were headed for
the big-money civil firms. And in the early days of my life as a lawyer
there wasn't all that much difference between the baby DAs and the baby
defense lawyers.

Of course, we thought the prosecutors took the easy way out. They
had the power, the money and the prevailing public sentiment on their
side. But I remember how imbued those young prosecutors of the seven-
ties were with the notion that they were entrusted with great power and
should use it ethically, to do justice. Conviction or acquittal to them was
not the true measure of a good prosecutor. A job well done was.

Nevertheless, I always believed that the defense had the greater challenge and had more fun to boot. It's more meaningful to have a real live
person for a client than the abstract "state."

In the last decade too much has changed. Right now, you can take the prosecutor's code and stick it in *Bulfinch's Mythology.* Winning is all that counts. Justice to a prosecutor these days doesn't mean discovering the truth, doesn't even mean fitting punishments to crimes. It means convict as many as you can and see to it that they get the max.

None of my crowd went into prosecution. My friend Carol Freis ultimately became a personal injury lawyer. Stuart Christenfeld—one of the smartest and most important members of our little study group—became an entertainment lawyer. John Weston, probably my closest buddy, and I became defense attorneys. For the most part, in any event, the people in the class ended up in civil, not criminal law.

It may sound as if those of us heading for the defense bar were political activists. We weren't. Who had the time? There were days when I was dead on my feet. I was taking diet pills as it was, to stay up late, sometimes studying overnight because the ordinary day just didn't provide enough time for all my responsibilities. The pills were a mild form of amphetamine prescribed by my doctor and supplied by my husband the pharmacist. I had taken them before, at Queens, to get through finals. I took them even when I was not in school, to be able to clean the house, nonstop, once the baby was asleep.

It was a very low level of speed but it had its pitfalls. Amphetamines, in general, affect you in all sorts of unintended ways. Number one, the drug kills your appetite. Number two, it eventually gives you back pain. And if you get distracted during one project, and shift to another project, you could spend many focused hours filling out new address books or doing crossword puzzles. It makes you very detail-driven and result-oriented and you've got to make sure you don't stray from the law books while you're on this junk or you'll wind up counting every rubber band in the house ten times and sorting them all into colored groups.

At UCLA, there were some people taking "black beauties" for mid-terms and finals. Serious amphetamines. I couldn't take those. Those were killers. Everyone who couldn't lay their hands on speed was on No-Doz. What's really scary is that all the medical students were doing the same things, while tending patients, whereas we were only buried in books.

Besides the speed, I was impelled by something more profound, more genuine and lasting: positive feedback. From my professors. From my peers. I was looked up to as a leader in class and in our clique's study group. The law itself, as it turned out, was one hell of a high. People look at me like I'm crazy when I tell them that I never had a better time in my life than when I was in law school.

On one early day at school, I'm hanging out with a girl named Diana— we women were the merest minority, only eight of us out of about two hundred, an almost invisible minority (compared to the 50 percent or so today). It is the season of campus politicking. The young men who imagine themselves to be orators and leaders, future Caesars of the nation-state, are campaigning for local office, that is, class president, a basically meaningless position. One of them is John Weston, who, with his dark Beatles bangs and self-important air, strikes me as particularly pretentious. And when we first meet in the student lounge, I don't make any effort to hide that assessment.

Sarcasm and superiority—that's the stance I like to take with John, and he eats it up then and for some years to come. Over time we become terrific friends. But at that very moment, chatting in the lounge, I think he's being attentive mostly because he's looking for a regular ride to school and back. He lives in Beverly Hills, too close to campus to get a parking permit, that's the problem. I live in West L.A., far enough away. And I become his ride, his buddy, ultimately his tutor. Nevertheless, we argue a lot and I frequently resort to the put-down—"Yeah, right, sure." But he is tough and smart, too, although a dreamer, a rich Beverly Hills kid who doesn't have to worry about much in the way of survival, or a promising future.

It develops that just about every day I go to his house, pick him up and we go to school together. I drive my car or he drives his car and we use my parking space. I have a yellow Corvette. Yellow is perfect for this car because it's a true lemon. And he has a car he calls "Steed." It's a Pontiac Firebird, blue with a black leather top. He loves this car. His fantasy, as the name implies, is that he can whistle and the car will come racing over.

Escape is an important part of our relationship. We lead lives where there are no weekends off. There is almost never a night off. And at the end of the school day, when I drag myself back home to be with my child, to be with my husband, to cook dinner and then to study, there isn't any opportunity for freedom and childish excess. And particularly in the spring, that routine can wear you down. When exhaustion sets in, that's when John and I go off and take an hour or two here or there, play hooky and pretend we are normal people. Sometimes we just head into Westwood—the section of L.A. that adjoins the campus—then much

more of a college town than it is now. We go in search of New York–
style hamburgers (which is to say, an unadorned chopped meat sandwich;
Californians have the idea that the hamburger was invented by McDon-
ald's). We go shopping. We do silly things.

One evening in spring in our first year, during a terribly tense period
as exams approach ("Are we going to flunk out? Are we going to get it
all done? Can we go five days straight without sleeping?"), we decide to
take off. It is a night made unusually warm by the Santa Anas, the easterly
winds, off the desert toward the ocean. We drive along Sunset Boulevard
to the San Diego Freeway and then the Santa Monica Freeway, west,
toward the Pacific Coast Highway.

"Have you ever had a chocolate-covered frozen banana?" John says.
The air is fragrant with the wildflowers that suddenly appear everywhere
in the temporarily green, soon to be kindling dry, Santa Monica Mountains.

You can get these funny bananas at Balboa Island in Orange County
to the south, out on the pier at a place called the Fun Zone. And that is
the usual place that bananamaniacs in L.A. go. But part of the enjoyment
of getting in the car is the ride north along the highway, with the stars
over the ocean to the west and the dark mountains to the east.

"But there's one place in Malibu," John says, and that, at the moment,
seems infinitely more interesting.

So we drive toward Malibu in my yellow Corvette, the top down. John
is at the wheel, and we aim for this place up near the Malibu pier. On the
road (which wasn't as traffic-clogged then as it is now and always had the
feeling of liberty about it) we sing Top Ten songs—the Turtles ("Happy
Together") and the Lovin' Spoonful ("Do You Believe in Magic?")—and
we shout into the wind just for the hell of it.

It is hard to miss this banana place, signaled as it is by a typical bit of
southern California culture, a fifty-foot-high doll. We buy our frozen
chocolate-covered bananas and we stroll out on the Malibu pier, a million
miles from responsibilities, in the warm evening.

As friends, we were a great match in those days. John never did want to
grow up (Peter Pan with an attaché case). Although his parents were
hard on him, childhood was otherwise a lark, beaches and sunlight and
music. And I, so far as I could tell, had never had a childhood at all, in
the sense of unbridled playfulness, until now. So put that top down, hit
the Top Forty button and we're outta here!

But the Pacific Coast Highway was also where I went to be lonely. On nights when the personal and academic pressure nudged me toward melancholy, I got in my car and drove alone; I imagined I was Maria, the protagonist of Joan Didion's *Play It as It Lays.* In the story, Maria compulsively drives one freeway to another. She drives "as a riverman runs a river, every day more attuned to its currents, its deceptions . . ."

My marriage no longer made much sense. Lew was a good guy, but we didn't belong together. He knew it. I knew it. And I was depressed off and on during those months. Driving was an escape. On the road, with the radio blasting, I identified with Didion's Maria, but I didn't intend to wind up like her. She was the helpless victim type. I was the angry fighting type. Although you could get down, you had to get out of it, you had to cope. As for the divorce, I didn't want to make it hard on Lew. We talked about it. He said, "Well, fine, if we can afford it, but I don't think we can." So I did some rather quick research at the dean's office, and the dean said, "I can offer you right now a $1,000 loan, a UCLA loan, and we'll help you make out the paperwork for a regular federal student loan and there won't be any problem at all—you can make it."

Lew agreed to provide minimal alimony and child support and he moved out to start a new and relatively comfortable life, while I went about mine. Finish law school. Make enough to support the kid. Help the poor and oppressed. And be a good lawyer, whatever that means.

My height, four feet eleven inches, is usually noticed at first and then, I believe, quickly becomes a nonissue. I stand straight, fight hard, and I believe anyone focusing on my size to explain who I am is making a big mistake. But there was one time when my being short was my defining characteristic, graduation day, June 1969.

The graduate students, including law students, are parading toward the track stadium next to Pauley Pavilion, down a walkway alongside the kids who are graduating from the college. The graduate students enter the quad from one direction and the undergraduates march in from the other, until we are paired off, striding two-by-two. As these two lines merge I, like a gear for a tricycle about to mesh with one from a construction crane, am paired up with Lew Alcindor, the seven-foot-two, soon-to-be Kareem Abdul Jabbar. I mean who wouldn't laugh?

I laugh, but mostly it's a thrill. I'd been a basketball fan all my life (a cheerleader for basketball players, in fact, in college), and this is one amazing athlete and decent person. His decency as a human being is just obvious, although he is painfully shy. I'd seen him on campus before and said the usual inane things to him, like "Great game." But he isn't much for conversation. You don't want to intrude. He seems more sensitive about his height than I do about mine. He has nowhere to hide and sometimes he seems to be walking scrunched over, like maybe he could get all the way down to six feet eleven.

In line, we aren't supposed to talk, but we do, a bit. I look straight up, wish him good luck in his pending professional career. He looks straight down, says thanks and then notices the contrasting cowl on my robe, "What's that? What does the purple mean?"

"Purple," I tell him, "means the law school."

"Oh, you're going to be a lawyer," he says.

"Yeah, I am."

4

The Bar

It's the summer of 1969 and I feel a little like a marathoner who has just stumbled and tumbled across the finish line, gasping for breath, only to learn that I have to pick myself up, steady my legs and run another race. I've just survived a wearying, dispiriting few months: divorce from Lewis in January, mononucleosis in the spring, final exams in a condition so weak I slogged through them spacey, like it was an out-of-body experience—and then looming, just weeks ahead, the dreaded bar exam.

It was an easy time to become distracted, too, if you weren't completely focused on your own objectives. The nation itself was still enduring paroxysms of violence. Following a spate of assassinations (Martin Luther King and Bobby Kennedy were both killed in 1968), we were now beset by a spectacularly gruesome event when Charlie Manson's cult killed the actress Sharon Tate and her houseguests. No one would know who the killers were until more than three months later, in December. Part of the story going around (false, as it turns out) was that the fetus was cut out of the stomach of the pregnant Tate. I found that image the most grotesque among all the others in what was already reported as the Grand Guignol of depravity. In those days I could still be shocked. I hadn't yet learned to be philosophical about evil.

In any event, as bad as the killings were, all my energy had to be directed toward recovering physically and mentally to face the looming dragon of the bar exam.

I started the bar review course a week late because I hadn't fully gotten over the mono. Fortunately or not, I didn't have to worry that my remaining strength might be sapped by some wonderful romance, because I wasn't seeing anyone. (Gerry Chaleff, who became a renowned criminal lawyer in Los Angeles, and I dated for a while, but it was a disaster; we argued constantly. The only way to deal with such an intelligent but competitive man was to call off the romance and become best friends, which we did.)

Mostly, I just wanted to run away to the beach.

The bar review course was offered in a bleak union hall on Robertson near Pico, just south of Beverly Hills. The instructors' tactic was to try to scare the hell out of you and make you feel that flunking was the usual outcome among those benighted students who did not take the instructors' advice to heart. Their advice, however, struck me as a mindless collection of tactics and formulaic approaches to answering typical questions.

All legal exam questions present hypothetical problems that raise a number of issues. Spotting the issues is half the battle. Coming up with acceptable solutions to those issues is the other half. That's all the bar reviewers wanted us to do. List the issues. List the solutions. They warned us not to try to argue persuasively that one solution was better than the other and not to offer analysis to justify any particular solution.

For someone with the soul of an advocate and the heart of a litigator, those restrictions were contrary to my very being, not to mention the opposite of what I had done successfully in three years of law school.

I concluded that their advice was aimed at the least capable among us, those who were in danger of going off on tangents and using all the limited time allotted to each question to argue the legal equivalent of the flat-earth theory. But I could spot issues in the phone book, I told myself. I didn't need their techniques. I decided that I'd sit through their stupid classes in the morning. Then I was going to the beach.

Nearly every day, I picked up my friend Carol Freis and we drove to Malibu, taking Lainie, still a toddler, with us. Along with a pail and shovel, peanut-butter-and-jelly sandwiches and suntan lotion, I dutifully carried the course outlines in my beach bag. But I never read them. I read escapist novels. Two weeks before the exam, never having looked at the outlines, I panicked.

"You've gotta look at this stuff," I exhorted myself. How embarrassing to be at the top of your class and fail the bar! The reality of this possibility hit home when I took—and massively flunked—a practice exam. It was actually my one halfhearted attempt to use the bar review method and it was a disaster. With time running out, I realized that at least part of my resistance to the instruction at the review course was a defense mechanism, a response to exhaustion and an inability to study long hours.

But there was no time to learn their method now. I'd have to rely on whatever talent had carried me through school, study their outlines just to relearn the legal rules, then take the exam my way using the tried-and-true law school—not bar review—analysis and language.

The night before the start of the exam, Carol and I headed off to Glendale—the exam was held in one of those cavernous civic auditoriums—and we rented a hotel room for the two and a half days of the test. I felt anything but ready as the fateful moment approached. And that deep unease delivered a lasting message to me about meticulous preparation. It isn't just that the process teaches you so much but rather that it shores you up psychologically, imparts a sense of readiness that diminishes anxiety. Anxiety, at one level, of course, aids performance, but if it is too high—as it might be when you believe you are not ready—it will cripple you for sure.

The test begins on a Tuesday morning, August 26, 1969. Like everybody else, I switch into exam overdrive. There is probably no other mental state like it. You're trying to do so many things at once. You're trying to understand a particular question and you're anxious because you know if you can't get over that initial hurdle—minimal comprehension—the game is over before it begins. You start reading the question, and fight off the initial fear: "Am I going to understand this thing?" Then comes the "Ah-*hah!*" You do. You go back to read it again to make sure you've spotted the issues ("Have I spotted *all* of them? Every single one?") Then you have to understand the possibilities that grow out of the issues. It's all so stressful because the precise substance of the question may be entirely new to you. And besides that, you're in this terrible hurry.

It is unreal: I'm lost in some prison camp for two and a half days. My entire life depends on what happens in this airless, shabby auditorium in Glendale. My intention is to work, long term, for the public defender's office as a criminal lawyer and if I don't pass this stupid exam, maybe I can't. (The next one is six months away.)

My pride's on the line, too. Nobody in the top 10 percent at UCLA has ever flunked the bar. (At least that's the official Bruin mythology.)

And, of course, I've got a nervous stomach like everybody else in the place. I race for the restroom every hour on the hour. The whole time I am taking the bar I hear the toilets flushing.

At some point—a break between sessions—some guy I know who flunked the test twice before starts carrying on about how hard the thing is and how everybody fails. And I tell him to go screw himself. I can't listen to that stuff. Not now.

Morning session. August 27, 1969. Question No. 13.

There is this fellow named Dan (D for defendant), it says here, employed as an armed bank guard. He suspects his wife, Ann (Dan and Ann, cute), is having an affair with another man, Victor (oops, Victor is going to get it—V is for victim). Dan gets roaring drunk. He goes over to Victor's apartment, forces his way in and finds not only Victor but also sweet Ann hiding in the bedroom closet. She is in a lounging robe. "I'll kill you both!" Dan screams. He draws the revolver issued by the bank and shoots Victor to death. He tries to shoot Ann, but the gun jams.

Later he testifies that he was so drunk during the assault he can't remember any of it, and his attorney requests that the jury be instructed to consider a verdict of manslaughter, a much lesser crime than first- or second-degree murder, because Dan wasn't all there at the time he did the deed.

Does Dan have a right to a lesser charge?

Answering, I realize that manslaughter, in any event, is the best he can do. He won't be acquitted. Even though he maintains he was virtually unconscious at the time, voluntary intoxication is not grounds for an acquittal. He probably can't support an insanity plea, either, based on voluntary intoxication because California does not acknowledge temporary insanity. The impairment, to work to his benefit, has to be a full-fledged mental disease or defect that rendered him incapable of knowing the difference between right and wrong or of appreciating the wrongfulness of his acts. On top of that the impairment must rob him of the ability to conform his behavior to societal norms. (That was the test then; these days you have to be under the impression that you're shooting a lemon to avail yourself of insanity as a defense.)

Analyzing the case on a theory of diminished capacity, you could argue that raging Dan was so drunk that he didn't have the ability to deliberate (which requires careful weighing of options) or to premeditate, as is required in first-degree murder. And he was not in that state of mind where he could explicitly harbor malice (which at that time required some appreciation that his conduct was wrong), another criterion. That would reduce the crime to voluntary manslaughter. You could even argue that he was so drunk he couldn't form a coherent intent to kill, further reducing it to involuntary manslaughter. On the other hand he did declare that he was going to kill them both.

It strikes me, though, that this case is like those described in criminal law as "Texas Justice," where men who kill unfaithful wives routinely got off. That code doesn't necessarily apply in California but "heat of passion" would. We had learned that the criminal law takes into account basic truths about human nature. When someone is provoked into that excited state called heat of passion by circumstances that would arouse reasonable people to act emotionally and rashly, they do not have the mens reas for murder. When a man catches his wife and her lover in flagrante delicto and shoots them it is the classic case of manslaughter. His being drunk at the time does not exclude him from the category of the "reasonable man" since in our macho society it is a matter of faith that any normal man, whether drunk or sober, would shoot to kill when his manhood is thus affronted.

So, as I think it through, my decision is that Danny boy should get both voluntary and involuntary manslaughter instructions from the judge and let the jury decide how far down the scale of criminal culpability his intoxication and his passion took him.

The other aspect of this case that's interesting—putting Victor aside —is whether, since Dan's gun jammed, he could still be charged with the attempted murder of Ann. He didn't even have the ability to do the murder once the gun jammed, did he? But that argument is a nonstarter —no way he could have known the gun would fail him.

Nevertheless, I think a realistic appraisal is that in the end Dan won't fare too badly. What with all that passion, craziness and betrayal in his relationship, he probably would, in fact, be convicted of nothing more than manslaughter.

On the exam, I handle this and others like it well enough. I don't know if my answers are right but I find I have a lot to say about the issues. It should turn out okay.

When the nightmare of the two-and-a-half-day test is finally over, my mind goes blank, as if it had given away everything it knew. I walk out into the parking lot to find groups of my obsessive colleagues standing around badgering each other: "And what did you put down for this one ... and what did you put down for that one?" Who cares? I don't want to talk about it. Don't want to hear someone else had a different take on an issue than I did. I walk away.

As it turns out, the smuggest of those people out in the parking lot, the most loquacious, the most cocky, are the ones who didn't make it in the end.

The day the results are announced, I am already working at the public defender's office as a clerk (on the assumption that I'll pass the thing), and someone, wide-eyed, tells me, "They're out!" Everywhere, clerks are scurrying.

In the hallways of the courthouse where I work, it's all you hear about. Some people are leaving for home, quitting early, their heads down, because the day has gone real badly for them. These are mostly guys, and they don't cry, not until they get home, anyway. I'm dying inside because I don't know whether I made it or not. It's worse than waiting for any verdict.

I can't find the time to get over to the *Daily Journal,* the law publication in L.A., two blocks away on Spring Street. The journal posts the results in the window of its office on the day notifications go out. But I do call. You're allowed to ask for three names over the phone, so I mention mine and John Weston's (he's in Europe and I want to tell his family so they can get to him). We're both on the list: We made it. It's over. I leave the building, grinning and jiving. Outside, you can identify those who have put the bar exam behind them and those who haven't.

As a practical matter it meant that those of us who were already working somewhere as clerks could now go on to jobs as novice lawyers, while everybody else would have to float in limbo for many months or even years.

A few weeks later, in the morning, I was sworn in at the L.A. Music Center with hundreds of others.

Back at the office, they didn't waste any time. They handed me some files. "Go do prelims" came the order. Fine.

Prelims are the hearings that, in California, usually take the place of the grand jury. A Municipal Court judge, rather than the grand jurors, determines if the evidence is sufficient to warrant forcing someone ac-cused of a felony crime to face trial. Preliminary hearings are supposed to serve the function of screening out baseless charges at an early stage of the proceeding. They somewhat resemble trials, except only one side, the prosecution, calls witnesses. But the witnesses testify under oath and are cross-examined, and documents are marked and admitted just as in a trial. At least that's what prelims were in those days. Now they are just rubber stamps for the police, and no real witnesses need be called. But in the late 1960s there was no better training for a young lawyer than to be given prelim duty.

You're assigned to a prelim courtroom and every client whose case is in that court is yours. You get ten minutes to interview the client and then the hearing begins. You do the best you can with little information; sometimes the case is dismissed but more often the client is held to answer to the charges and the case is sent to Superior Court for trial. On that first afternoon, I did two prelims. It was my first work as a lawyer.

In the historic sense, it meant that now, in the courtroom, I was officially permitted to pass through the wooden barrier separating the public from the official business on the other side; that is, I was finally, literally, allowed to pass the bar.

As for John Weston, his civil libertarian viewpoint and valuable family connections take him into First Amendment law. We talk a little after law school and the bar and then drift apart, great friends who seem to have little in common anymore. I am going into the public defender's office, he is going into the lucrative business of defending freedom of expression —the freedom of pornographers, as it turns out, their inalienable right to be smutty. The career goes well, I suppose: he's now argued five times before the Supreme Court.

After a long silence, more than a decade, he calls.

He knows someone who needs help and he's not in a position to give it. His own clients are in deep trouble for, among other things, employing the services of an underage porn queen. Her name is Traci Lords and it looks as if she now needs representation, although her troubles seem trivial compared to those of her former employers.

John is principled about this: he knows that this young girl is under a lot of pressure from competing factions. Will she help the government lock these guys up because they employed her before she was legally old enough for on-screen sex? Or, if out of loyalty to her former friends, she refuses to cooperate, will she be charged with crimes, albeit petty, stemming from her lying about her age on official documents?

One reason that I come to John's mind, of course, is that he's looking for a woman lawyer to defend a woman client. Ordinarily I resent such appeals and think that gender is one of the dumbest criteria for choosing a lawyer. You choose a lawyer because he or she is good, and that's all. But once I meet Traci Lords I know John is right.

"She's the Elizabeth Taylor of the porn industry," John tells me.

I say, "Swell."

And then she shows up in the anteroom of my office on Wilshire Boulevard, this truly gorgeous eighteen-year-old kid, born sexy—with one of those Barbie Doll faces, pouty lips and a body that defies ordinary experience. She arrives with something of an attitude, not trusting me much, afraid that I might be judgmental somehow. But I am not. I want to know what she expects me to do for her.

Traci Lords, although very young, is more mature than her years and more clearheaded about who she is and what she wants than you might expect. She is certain that she wants me to keep her out of court if I can. The Justice Department is in its anti-sin mode, prosecuting the purveyors of pornography all over the country. Traci (her given name is Nora Louise Kuzma) is absolutely not going to allow herself to be the star in a traveling freak show in one state after another. She says she plans to try for a legitimate career and she just can't tolerate being used this way.

At a meeting with the U.S. Attorney, I maintain that the government is trying to exploit a kid for its own prosecutorial purposes. After many tense hours in which each side claims the moral high ground (from them, "Don't you want to stop these slime balls who are exploiting kids?" and from me, "Don't you see you're putting her life in danger and she can't be a film star in the witness protection program?"), we work out a deal.

As I point out, all the government really needs to prove is that Traci Lords was still a child when she starred in each of these sex productions. I persuade them that they don't need Traci; her mother can be the witness. She can look at stills from the movies and tell the jury how old her daughter was at each stage. It's a courageous thing for a mother to do and in testimony she acquits herself bravely and well.

It was the first and last time I ever got involved in a pornography case. I have nothing against the sex industry per se. But I don't think this kind of First Amendment lawyering is particularly ennobling. I know some people will respond to that stance with an "Oh, yeah, is defending killers better?"

I think so. Pornography is petty stuff. Yes, it is about the First Amendment and the Constitution, but where does that take you? All the way to the rights of individuals to make dirty movies.

But killers, I maintain, are really interesting. They never just spring full blown from the womb. What draws you in is the search for the solution to the puzzle: How did this happen? Where did he come from? What made him what he is? What, indeed, is he? (There's no one profile of a killer—some are true criminals, some are victims, some, and this is the scariest part, are just like you.) If you're doing your job right, you learn about family influences, opportunity in life, individual resilience in the face of deprivation, mental illness and, every once in a while, about evil.

In homicides you are learning about human nature at its most explosive. You are defending people charged with crimes that carry the harshest penalties that society will allow. And your clients—their lives on the line one way or the other—may actually be innocent, or not as guilty as the charges imply.

But the dirty-movie business? No thanks.

5

Clerking Days

The old, now-condemned Hall of Justice in L.A. stands empty these days just a few steps away from the scene of many of today's big and notorious trials at the relatively sterile Criminal Courts Building, where the Simpson trial was held, for instance. In fact, the parking lot behind the old hall became the television broadcast center for the Simpson trial. It's there I would report to work during that case—as a commentator for ABC. The lot looked like an Old West mining town, full of temporary trailers and broadcast platforms. The television folks dubbed it "Camp O. J." The 1925 building itself remained locked and darkened, and rats ran out of it into the shadows of the glamorous slum the TV people built.

In the sixties the building was never well-lighted either, but it was a wonderful place, full of commotion, confusion, camaraderie and life-and-death business, a mad place (we called it "the Palais du Justice"). It's a rectangular building with an elaborate lobby, high-coffered ceiling, long dropped chandeliers. You got up into it via creaky, whooshing old hand-operated elevators. It was always gloomy inside. A central airshaft—with grating on the bottom meant to prevent inmates from bailing out through that route—was supposed to contribute light but didn't do all that well. Philip Marlowe could have strolled in here at any moment, looking mysterious and perfect, his weary face only half-lighted in the gloom.

The building was a self-contained organism dedicated to the lawbreaking industry; it was Crime Central. The public defender's office was on the fourth floor. The district attorney was on the sixth floor, the courts were on the fourth, seventh, and eighth. On top of the building was the men's jail, and at one point even the women's jail occupied one half of one floor. It was one-stop shopping for the legal system. The morgue was in the basement.

My interview for a clerk's job with the public defender, while I still awaited the bar exam results, took place—where else?—there, at the gritty Hall of Justice.

The public defender's office had a lot going for it. The pay was good, and the training was great. If you joined a firm, as many other graduates did, it would be years before you got any really intense courtroom experience. But in the government, they throw you right into it, and you damn well better learn. I was also drawn to the mission of the PD, of course, defending the poor, the people without the resources to pay for their own defense. The public defender—like the district attorney's office— is an arm of the government. It is responsible to the county for its budget, which is the one tool politicians have for controlling it. Otherwise the PD can be, and often is, defiantly independent, a remarkable American institution that takes public funds to fight the very lawyers who call themselves "the People" as they bring charges against the indigent.

Our agency, the first public defender's office in the country, was in the process of transforming itself from the hardly noticed operation it once was into an arena for idealists—committed, fervent people. Public defenders before the mid-1960s were especially hampered by the relatively free hand the police traditionally had. Before that time there were practically no search-and-seizure restrictions, and the state police usually didn't need search warrants. A lot of the process was not formalized in writing —on either side. Private defense lawyers scribbled down a few notes on a piece of paper and slipped it into their pockets—they were called "hip-pocket lawyers" then—and they did not have a reputation for preparing their cases well. They were often very capable and very charming, it's true, but they didn't approach the defense with the intensity that the new lawyers in town in the middle and late sixties did.

Almost from the beginning of its history in the 1920s, the Los Angeles public defender's office had women on its staff of lawyers. But they were very, very few. And they tended to linger in niches. Invariably a woman lawyer would find herself working on domestic cases or others that seemed suitably maternal. But only occasionally did women find themselves on the front lines. Now the times had definitely changed and the office was eager for women who could fight like men.

So, for that initial interview, I'm in this tight little office, confronted by three men, one from the PD's office, one from the DA's office and one from the county counsel's office. Theoretically you interview for all three positions. But I tell them during the interview that I'm only interested in the public defender job; I won't go to work for the district attorney, so don't ask me any more questions in that regard, thanks. The public defender interviewer is John Moore, the number-two guy in the office. And he focuses on a few ethical questions.

It's a narrow room with grimy windows and ugly county decor: a little Formica-top table, green walls. Drab as hell. The interviewers are very businesslike, matter-of-fact civil servants. Suits. They're asking me questions about dealing with specific situations. But the answers can mostly be handled with a well-schooled attitude, an approach that demonstrates an understanding of what it means to be a defense lawyer, and I had that down reasonably well then (and soon would have it a lot better).

The right posture is, number one, everyone is entitled to a defense or the whole system breaks down, with government rolling right over people. Everyone is entitled to an advocate, someone on his side, guilty or innocent. (California was a pioneer in public defense, but now the nation as a whole was embracing the concept, partly at the forceful prompting of the U.S. Supreme Court.)

Number two, guilt is a very subjective term. A defense lawyer has to remember not to be lofty and judgmental (that's for the others).

I understood early, and had it drummed in for years during my practice, that most people accused of petty crimes are not criminals—in the sense that some people are bankers and others are Jesuits—but merely losers of one kind or another. Often they are stupid people, foolish people, deprived people, uneducated people, poverty-stricken people, immature people, or all of the above. None of the people I ran into in the first few years was anybody's idea of a worst nightmare. Most of them weren't dangerous, most of them weren't evil. They were just screwups. In fact, even society's winners—the people at the top of the heap—can get caught in the criminal law net sooner or later. We've got a zillion laws and the legislatures keep grinding out new ones. (In Santa Monica, it's illegal to have a dog leash longer than six feet.)

Personally, it does not deeply offend me if some kids steal a car. I don't want them to do it. It's wrong. It interferes with other people's property rights and causes a lot of aggravation, but it does not somehow tear at the fabric of society. I can tolerate this at some level and I can try to understand why they did it. So they got caught, so slam them for a little bit and then let them go home. Let them learn their lesson. If they don't learn their lesson, you'll slam them again next time.

But there are many levels of crime and criminals here. At one extreme, there are despicably evil people, it's true. Some lawyers cannot represent them. They are, in fact, too judgmental to be advocates for someone of whom they disapprove so strongly. I don't have that problem. As judgmental a person as I am in private life, I don't need to like clients or approve of them to defend them (I prefer to, but don't need to). I understand my role as an advocate and as a lawyer. And it gets your juices going, too, fighting the side with all the power. I never thought it was fun to root for the Yankees, remember? Where is the exhilaration in having the bigger boot and kicking somebody in the butt with it? I just don't find that morally interesting. I don't find being the schoolyard bully a great role. And most prosecutors act like the schoolyard bully.

During the job interrogation, my attitude was fine, feisty. And two days later I got my grade card and it was a ninety-two. So I was hired. (The minimum grade was eighty-six.) I called and said, "When should I report to work?" And they said, "When can you come?"

On my first day, nervous and hyper, I was dressed in the uniform of the day, white boots and a miniskirt, and a long straight blond fall. I felt like the greenest clerk on earth.

Mark Horton was my first boss, a man who had been defending the poor long before it was as respectable as it is now. He had small bright eyes and sandy hair, a little like Roddy McDowall. Horton was in charge of kindergarten (the clerks) and first grade (the newly appointed young lawyers). His way of communicating was to roll his eyes and mug. He had a silent, Socratic method of conversing. Horton would look this way and that, up and down, like a mime from the silent movies, looking up, looking down, shrugging his shoulders, wiping his face and brow. I always felt I was deaf in his presence. I didn't understand him from day one. It was like trying to conduct a dialogue with a Freudian analyst, no response. Who needs that? Give me some answers, for crying out loud. Talk, you mother. But the boys loved him. My young male colleagues adored him. It was still a very sexist world at this time, although I didn't yet know enough to characterize it that way.

If I didn't get Horton from the second I met him, I think he was equally baffled by me. I may have come on stronger than he could handle. (It took me years of therapy to realize how I often appear to people—so aggressive and unyielding—while on the inside I'm feeling like a little bird flapping my wings as hard as I can to stay in the air.) On the first day, Horton brushed me away like so much debris on the road. And what a break that turned out to be! He tossed me over to Paul Fitzgerald, an intense, garrulous man whose Irishness was accentuated by a nose broken during Golden Gloves matches and, of course, in the street fights of his youth. As a lawyer, Fitzgerald was the most eloquent sort of brawler, a man who relished the toughest cases the system could throw at him. And the system gladly did just that, putting him in charge of the "specials," the big ones.

Horton approaches Paul, his eyes rolling in what must have been frustration or despair, and says, "Paul, keep this young lady with you, will you? And show her around."

Paul seems to genuinely love the public defender's office and he's excited by the ethos of the 1960s. He's trying a case called the *People* v. *Duren*.

"Okay. We're going over to the Brunswick Building to try this case." He carries his books under his arm. He's six feet tall, maybe a little more, bowlegged, and he walks with a hunched gait. He's got a crew cut and he's wearing a white shirt with a little narrow tie. He looks so conservative, although he's one of the wildest human beings I've ever met—ready to dip into almost anything the libertarian sixties allows.

He's got this distinctive nasal voice. Later on he develops the habit of having a pocket full of quarters, three or four dollars' worth, and he rotates six of them in his hand à la Captain Queeg. He's a fascinating person. I'm enthralled by this guy at once. Crazy as a jaybird, but charming and brilliant.

As we walk to the Brunswick Building, I don't know anything about him yet except that he is, by reputation, a very skillful trial lawyer.

I avoid looking him in the eye while he talks a mile a minute. He's funny. He's knowledgeable, and he's telling me what he's doing. He's picking this jury, that's the main thing at the moment, he says, talking in the kind of streetwise way that defense lawyers in criminal law talk.

Paul is representing a guy by the name of Robert Lee Duren, charged with five separate and distinct murders, about four attempted murders, two assaults with a deadly weapon, and about ten armed robberies. Mr. Duren—Paul always uses the mister—is a black man, about thirty years old, fairly well educated and bright. He's married and has a child. Unfortunately—as Paul puts it—he has a prior felony conviction for robbery, armed robbery, for which he served a term in the penitentiary. Looks bad.

This is a death-penalty case during the period before the U.S. Supreme Court ruled unconstitutional the death-penalty laws of many states (and like all the others, California brought back a revamped version later). We're walking from the Hall of Justice down the hill to New High Street (typical of Los Angeles, there is no "Old" High Street anymore), where the Brunswick Building takes up the whole short block. Paul is hunched over in his flappy suit. He's like the Paul Newman character in *The Verdict*. He's carrying the books under his arm, his head held forward like Ichabod Crane, but lithe and sexy more than awkward. (Only I don't see the sexy then; I see the sexy later when I get to know him—and one of my girlfriends ends up going with him for a long time.)

This, Paul explains, is what they call in the office a "Pill Case," referring to the cyanide pill that drops into the bucket of sulfuric acid, giving rise to the lethal gas in the green room at San Quentin. And people are saying, "If ever there was a pill case, this is a pill case."

Two of the counts of murder that Duren is charged with involve a husband and wife, an Asian couple who ran a very small shrimp restaurant near the USC campus. He made them kneel down and then put a gun to the back of their heads and shot them. The photographs at the trial will show these hardworking people on the floor just drenched in blood.

In a couple of other robberies, he shot people but they didn't die; they lived to testify against him. In other words, there are the most sympathetic sort of eyewitnesses, survivors, for half of these robberies.

Then an additional problem with the case, as Paul puts it, is that Duren used a semiautomatic pistol. He used the same pistol for every robbery and every shooting and wore the same long leather coat each time. A semiautomatic pistol ejects a shell, so he left his calling card at the scene of each crime. When he was caught, wearing that coat, he was also carrying the gun. Ballistics people could easily tell the crimes were committed by the same gun. Even the lab at the LAPD was up to that.

Moreover, he'd confessed to the LAPD. Paul would contend later that the confession was coerced, but even if it was, this was not an innocent man. And this case was not a who-done-it. They had the right guy.

The only question—as long as the prosecution's case didn't implode through an excess of stupidity and malfeasance—was not whether Duren was going to be convicted of five or six counts of first-degree murder; that was a foregone conclusion. The question was whether he would die. Was he going to get the death penalty? (Yes and no: the jury gave it to him, the judge imposed it, and the U.S. Supreme Court invalidated it in 1972.)

As we walk, Paul is talking quickly. He starts, "The problem in this case, for us . . ."

Right away he takes me into his circle. That's the thing that was most endearing about him. I'm not a baby, I'm a public defender now. I'm part of the crowd. It's our case. It's our client. It's us.

"The problem in this case for us, with this client of ours, is that he has a very distinctive physical characteristic, a dermatological defect (Paul speaks in very explicit scientific lawyer terms). He has these big white areas on his lips. And most of the eyewitnesses remember this white defect on the lips of the perpetrator." (On top of all the other evidence!)

At no time is Paul Fitzgerald talking as if he is anything but this man's advocate. He's talking about the problems, from a lawyer's standpoint, of defending this man, achieving the best outcome, at least saving him from the gas chamber.

None of the conceptions that the public holds about these cases reflect the way the good lawyers analyze them: here's your problem, how are you going to deal with it? There are no judgments, and there's no moral jumping up and down. At trial, we like to try some showmanship, and sometimes we even obsess over all the gruesome details, but none of that is ever the central focus. You may as well be a pathologist, if that's where you're coming from. (Moreover, it's not dignified to admit that the gore interests you, even if it does.) The main job is to figure out how to represent this man given these issues.

So we get to the courtroom.

These old courtrooms are terrible for observers, with huge pillars in the middle. Later, as a lawyer, I couldn't see the jury half the time because of these pillars. Now, observing, I'm at the back. He tells me to sit in the back row and watch. And he's questioning the jurors, he's doing voir dire. I'm blown away by his poise, his gestures, his Irish eloquence—and he's trying the case against one of the town's legendary prosecutors, Roger Kelly.

Roger was one of the old-time guys, a quirky, independent prosecutor who actually wanted to dismiss the Hillside Strangler case because he believed that his lead witness, Kenneth Bianchi, was an unreliable, lying sack of manure. (I never tried a case against Roger, but I did get to know him over the years. I admired him a lot. He died of a heart attack, fifty-three years old. Roger was a bulldozer, but he was a good lawyer. He and Paul liked each other. They respected each other.)

The attorneys then were businesslike; they never got personal in court. You just tried your case. There was none of this nonsense that was so common during the Simpson case where attorneys started calling each other names and then recanted: "Oh, I love you, Mr. Cochran." I'd be tempted to say: "Screw off! I didn't ask you to love me! Don't you dare love me." Anyway, there was none of that back then.

The lawyer is there to represent a client. It is business. I mean, the prosecutors could be pushing on a case they should dismiss, they could be vicious in their cross-examination, they could hide evidence and play other games, but nothing is personal. All business. All professional. Prosecutors like Roger Kelly knew how to try a case.

In Duren, he's playing it just right. Duren is a dangerous man. Killed a whole string of people. Right? But there are no personal attacks directed at Duren as the Simpson prosecutors did with O. J. They hated Simpson. They wanted to get him. They made it personal. It's all their little egos and their little temper tantrums coming out in court.

But that's not what's going on here. This is a fight, combat of a very serious order. Initially, Kelly and Paul are questioning jurors, a tedious business for casual observers. But for me it's compelling. Why is he asking that question? What is he trying to know? It's a real clinic for me, and I'm not sucked into the more ordinary response: "Oh, my God, Duren is sitting there and I can see his white bloody lips!" No, I've got to learn this job.

Over the lunch break, we go back to the office. Paul says to me, "So what did you think of that lady in the front row with the white hair? What did you think of her? Should I keep her?"

I say, "No, I don't think so."

"Why not?"

"She looks really mean. She looks like she's afraid of the client, too, you know."

He says, "You're right. You're right. I'm not going to keep her."

And then he brings up a couple of other people. "And what do you think about the guy in the back row?"

And I say, "Well . . .," and I'm answering his questions with a lot of strong opinions. And then it occurs to me, "What are you telling this guy? This guy's a senior trial lawyer. You don't know shit. What are you telling this guy?" But then I'm saying to myself, "He asked. Right?"

Well, he did ask. And he meant it. And he agreed with me. And the next day, he says to me, "Kid, I'll tell you this right now. You are a natural." Bingo.

Now if Mark Horton had given me that kind of feedback maybe I'd go and sit in his office and talk football with him, but I wasn't hearing a thing from Horton. Paul Fitzgerald knew more about me in those two days when I was observing him in trial and gabbing about his case than Mark Horton was ever going to know, with his little Socratic games in the office.

So I no longer cared what happened in Horton's kindergarten.

A clerk's job is to organize the paperwork for the lawyers, conduct initial interviews with prisoners in the tank—a dimly lighted, huge jail cell a few steps from the courtroom—to see who qualifies for court-appointed counsel, who can post bail and the like. I interviewed most of the clients on their bail: "Can you make bail? How much? Do you work?" Some of the time, the cops had simply brought in the wrong person. A few of the people in the tank were certifiable and needed hospitalization more than they needed arraignment. The crimes were, on the whole, less serious in those days—a lot of burglary, some bookmaking. The great explosion of drug-related violence was still only the whispered sound of a lit fuse.

In large measure, the clerk is learning on the run, getting a head start on nuts and bolts lawyering for when the day comes. Around the edges I'm trying to read the law books. Whenever there is a lull in the action, I'm reading cases and taking notes and making up cards that will serve as a quick reference later. But I do a lot of that at night and on the weekends, too.

I'm learning the penal code. I'm dropping in on Paul's cases whenever I can and I interrogate him later—"What was that about?" or sometimes just "God, you were great." And I'm reading the advance sheets, automatically. The advance sheets are the state appellate case decisions that come down every week in the form of a paperbound volume about the size of *Webster's Collegiate Dictionary*. So every week there's a thick new book of decisions to read. In effect it's intense continuing education. By staying up on the law, I am, in fact, keeping a step ahead of a lot of the judges and some of the prosecutors.

It's hard to realize how much learning—just in basic material—is required after law school. In school, we studied criminal procedure, including the expanding area of search-and-seizure law, and the constitutional prohibitions against coerced confessions and forced testimony. We had a course in evidence. We learned the fundamental evidentiary rules. They're the same basic rules of evidence derived from English common law that most states and the federal courts adopted. Basically, the California Evidence Code's definitions of such things as what constituted admissible evidence, and the hearsay rule and exceptions to it, fit the general pattern.

But in law school in those days, they didn't teach the nuts-and-bolts stuff you needed to actually practice criminal law. There was no course called Grand Theft Auto 101, for instance. To learn what kinds of facts have to be proven in court to nail someone for a crime, you have to hit the books yourself.

So right now, as a clerk learning as fast as I can, I have to dig into exactly that sort of material. Ah, let's see: Grand Theft Auto? You need a "taking" of a vehicle and an intention to permanently deprive the owner of his property. If the defendant is just "borrowing" (without the owner's permission) to go for a ride, it's only a violation of the vehicle code, called "joyriding, 10851." Rarely is someone caught in the act of stealing a car. Most car thieves get caught while riding around in the booty. It helps, from the prosecution standpoint, if the defendant is, in fact, driving the stolen car at the time he's arrested. But the prosecutor also has to show that the driver knows it was stolen. Hot wires dangling from the ignition are usually a pretty definitive clue.

But the learning is in my spare time. I am working my tail off, mostly. This is assembly-line justice, necessarily. I walk into the tank and I'm surrounded by all these guys, 110 of them in a place that reeks to high heaven.

Since the court I'm working in is a first stop in the assembly line, most of the men are recent arrestees who have been held in police department custody before being brought to the courthouse. Downtown L.A. is within the jurisdiction of the Los Angeles Police Department, a city agency. The court personnel call these men caught by the city police "LAPD fish." Those who remain incarcerated after the court appearance shift over and become the property of the Los Angeles County Sheriff's office, which operates the county jail system.

The men are not wearing much in the way of clothes, sometimes just pants, sometimes they're naked (only the county jail issues uniforms). Occasionally, there's a white-collar businessman, his face a mask of mortification. But mostly they are poor, and they're very dirty. The cell is dark and musty like a cave. I can't quite make out the features of all these men. It crosses my mind that this is disgusting but, aesthetics aside, these are my clients. I'm thinking, Please, guys, don't be peeing when I walk in. If no one's on the toilet we can pretend I'm not a woman and get through this thing.

There is joking and commotion. "You have to be quiet or we won't be able to do this!" I yell. Sometimes, in desperation, "Shut the hell up, you guys, please!"

We weren't dealing with the Crips and the Bloods then—they never shut up. It is 1969, and if I manage to be pleasant and respectful (in a loud sort of way), the inmates always seem to listen in a civilized, intent manner.

They get their rights en masse. I give the same fifteen-minute rap every day. I say, "Okay, I'm Leslie Abramson and I'm with the public defender's office and you're all charged with a felony. I have to tell you what your rights are: You have the right to have an attorney represent you. If you don't have the money to hire a private lawyer an attorney will be appointed by the court to represent you. Today you're going to be told what the charges are against you. The judge is going to ask you how you want to plead. Unless there is something very unusual about your case that I don't know about you're going to plead not guilty. A date will be selected for your preliminary hearing and we will be talking to the judge about bail. I should also tell you do not talk with anyone but your lawyer about your case. That includes the police, if they haven't already talked to you. It also includes the other inmates at the jail. The jail is full of informants, snitches, rats who will try to beat their cases by making yours. Unless you get out on bail your next court appearance, the preliminary hearing, will be within ten days." There's more, but I consider it lucky if they understand that much.

This pitch, by the way, is given inside the tank without any bars or doors separating me from the arraignees. Once in a while a new bailiff throws me a "You're not really going in there" look as I head for the tank. But despite what I might look like, I'm not identifying with other girls. I'm not demure. I think of my intellectual self as 80 percent gender-neutral. And, very quickly, I am comfortable in the tank, grow to like the clients. These guys need help. And I believe that they, at the outset, can tell I want to help them.

The clerking job is only partly practicing law; it's also social work. I have to make a quick assessment about who these people are. Many of them don't have a clue about what's going on. They're not sure why they are there or what's going to come next. They are pretty much helpless in this scary, Dickensian system. There is also the issue of trust. Most of the black defendants never had a white person stand up for them before.

In those early days as a clerk, I believed that what I was doing was important—and still do.

I was at the very beginning of a career in the PD's office but Paul Fitzgerald's days were about to end. It was the Manson case that did it. I was in the courtroom the day the first defendants were brought in for arraignment. I stood back against the wall of the crowded courtroom as the young women who did the killing were herded in, like the witches of Salem, sickly and pasty and surrounded by an aura of evil. They were acting inappropriately, laughing and smiling and carrying on, as they would throughout their trial. I had nothing to do with this, I was just watching. I was assigned there. But I wouldn't have left anyway.

The place is always full of hustle and bustle and confusion but this was a circus, the press and the public cheek by jowl and the whacko defendants standing before them all.

Even with the little knowledge I had then, I knew that it was more than it seemed to be, that this Manson guy had not only created the circumstances that led to horrific murders but had also, effectively, deprived these girls of their lives. It took a long, long time for the girls to deprogram after the seductive brainwashing of that vicious, wild-eyed man. And they never got much help with it from the authorities. They just deprogrammed themselves in prison, but, boy, they were loyal to Manson for a long time.

Charlie Manson, to me, was the most extreme and repugnant extension of the craziness you saw often during this period. (I remember, back in law school, some naked, bummed-out lunatics showing up one day to dance on the lawn—what are these people?) Clearly, we had a situation where there were too many drugs in the hands of ignorant lowlifes and others who were just too vulnerable. That's why I always drew lines—I'd used drugs from time to time, but I wasn't about to come out with a manifesto that everybody should drop acid. There were a lot of sick chickens diving headfirst into mind-altering substances at the end of the sixties, and if you take the very worst of that scene—communes where middle-class kids and lifelong criminals sang the song of freedom and acid—it might just turn into this kind of nightmare. Manson exploited his whole group of young people. And he did it easily. I could understand how a charismatic druggie could brainwash people with dope. Easily.

•

Over the years, I and many other interested observers would learn a lot more about the malleable mind. If you think about the Patty Hearst kidnapping case, which was a few years after the Manson murders, you begin to understand the true nature of mind alteration. You saw this rich kid become emotionally bound to her tormentors. And, later still, as I worked with abused women and children, I understood how brutal domination can lead people into acts of violence. Even now, I have empathy for the Manson girls, no matter how scary they seemed at the time. I see that Charlie Manson destroyed them. And they connived in it, destroying what was left of themselves. Now they've come back to sanity, in prison—for all the good it will do them.

I always knew at the time it was happening, too, that during decades in prison as middle age and then old age closed in, the most horrible moments that these "girls" would experience would be when they realized what they had done not only to others, but also to themselves.

I do believe in rehabilitation, particularly in a situation where, in an aberrant and temporary period of life, one is lured into an abnormal, violent act. I had no doubt that most of the Manson people would come to a point where they would want to erase the scar.

This is, in fact, what's happening to Leslie Van Houten and to Susan Atkins and some of the others. Nevertheless, they'll be locked up forever because of the notoriety of that case. They did terrible things, but many other people have done equally horrible things, gone through the system in a more ordinary, unspectacular way and ultimately been paroled back into the world of the living again. These women never will because everyone was watching.

Paul Fitzgerald fell into it. He was fascinated by that case and couldn't let it go. I can see now that there is a brand of criminal lawyer (I do not include myself) who finds these stark and hideous things totally fascinating. I try to understand this aspect of human nature, it's true, and, professionally, I am attracted to the challenge, but the cases don't grip me as powerfully as they do some others in the lawyer business. Evil is evil. It is not romantic. It is not fun.

Paul, in a legitimate sense, became the head of the Manson family for a while. He was the senior member of the defense team and everybody looked to him for answers. There was a point when some of us thought he was a little drunk with the power of it.

Paul's entry into the case came at a midstage, just as the jury trials were about to get under way. Susan Atkins had already testified in front of the grand jury as to how the killings took place. Manson was brought down from Inyo County, where he had been jailed on charges—regarding the burning of government property—that were overwhelmed by these.

He wore a tattered buckskin outfit and moccasins; his beard was full. In the courtroom, now Department 100, it was standing room only. Literally. There were no people sitting. It was a mob. It reminds Paul, when he thinks back on it now, of the crush around Oswald after the Kennedy shooting. When Manson came in, it also reminds Paul—in what he realizes is a warped image—of a self-selected Christ being brought up before a bewildered Pontius Pilate. Even Paul had never seen anything like this in court before. But, as always, he was in his element. This was his court, after all.

At that moment I don't know how many people on earth were real worried about whether or not Charlie Manson and his murderous friends were going to get a fair trial, but Paul was working on it full-time. The publicity surrounding the case was going to militate against the defendants. A definite problem. The prejudice against the hippie culture would also. The fact that Manson was both a counterculture figure and a decided bigot inclined toward race war—"helter-skelter"—was a double whammy of prejudice.

Paul swung into action, representing each one of the cult members—an obvious conflict of interest, but he could persist in doing it until he, in the name of the PD's office, formally declared that the conflict existed. He was determined to buy time, create a delay of several days until capable lawyers could be appointed to take his place. This was his court. He could make it work for the defense. No one was going to steamroll him.

"They're not going to fuck with me," Paul says to himself and anybody else. "We're going to do this thing right." For a week, he puts the whole crazy event in a holding pattern by skillful use of the court calendar. He knew that each of the defendants was going to get a much better crack at obtaining a good lawyer if enough time elapsed.

Paul despised most—not all, but most—of the lawyers that judges appointed when the PD had to "conflict out." He saw them as the "old boys' " cronies and hacks. But if he could slow this thing down for a few days, that would do it. That would allow top defense lawyers to show their interest and maneuver in.

Paul stands up and says, "Your Honor, Mr. Manson is qualified to obtain the services of the public defender. The public defender should be appointed. We'll determine whether there are other people in this multicount indictment that are going to appear in front of Your Honor. We want to put this case over until such time that it's appropriate to declare a conflict."

He takes each of the Manson group individually and does exactly the same thing, putting them over that week, letting the dust settle, knowing that the public defender is only going to retain one of these people in the end. Susan Atkins gets two lawyers early, Leslie Van Houten will pick up a lawyer. (His name, by the way, is Ira Reiner, a man who will later in his career switch over to the prosecutorial side and serve as the county district attorney.)

Manson, ultimately, will go "pro per," defending himself.

Paul ends up with Patricia Krenwinkel, the daughter of a suburban insurance agent. He takes her on because he wants to make sure he stays part of this huge, tumultuous case. But it turns out that even handling that one client poses a conflict for the public defender's office since some of the witnesses in this trial are already being defended by the office in other matters. Rather than be forced to abandon this client to whose cause he was committed, Paul quits the office and enters private practice. In a way Patricia Krenwinkel was his ticket out. Paul had always called county service the long gray life. This case, red with blood and black with evil, was anything but gray. And Paul followed it into a new life.

Division 30, the scene where the Manson circus began, was also the setting for one of the most bizarre incidents of my clerking days. The light was particularly variable and strange in that courtroom. Sometimes you couldn't see things because the sunlight would be streaming in, blinding you. More often everything was indistinct because of the gloom. It was like the feeling a schoolchild has, as the classroom with its big institutional windows blinks from brightness to darkness and back again. Mood changes as rapidly as the light does. In Division 30, it made all the difference in the world if you were in court on a rainy day versus a sunny day.

It was there that we kept herding in the custody defendants every morning for arraignment or dismissal. We processed over one hundred people a day. They were always called—by the judges, the lawyers, the clerks—"the bodies."

"All right, bring in the bodies. Are the bodies ready?"

Occasionally, there were inmates brought in with health problems, often in wheelchairs. The well and the sick together are given their rights all at once (they've all heard it before from people like me back in the tank), and their lawyers stand up and respond with not-guilty pleas for everybody.

The defendants never have to say anything during an arraignment. Their lawyer says it all for them. "Waive reading of rights, Your Honor," "Enter a plea of not guilty," "Ask that the preliminary hearing be set on such and such a date." One right after the other.

Comes the day when the bailiffs bring in a man in a reclining wheel-chair. He's wheeled to the front of the pack of about fifty, off to the corner.

It isn't a day with light streaming in. Hard to see well. But I conclude he looks pretty peculiar when they first bring him in. I don't know why we're arraigning somebody who seems to be in such bad physical condition. He can't possibly know what's going on.

A few minutes after the mass pleading, one of the public defenders says he wants the man in the wheelchair returned because he suspects this one actually needs some personal attention, that he should, at a minimum, check with the guy to see if he's going to be healthy enough to go through a preliminary hearing on the date scheduled.

This guy hasn't just been arrested. As I recall it, they had tried to arraign him before but couldn't get him out of the jail ward of the hospital because he was too sick.

So the PD has the marshal bring the guy back in.

He's returned. He's in exactly the same position. He hasn't moved a muscle since his exit. The public defender goes over to him and tries to talk to him, and he's not giving him any answers. And then the lawyer touches him and the guy is stone cold. The guy is cold! This is probably two o'clock in the afternoon. The man in the wheelchair had probably boarded a bus at six that morning and then been in a holding area for hours.

The public defender says, "Judge, I don't think this client's with us anymore." And the judge says, "Well, that's a first. We've arraigned a dead man."

And I remember thinking, how would you know that was a first? There's so little personalized service going on here. Half of these guys could be dead given that they don't say anything or do anything and they have no idea what's going on, by and large.

As for my role in this foolishness, I never had talked to this man because after he arrived at court from the hospital he was kept apart from the rest in the tank. If any of us had tried to talk to him that morning we might have noticed he was dead, or we might not have, in the usual commotion. But the weird thing is that the sheriff and the marshal, who actually had physical contact with him, didn't notice. Now I don't think he croaked in the ten minutes between appearance one and appearance two. He was cold. He was a stiff.

At the moment all this is becoming apparent, I'm upset. I don't get totally enraged but I just think, We're not paying enough attention to these people if we could arraign a dead man, if we don't even notice that one of our clients has already gone to his reward.

After this wheelchair-bound man opts out, one of the lawyers says, "Does this mean we should withdraw the plea of not guilty?" And the judge says, "Yeah, I think we better do that. I'm inclined to dismiss the case. Is there any objection from the People?"

Joking. I suppose it happens in all the grimmest lines of work. But the fact is, at this preliminary stage of the process, we never truly knew any of them, and that ignorance is fertile ground for some heartless humor.

For the overburdened public defenders the running joke was that a death certificate was one of the best ways to get rid of a case. Your client's dead: "Phew, one less on my caseload." You file the death certificate with the court as fast as you can, and the case gets dismissed. "Hurray! I've won again!"

6

Judges and Cops

In my first days, after clerking, some preconceptions were shattered fast. One was that judges are wise and capable—how else do they become judges? They're put in charge, right? They're powerful. At a minimum, I assumed, they knew the law.

But from day one of doing preliminary hearings, I realized that an astonishing number of the Municipal Court judges I encountered (in L.A., the Municipal Court holds the preliminary hearings before Superior Court takes over with a trial) were remarkably stupid, totally crazy or deplorably lazy. If the attorneys don't know the law any better than the judges, as sometimes happens, the ship is completely adrift.

Of the eight or nine judges assigned to preliminary hearings when I began, one was clearly bright: Bonnie Lee Martin, who later became a Superior Court judge. A few were probably sane. The rest were a joke.

Some of the rules of evidence are complicated. Judges have to be able to concentrate to figure them out and keep a hearing moving along in a legal and just fashion. But the hearsay rule, to take just one example, was something that gave this bunch of judges fits.

A hearsay statement is any statement made outside of the court proceeding, and it is usually not admissible as evidence because it can't be challenged by cross-examination on the stand. Its reliability can't be tested, except if the person who actually said it shows up to testify.

Let's say that you're charged with burglary. A witness has told the police that he saw you at the victim's house. That witness is not in court, however. So the cop, according to the hearsay rule, is not allowed to testify to what the witness said. If the witness subsequently comes to court, takes the stand and says, "I saw him outside the victim's house," that's fine, because on cross, an attorney can doggedly attempt to find out whether the witness is really sure it was you, whether the witness had an opportunity to really see the person outside the house, or whether there might be some bias or other motivation in this instance to make a false identification.

There are a few major exceptions to the rule that will allow a hearsay statement in, even in the absence of the person who said it. If the witness told the police out of court that he saw you outside the victim's house but then the witness comes into court and says, "No, I didn't see him," he can be challenged with the original out-of-court statement. It's still hearsay, but now it's being employed not as an assertion of fact but as one more way of testing for credibility. So the prosecution can say, "Didn't you tell the officer that you did see the defendant at the victim's house?"

It makes sense, on the surface, because it is playing out in its entirety openly in court and the jurors can come to their own conclusions when all is said and done. For the attorney in pitched battle, though, it is a minefield. If the witness on the stand denies ever making the statement out of court, that means it's now actually being introduced in court through the denial, and the jury can consider it as evidence that, yep, the defendant might have been at that house (and the witness is just denying it now).

It takes a good judge to keep the contest clean.

Here's an exception to the rule that turns out to be particularly nettlesome. If someone says something accusatory directly to you—"I saw you kill the victim"—the expected response, if you're innocent, is a denial right there on the spot. The same would be true if you overheard someone say it to someone else about you. But if you don't respond with a denial, that's considered an "adoptive admission" on your part. And now because of your presumed silent admission, that hearsay statement can come in against you even though that witness is not actually in court.

Like many other aspects of the rules of evidence, this exception to the hearsay rule is based on an old-fashioned and mainly fictitious view of human nature, in this case, that no one would fail to deny a false accusation. But there are lots of situations where even an innocent person would say nothing. What if your accuser is another inmate in the jail, and you've been warned by your lawyer to say nothing to anyone? What if you believe someone else in the room is the guilty party but you're afraid to speak out?

In any event, it's supposed to be a very narrowly defined exception. It's supposed to require an actual accusation and conduct on your part that demonstrates agreement with the statement.

But in the real world, judges often ruled that *any* statement made by anybody in the presence of a defendant is admissible against him without proof that he even heard, let alone agreed with it. All of these goofy judges were ignoring a core requirement of the exception, making up a new rule that just seemed to suit them.

It suited the prosecution well, too, especially when they'd dropped the ball and forgotten to subpoena a necessary witness. Then, likely as not, they'd use a cop to testify to the statement of the witness who should be in court but isn't.

At which point, I—as would any defense lawyer who isn't comatose at the time—have to jump in and say, "Your Honor, I object. Hearsay." And, invariably, the judge turns to the police officer and says, "Now you say Mr. Doe was in the police car right next to you and the witness when she made this statement?"

"Yes."

"Overruled."

Incredible. And that was only one of the many, many quirky aspects of practicing law before this disappointing group. Once in a while you'd get a case kicked out based on a judge's inclination to make up rules. But most of the time it was just an Alice-in-Wonderland experience.

One of the most notorious cuckoos of the lot was a judge named Noelle Cannon who, as it happens, liked me a lot from the very beginning.

On my second day as a lawyer, I'm doing a prelim in front of Judge Cannon, a petite woman, perhaps in her late thirties, with platinum-blond short hair, fastidiously made up and manicured, bejeweled, beautifully dressed under the robe. Her chambers are pink. The decor is personally chosen, none of the county-issued junk. Her miniature poodle is in chambers during all proceedings. The prosecutor in this case—it is about an assault, a stabbing—is a whiny woman who never should have been a prosecutor. This sad-sack lawyer asks the victim of the stabbing to describe where he was injured. He tells her he was stabbed in the stomach.

"I object, Your Honor." This is a pretty technical objection on my part—and a little ridiculous. The witness means he was stabbed in the abdomen, not the stomach, because, in a literal sense, he can't know about his stomach—it's an internal organ, out of sight. You cannot testify to something that's beyond your personal knowledge.

I am a baby lawyer at this point, learning. And the way you learn, before you fully understand the strategic use of objections, is to object on every conceivable theory; you become extremely familiar with the rules that way. Of course, it's a terrible nuisance for the prosecutor. But this one was more than annoyed; she just didn't get it.

I object, and the judge sees the point and sustains. The DA, rather than rephrase the question or obtain the information some other way, asks the same question again. The same answer. I object. The judge sustains.

Three times this happens. Judge Cannon is exasperated. She slams a book down on the bench and calls a recess. The prosecutor bursts into tears. This is the DA in the case! Crying. The judge is disgusted, strides into her chambers—with its French Regency chairs and floral prints and china teapot—and calls me in. She is tough and angry despite the frilly surroundings she loves. "I can't stand these silly little girls that the district attorney's office sends in," she says. "They just don't train them in evidence."

I say, "I was just making a 'beyond personal knowledge' . . ."

"I know exactly what you were doing, but she doesn't understand that you can see an abdomen but not a stomach."

So she calls the prosecutor in. Still weeping. The judge says, "Have you ever heard of the personal knowledge rule?"

"The what?"

"The personal knowledge rule. The stomach is not within your personal knowledge. You can't see it. That's why I was sustaining her objections." The prosecutor is vacant. Helpless.

I know the episode comes across nasty. But, look, I'm representing my guy. It's not for me to help the DA's office if their people aren't up to it. And this girl is such a miserable lawyer that we all benefit here, because what she is actually learning is that she doesn't belong in a courtroom. She doesn't know what she is doing, a twit who's an obstacle in the proceedings. For goodness' sake, she's got this guy's medical records. There are all sorts of ways she could have established where he was stabbed.

Noelle Cannon was always particularly offended by women she regarded as incompetent because, I think, she believed it reflected on her. But my tormenting of this poor young woman lawyer evidently endeared me to Judge Cannon as someone who could handle herself. I became her pet.

So far as I know, I didn't do anything special to encourage her beyond being the hardass in court I thought I should be. But she befriended me, often inappropriately. She'd go into chambers and invite me in for tea. We'd sit there and chat while I'd listen to her crazy rap.

I'd walk in for some reason, maybe to give a message to the public defender who was there, or to check something on one of my upcoming cases, or on a case I had already done. Usually, just a few people would be there—one or two DAs, one public defender, a sparse audience, a clerk and some other court staff. She'd look over at me, nod her head and say, "Court's in recess," beckoning to me as she left the bench. Sometimes she'd say, "Got a minute?" And I'd apologize quietly to the people in the room because my mere entrance had brought the proceedings to a halt, "Sorry about this." And I'd follow her back to chambers.

I can't say no.

I settle into a regal guest chair. She has a pot of hot tea on her desk and a china teacup and she's got little things of sugar. The tea setup is sitting right there on her desk. (She has a hot pot to brew water and she makes the tea herself or has a clerk make it, even though you're not supposed to use clerks that way.) And she never asks me anything. It is, essentially, a one-way dialogue. I am a prisoner, watching my step to keep her on my side. She launches into a tirade, as is her habit, against a member of the police.

"I'm going to have an officer thrown off the police department," she tells me.

"Really, Judge. What happened?"

"He had the effrontery to try to give me a ticket and was rude and disrespectful."

She tells me some story about how she had been shopping somewhere and she was driving home in her car and she got pulled over by an officer who was exceedingly surly and even after she told him who she was, she says, "He had the effrontery to lecture me—me!—on the vehicle code. And I've written a letter to the chief of police. . . ." And she's just off the wall about the impudence of this cop.

In court, her favorite sport is catching a cop in a lie. Particularly after this incident with the cop who was rude to her.

•

I'm in her court doing prelims. It's a drug case, as I recall, and there's this young cop on the stand and he's into his young-cop bravado act, a total asshole, defensive in his testimony and telling one of these fairly typical, unbelievable search stories. In the middle of his testimony she looks at him and says, "Get off the witness stand."

"Excuse me?"

"We're not hearing any more testimony from you. You are a liar. Get off the witness stand."

Bam! Case dismissed! No one says a word. I, of course, would like to credit my wonderful cross-examination. But that isn't it. This cop is no worse than a million others. It must be something about his demeanor. Maybe he resembles the cop who gave her a hard time.

Judge Cannon storms toward chambers, beckoning me with her finger, me alone, which is really improper. (The DA is supposed to be included.) "That liar! That little monster! That beast! How do they train these people?"

And I say, "Yeah, he sure was telling a story."

The DA's sitting out in the courtroom fuming.

Eventually, she calls him in and tells him he should be ashamed of himself for putting such an officer on the stand. She's gone off into never-never land, uncontrollably whacko, in light of the fact that the cop was not so far out-of-bounds.

She is ranting and the DA doesn't say anything. We walk out of there together. He turns to me. "She's just crazy, you know that?" I point out that she's an equal-opportunity nut, often doing harm to both sides.

My client, of course, is delighted by the nuthouse turn of events and I say, "You got lucky. That's all."

I learned to stay out of Judge Cannon's court except when I absolutely had to be there. Years later she was removed from the bench by the State Commission on Judicial Performance, and none of us were surprised.

Now Leland Geiler was a nut of a different species, a sex-obsessed man with way too much authority for anybody's good.

Earlier in his career Judge Geiler had been on the vice squad as a cop, an assignment that made about as much sense as hiring a pyromaniac for the fire department. He was jowly, with thinning hair, and fat, his stomach sticking out of his baggy suit. I think he was now in his forties. Judge Geiler had an absolute talent for bad rulings, and that made him odious enough. But the worst time I ever had with him centered on Thanksgiving festivities. It was just before the holiday break and the deputy sheriffs who were the bailiffs in the prelim courts produced, as was their custom, a turkey dinner for the people who worked in the courts—the lawyers, the bailiffs, the judges, everybody.

I'm invited back to this kitchen-type room behind Division 30. There are two tables and Judge Geiler's at one of them. He calls me over. People are coming and going and the judge is laughing mightily as he recounts some of his days in vice, particularly the time they arrested "faggots fucking the ponies in Elysian Park." I'm sure he's told this story many times and now he's telling it mainly for my benefit, and I am having a terrible time tolerating it.

The time of the park incident, I believe, is in the fifties, when there still were some wild ponies living there, and Leland and his merry band of vice cops go to the park and "catch the faggots up there fucking the ponies—preeverts, preeverts—and we'd round them all up and those faggots would go back down to the park as soon as we set them free and every time they'd be doing it again."

He just can't get over how funny this is. And the bailiffs are all dutifully laughing, too. He also tells stories about prostitutes he's busted. Equally hilarious.

One of the sheriffs evidently catches on that I am very uncomfortable with this guy and his creepy stories, and the sheriff says, with the required deference, "Gee, Judge, I think you'd better get back. You know, your session is going to start soon." And he says to me, "Don't you still have an afternoon calendar in 30?" And I say, "Yeah."

Geiler leaves first, and this sheriff comes over to me and says, "Sick bastard, ain't he?"

And I say, "Does he do this often?"

"We've all heard these stories many times," he says, confirming what I believed. "That is a very sick guy. He shouldn't have been telling those stories in front of you."

And I'm wondering, How do these lunatics become judges? How do they pick them? Because he was a cop? Because he was a vice sergeant? That's a qualification to become a judge? This is a demented human being.

Over time, he, like Noelle Cannon, is kicked off the bench after a disciplinary hearing. I testified against him. It's a long time ago but I believe I had something to say about the remarks he liked to make to me about my skirts. "Bend over and we'll get a better view" was more or less typical. But he should have been thrown off even if he wasn't a dirty-minded man. He was, more important, intemperate on the bench, cruel and unfair.

Later, as I moved away from this preliminary panel of judges, I ran into judges whom I could respect enormously. Judge Tom Fredericks, for instance, was a saint, a fair and candid man. And then there was an extraordinarily conservative judge who was somebody I could look up to, even if he was the scariest-looking judge on the bench with a reputation for arbitrary, albeit creative uses of the law. (A rumor has it that he once sentenced someone to death *after* the death-penalty law had been struck down as unconstitutional.)

Judge Julius Leetham was a terror to defendants. He was undoubtedly the harshest sentencing judge of his era. Pale with sunken cheeks, a grim reaper if ever there was one, Judge Leetham could throw a young person away forever and not bat an eye. Normally, I detest people like that. But I loved this guy, primarily because he could cut through all the crap, all the pomposity. He was extremely funny on the bench, too, sounded a little like W. C. Fields: "Well, Counsel, what little treat of grim and ghastly crime crosses the floor of this courtroom this morning?" That sort of thing. Got to me every time.

He was flowery in his solicitude. "Mr. Chavez, sir." (Mr. Chavez is a glue-sniffing, brain-blown nineteen-year-old.) "Mr. Chavez, sir, thank you for gracing our courtroom."

Most lawyers I knew were terrified of Judge Leetham. He was hard, it's true, but he was more or less under control depending on what the case required, and he had a fine, crisp mind. What they didn't understand was that as tough and arbitrary as he could be, there was a strong, admirable strain of morality there that he disguised as pragmatism: "Well, this case is just going to take up too much time," he'd say when he thought the prosecution was being vindictive and excessive in its charges, "Let's work out a disposition." And he would break the DA's arm to accomplish that, which none of the other judges ever had the guts to do.

Judge Leetham was driven to extremes by certain kinds of cases, crimes of violence and drugs in particular. You just knew he was going to be outrageously severe if you took them to him. So you had to get him removed, if you could. In California (unlike in federal court) you get one chance per case to remove the assigned judge. It's called an affidavit of prejudice but you don't have to actually prove prejudice. It's like the peremptory challenges you can use to remove jurors you don't want to have on your case. I'd go in there and I'd affidavit Leetham.

"Now, Judge, I'm about to file one of these nasty papers because, you know, this is not the kind of case that you should hear."

And he'd say, "A very astute observation. A fine lawyer knows when to, shall we say, proceed elsewhere."

On the other hand, there were certain cases where he'd actually be a better, fairer judge than any other in the courthouse. He wasn't impressed with car thefts or nonviolent burglaries, in light of what else was out there, even if the prosecutors might be all worked up. Because we understood each other, Judge Leetham and I had a fine, long working relationship.

A few years later, when I am in private practice following seven years as a public defender, Judge Leetham handles a major case of mine involving the Weather Underground. It was a bombing case that came to me when I was already some months into private practice. I represented a woman named Judy Bissell. She had been married to a guy who was related to the Bissell vacuum cleaner family. She was an activist at the University of Washington in Seattle and, along with her husband, had planted a bomb on the porch of a military office on campus. The bomb went off but didn't hurt anybody. The incident drove her underground and into the shelter of the Weathermen.

The Weather Underground had an aboveground support group called the Prairie Fire Organizing Committee that was conspiring with the fugitives all over the place but the FBI could never get the drop on them.

Judy and her friends had been underground for seven or eight years. Their underground cell consisted of Judy; a friend, Leslie Mullins, the daughter of an army colonel; an older guy who was their guru (Clayton Van Lydegraf); a gentle-seeming guy named Mark Perry; and another young man I remember as being extremely nervous, intense and thoroughly lacking in social skills. There were five of them, along with two FBI agents who had infiltrated their cell two and a half years before and actually lived with them. Nothing happened until—at the instigation of the FBI, some believed—the group, one Sunday at 3:00 A.M., planted a bomb under the empty offices of a notorious right-wing, racist, homophobic California state senator. The whole operation had been plotted over late-night dinners at Cantor's twenty-four-hour Jewish deli on Fairfax Avenue.

The FBI members of their group had, of course, made sure that the location was thoroughly staked out. The cell was rolled up, their cache of dynamite found and seized. It was sitting in a dilapidated garage in a residential neighborhood. (For people who professed solidarity with poor people of color the fact that it never occurred to them that their explosives could accidentally take out a substantial number of brown babies disturbed me.) Even they figured out that they had been set up. Four young people and the old guru were in jail by the time I was hired by Judy's brother, Daniel, a lawyer from New York.

The case progressed slowly. I was in front of Judge Leetham's court for about eighteen months filing a variety of motions, many of which he granted in our favor. Somewhere along the way, I felt he got to know these clients. Impotent political plotters did not seem to push his buttons. I suspected that he saw our clients as a bunch of wrongheaded but once promising kids who had been led astray and brainwashed by an aging megalomaniac—just like the members of many of the other cults that flourished in America then. A true-enough observation: When I first met these people it was like talking to prisoners of war emerging from long isolation. They were twisted by their cultish life. As bright as they were, they had simplistic and paranoid ideas about the world—that's what you get from spending too many hours reading Mao's *Little Red Book*. (The image of those two rigid little FBI agents meeting at Cantor's deli to imbibe Mao's wisdom along with the chopped-liver sandwiches struck me as really funny.)

We on the defense came to believe that—given Leetham's seemingly benign view—we could do something that was outrageous on its face, plead them guilty to everything and still win. Much to the shock of the prosecutor who had no idea what was going on, we waltzed into court one day and pled them guilty straight up, as we say. No plea bargain whatsoever. The clients trusted us and were willing to go with our intuition, our faith and our knowledge of Judge Leetham. They took a chance on "Julius the Just," a nickname some attorneys used sarcastically, but the fact is he could be exactly that. He did give a totally fair low-term sentence to these people, which made the prosecutors crazy. And off the defendants went to prison for a couple of years.

Judy still had to face the music in Seattle after serving her California prison sentence. So her friend, Leslie, got out first. I picked her up when she was released. She wanted to settle in L.A, now that her notoriety as a bomber was fading. She stayed with me for a couple of days, and, as it happened, my toaster oven was on the fritz. She said, "Oh, I can fix it. I'm very good with electrical circuitry."

I said, "Right. We know that."

And then I said, "Okay. Fix the thing."

•

During my training years as a public defender, the cops proved to be just as astonishing and disgraceful as the judges, in their way. It wasn't just their lying—it was the degree of it that got to me. As a young lawyer, I just wasn't expecting it. The cops, many of them, lie to the point of self-destruction.

It stands to reason that an arrest should not hold up if the officers responsible for the arrest and investigation, under oath, fail to tell the truth about what they did and what they learned. But that happened as a matter of routine. Mostly they'd lie in small ways—about how they spotted the evidence, for instance—not in large, implausible ways as we saw alleged in the "conspiracy" against O. J. Simpson.

Cops' lies were the leitmotif of all my early years. And in the kind of preliminary hearings I worked then, the police were even more significant on the stand than they were in complicated, full-fledged trials. In some cases—ones involving dope particularly—the cops are the only witnesses. And I did a huge number of dope cases in those early years.

Cop credibility *was* the case a lot of the time. And I was just left reeling by the amount of lying, the pettiness of lying, the consistency of lying—the nickel-and-dimeness of it all.

Part of this pathological behavior was just bullheaded resistance. The cops had a deep, angry philosophical disagreement with the evolving search-and-seizure laws. They wanted to roust people, follow their own instincts (and their prejudices); they didn't want to be fettered by rules that tried to make this a fairer, less brutal, more civilized society. And they were furious that in those days the laws, evolving constantly, were getting better.

The Warren Court kept coming down with rulings that restricted the cops' right to search people on whim, instinct or malice. The Court had a very grave concern about the potential for violating people's privacy rights. The rulings addressed practical, mundane and yet profound issues. How great an intrusion into a person's privacy is rational when you issue someone a ticket for a busted taillight? (So often that it was laughable, cops said the reason they pulled a suspect over in the first place was that a taillight was busted—there was an epidemic spreading through the ghetto, we decided, called kickitis; it caused black men getting into their cars in the morning to first kick out one of their taillights.) Well, even if it's true that the taillight wasn't functioning, the Court was saying, that doesn't give you the right to invade the driver's privacy. That busted taillight doesn't tell you anything about criminal activity. Therefore, if you don't have any reason to believe there's criminal activity, you've got no reason to search the driver, or the inside of his trunk.

If you approach the car with the busted taillight and you see the butt of a gun sticking out under the seat, then you can get the guy out of the car, pull out the gun and pat him down for weapons. But you still can't go in his pocket looking for heroin. Unless you decide to arrest him. Once you arrest somebody, you've got a right to keep contraband—that he might have in his possession—out of your police car. You've got a right to search his pockets then.

The procedure is supposed to be orderly and reasonable. Not to protect some armed lowlife with a pocket stuffed with heroin but to protect the rest of us. Do I want to get stopped when I'm trying to go somewhere —because my taillight might actually be malfunctioning—and then have these guys search my entire car? Read my private papers? Probe around in my personal things? (When these guys search, they make a mess out of everything, besides.)

The cops have hard jobs. Often they're frustrated. There's a great temptation to cross the line. You've got to restrict them to a right to search only when they have a reason to believe a crime is going on. And a busted taillight is not enough to allow the search of a car. Neither is an illegal left turn. Neither is speeding. Or being black.

Now most white people don't understand the difference between a traffic stop in Brentwood and a traffic stop in South Central Los Angeles. In Brentwood it's a minor pain in the ass to be pulled over. In South Central, you wind up spread-eagled on the hood of your car, the interior and the trunk are searched and trashed, and some cop's got his hands in your pants pocket. This isn't "Let me see your license and registration, sir." This is "I've got the power and you are scum."

I had a case once where a cop said he had probable cause for arrest because the defendant was holding an open container of beer in his hand, which is illegal in public. So the cop approached him to cite him for the open container, and when he came upon him he first noticed the signs of intoxication so he arrested him for that, and then patted him down and found the drugs.

But the key to all this is whether he's lying about seeing that open container which caused him to approach the guy in the first place and initiated the chain of events.

So, on the stand, I make him give me the exact distance that he was from this person, as well as the lighting conditions at the time and the size of the can. And he testifies that the can was in a paper bag pulled down, which is how a lot of people booze on the street. He is very specific. He could tell that the bag was partly down, that it contained a beer can and not soda pop.

In the hallway of the courthouse, we ask the bailiff to measure off the exact distance that this cop testified to, and it is far away, the other end of the hallway. I have the client poised with a can of Coke in his hand in a paper bag, the paper covering the can only partly, just so.

My client goes down to the end of the hallway. We're all out there, the court reporter and the judge, the attorneys. I ask the cop, "What is my client holding in his hand?"

"I can't tell."

"Is it soda pop?"

"I can't tell."

"Anything happen to your vision between that day and this one?"

"No."

Case dismissed.

You don't have to be a genius to do this stuff. Just keep in mind the story the cop is telling and then demonstrate it couldn't have happened. There is a real world where the laws of nature still apply, not just the world of the courtroom.

A lot of my early cases got dismissed because the cops didn't know enough to lie enough. They knew all about rules A, B and C and they would tell the court that, yes, Your Honor, they had complied with those. But they didn't know they also had to comply with the newer rule, D— and therefore couldn't lie about it. Ah-*hah!* Case dismissed.

The fact is that all they had to do, really, was keep up with court rulings (I mean, these guys are in the law-enforcement business), conduct lawful searches and then tell the truth. Sure, you might not be able to get the goods on all the bad guys. But at least you could hold onto the cases of the ones you did. But the arrogance of many of these cops was such that they just believed they could get away with anything. Sometimes they did. Sometimes they got caught.

The fact is that while many cops never changed the way they behaved merely because the law changed, they thought it was clever to say they had. And you still see that attitude today. Somebody really has to drive it into their thick-skulled culture that when cops lie and get caught the case often goes down the tubes.

I had a considerable disdain for these guys then, treated them all the same at first, and as you might imagine they weren't too thrilled with me either. They were surly, wouldn't talk to me in private and were even more defensive than usual on the stand. And then I decided to exercise my mother's adage that you get more flies with honey than vinegar. Not all my mother's clichés were wrong, just annoying.

I started to be chummy, a little flirtatious even, with the ones who seemed to be human and reasonably honest. Those tended to be the more experienced ones; they've seen it all, and many of them don't have that big chip on their shoulders. (The youngest ones can be terrible little creeps, and if I get them on the stand I try to smack them around a bit.) That gentler approach resulted in cops calling me up, as one did in a drug case I had pending in Judge Bonnie Martin's court. A report at issue said that the defendant had consented to a search.

"Leslie, I have to tell you something. That report stinks. That report's not exactly accurate."

"Oh, yeah?"

"Ask me if my gun was drawn when I approached the car."

(It is not considered true consent if the defendant said, "Gee, Officer, sure go ahead and search my car all you like"—while looking down the barrel of a Smith and Wesson.)

The cop didn't mean ask him right then on the phone; I knew the answer now anyway. He meant ask him on the stand. The fact is this is a decent cop who made a million arrests that week. And he doesn't feel comfortable about this one. I also know him by now.

So he's up on the stand and he's telling the story, and I painstakingly go through the usual line of questioning so the DA won't know the cop tipped me off.

"Then I approached the car," the cop says, "and I asked the defendant if I could look in the trunk and he said, 'Sure, go ahead,' and I opened the trunk and observed three small plastic baggies containing a white powdery substance resembling heroin."

And I say, "Officer, when you approached the car did you, by any chance, have your gun drawn?"

"Yes, I did."

"And was that gun pointed in the direction of my client?"

"Yes, it was."

"And did you do that for your protection?"

"Yes, I did."

Well, that's fine. Now I've given him an excuse for doing it. There's nothing illegal in a cop pointing a gun when he thinks he should.

"And when you asked him for permission to search the trunk of the car, was the gun still pointed in his direction?"

"Yes, it was."

"No further questions, Your Honor."

I saw that cop again and he was always honest on my cases. Always.

If you just ask the right questions (and it's a big help if your client has told you the truth about what really happened), some cops will give you a straight answer—especially if they like you more than the DA. A lot of them aren't all that fond of the prosecutors, who treat them like servants, gofers.

But lying was endemic. And none of this righteous protesting we always hear about one bad apple will dissuade me from what I know to be the situation.

The general rule is cops lie, especially about their reasons for stopping or searching. They don't jump over walls in Brentwood to notify ex-husbands about their ex-wives' deaths or look for additional victims miles from the scene of the crime. They jump over walls because the ex-husband is the prime suspect and they want to question him and search for evidence before the sucker hires a lawyer and starts asserting his rights. They lie even when the truth will serve them better. They outsmart themselves, and the "bad guys" get off.

7

The County Run

After just a few chaotic, stimulating months in the hub of the L.A. criminal justice system downtown, I got out. Some of my colleagues thought I had jumped off the fast track, fallen off the world, removed myself from the big time. But all I was trying to do was be sure I could pay proper attention to little Laine, who was going on five now. In fact, I had begun to regard the operation downtown as a safe cocoon. It was the kind of easy-relationship place where you always knew you could drop into one of the offices of a senior public defender and get some advice or a pep talk, maybe a bit of gallows humor to pick you up when things were going badly.

I knew I was gaining their respect downtown. I knew that, as long as I was assigned to prelims, I was relatively safe. It's hard to make a big mistake. At worst, you fail to get a case dismissed that should have been dismissed and the defendant is held for trial when he should have been let go. But, presumably, the prosecutor's cruddy case will be exposed at trial for what it is anyway, and dismissal or acquittal will come then.

The problem was Laine's schooling. I had just decided on an elementary school for her, and the criteria didn't include professional convenience: I wanted the best that I could find and chose a private school far to the west from the courts downtown. When I approached Mark Horton for a transfer—I was emotional and pleading, despite the fact that we never had connected in any real way before—I wasn't looking for a plum assignment, but just to be close enough to Laine to take her home at the end of the day whenever I could get out of court on time. Astonishingly, he did give me a plum: the Malibu–Culver City county run—a dual court assignment where you split your week between glamorous Malibu and working-class Culver City.

This was during the period when the public defenders' role had expanded to every level of trial, even misdemeanors (in earlier years the PD handled only felonies). The PD office had stretched its manpower thin. I didn't realize it at the time but the central office had concluded that it had no choice but to send some of its less experienced attorneys out to the peripheral courts, the little munis, where misdemeanors and prelims were the focus (rather than the felony trials in the superior courts around the county).

In Malibu what you had was a lot of beach crime, a lot of drunks, a lot of drugs and a lot of accidents along the Pacific Coast Highway. It was where I first encountered officers of the California Highway Patrol. They were a refreshing change from the hardnoses of the LAPD and sheriff's department, more honest more often.

Culver City was the busier court, with more varied petty crimes showing up and the most accident-prone police department I ever had seen. They had a penchant for running into each other during high-speed chases. Culver City was also the site of the old major motion picture studios. Naturally the CCPD became known as the "Ceystone Cops."

And so there I was, the only public defender in sight and responsible for virtually all the defendants in both courts, still wet behind the ears. The PDs were especially influential in these outlying courts. First, because we were on our own with little accountability to any supervisors. And second, by representing most of the clients we could control the court's calendar by determining the flow of cases. (A well-staffed PD's branch office can literally bring the system to a halt by declaring more cases ready for trial than the courts can handle, but for political reasons —like protecting their budget—they rarely engage in such guerrilla warfare.)

We learned from the earliest days in the public defender's office to take control of a courtroom. Don't let the judge set the agenda. Don't let the prosecutor, either. And for the nine months I engaged in shuttle lawyering I did my best to run things there, as well as in my next assignment, to the municipal courts in West L.A., where I did similar work as part of a large team of public defenders.

Mark Horton obviously did know something about me. He knew I could do my growing up as a lawyer on my own, and for that the Malibu–Culver City run was fantastic. I was honing my ability to work the judges, plea bargain and pick my fights. But my handling of my first jury trials, from voir dire—the questioning and choosing of prospective jurors—to direct examination in putting on a defense, was less than brilliant. The prevailing wisdom in the PD's office was that the only way to learn how to do a trial was to do one. I disagreed with this philosophy. Besides guaranteeing a terrifying experience for the baby lawyer, this practice was unnecessarily tough on the clients. But we had no mock trial training. And in my first trials it showed.

Two disasters involved Latinos and both demonstrated the conspicuous bias of the jury. In Culver City it was the case of a middle-aged Mexican-American woman who did not speak English.

She is accused of shoplifting at a Ralph's grocery store. As I recall it now, she put something in her purse after she paid for it and the store's people searched her purse. She didn't have the receipt in her hand because they'd confiscated the bag of groceries. They later turn the bag of groceries over to her and this time she finds the elusive receipt. So, at trial, we have what any sensible person would agree is reason for acquittal, the actual receipt for the items that she was supposed to have stolen.

The prosecutor trying the case is a very nice man, a part-time city attorney and part-time private-practice lawyer. (Culver City didn't have a full-time city attorney at that time.) I'm sure he pulls the wool over my eyes somehow. I'm so green. The voir dire I conduct, the jury selection, is poor primarily because I'm questioning the jurors from a list that Paul Fitzgerald had compiled years before for the office. These are all closed-ended questions—essentially asking these people to say yes or no about their prejudices and experiences rather than probing for the truth. I didn't yet know enough about how people think—and didn't have the voir dire skill to learn on the spot—to realize that this all-white jury was going to hold it against my client because she had to testify through an interpreter.

The horrible thing is that, even though she never went to jail and was merely fined, as I remember it, she was emotionally wrecked, a convicted thief—who was, in fact, innocent.

Maybe I didn't make a coherent argument. Maybe I didn't make it clear enough that this receipt reflected the items in question. Or maybe the jury was just such a collection of racist pigs it would have convicted her no matter what. It happens. This sort of thing happens all the time.

•

The second case is in Malibu, and I end up with jurors who are also all white and don't like anybody passing through Malibu (mostly they are rednecks, not the resident movie stars and industry moguls who always manage to talk their way out of jury duty). My guy is a truck driver. And he's accused of drunk driving, driving his truck in some conspicuous way on Malibu Canyon Road, which twists enough to give pause to many an experienced driver. At the time, he refused to take the sobriety test. So the cops didn't have a blood alcohol reading on him. But he did walk the line, touched his finger to his nose and passed those tests. He refused the other, as I remember it, because he got angry at the cops who called him a wetback or a greaser or something equally pleasant.

And his driving was not really erratic, it was just slow. At trial, he explains the slowness well enough by describing the challenging braking system on his truck.

The jury votes eleven to one for conviction anyway: a hung jury in what should have been a flat-out acquittal.

I was really confused. "How did this happen?" I ask the one juror who voted for acquittal. He says that other members of the jury had been reading a *Reader's Digest* in the jury room; it included a piece about the scourge of drunk driving and how we have to do something about it. So they did. Never mind that this particular driver was innocent of the charges.

When the trial is over, my client calls and apologetically explains that he's going to hire a private lawyer for the retrial.

I say, "I think you're absolutely right. I obviously didn't do a good enough job for you."

He was very nice about it.

But I was hard on myself. I felt that I was pretty good at doing prelims and I was learning to plea-bargain with the best of them, but I still wasn't making enough progress.

I realized, too, that some of my difficulty grew out of who I was. I was in a system where women lawyers were very rare. Not only that, I looked about twenty (although I was twenty-seven). I'm sure I was not an authority figure to the jury. I decided at that time that over the next few months, I would make a dedicated effort to lower the range of my voice, so that I could speak with more impact. It wasn't until later that I learned that I had to slow down some more, too (mostly, for the sake of the court reporters). I got rid of whatever New York accent was left in favor of

Middle American neutrality. I just couldn't allow my speech patterns to erect a barrier between me and the jury I was trying to win over.

I did tell my superiors that the jury trials were going badly. And one of them told me, "Don't worry about it. You've got to learn somehow."

"But I'm learning at the expense of these clients," I said.

"Well, nobody went to jail."

These days we do train lawyers better; we do it in courses and we do it in seminars. I can, in fact, teach people how to be effective in voir dire, how to draw out the meaningful answers from prospective jurors. It's no longer sink or swim—with the client in your arms.

One particular episode in the Malibu experience reinforced my skepticism concerning law enforcement, an incident starring a bunch of rogue cops. In this case, it was an elite group of sheriff's deputies called the Special Enforcement Bureau, or SEB, assigned to police that summer's Renaissance Pleasure Faire. Every year, this good-natured event drew revelers in droves to a bucolic piece of real estate called the Kanaan Ranch in Agoura, part of the Malibu jurisdiction. It featured the usual stuff: costumes, music, food, crafts and kiddy rides.

It had a pseudo-Elizabethan air to it that appealed to the counterculture of the time. It attracted throngs of hippie-trippy kids with flowers in their long hair, who looked, with their long dresses and bare feet, as if they were in period costume, except they were just being themselves. That particular crowd also meant a lot of drugs were being used there, mellowing out the festivities.

The fair that summer probably wasn't much different than the one before. But as this Pleasure Faire progresses, an enormous number of arrests are coming out of it. There are close to one hundred a day!

The reports on these arrests that the sheriff's deputies file are remarkably similar. They claim people are throwing the drugs out the window as they drive down the road. (What, they suddenly decided to just say no?) Or they claim the pot is out in the open (the roach-in-the-ashtray ploy) where it can be seen. Or, their favorite, they smell the aroma of marijuana coming from the car and, therefore, they stop and search it. Given that cop presence, and the number of arrests in the face of it, it seems that so many fools have come to the Renaissance Pleasure Faire that I expect the clients to show up in court wearing particolored hose with bells on their caps.

But, of course, I don't believe a word of these reports. These cops have thrown the rule book away. They are conducting illegal searches and making illegal arrests and I'm determined to prove it.

This may be only a legal technicality in some people's minds, but how many fairgoers were hassled on that road who didn't have any drugs in their cars? How many were humiliated and violated for no good reason? It's not for the benefit of the dopers that these out-of-control cops have to be stopped, but for everyone else just trying to enjoy a day's outing.

As the cases start reaching court, just after the fair ends, the prosecutor and I go to lunch every day with the judge (this kind of fraternizing is ethical and useful as long as both sides are part of it). This judge happens to be a friendly, open guy. He tells us that he's troubled by the number of arrests coming out of the Pleasure Faire. He's disturbed that the defendants uniformly claim that they were rousted.

"The drugs were in my bag in the trunk of the car," they say, "and the cops are claiming that the bag was open on the back seat and they could see pot."

We all know what's going on here. You don't propagandize the judge at lunch, but I'm saying things like, "There's a tremendous similarity to a lot of these stops, Judge. We're hearing the same things over and over again."

He says, "Yes, I know. But, of course, I have no reason to believe that these officers aren't being honest. But I guess if we hear this a thousand times, it's going to be perplexing, isn't it?"

The DA is muttering something like, "Oh, they're just doing a vigorous job of law enforcing."

We—the judge and I—aren't having any of that argument, though.

At this very time, as luck would have it, there is a growing student protest movement up the coast at Santa Barbara, near the University of California campus. Sometimes the protests there get out of hand. A bank is even burned in one of the melees. As a result, an overwhelmed Santa Barbara County asks for help from Los Angeles County, which sends the same group of efficient SEB officers who policed the Pleasure Faire. This time they go beyond illegal searches—they proceed to beat the hell out of the protesting students. SEB goes berserk. Kids get hurt. It looks like Selma, Alabama. The publicity the sheriff's department receives is so bad —calling the deputies bullies, likening them to the SS—that it leads ultimately to the whole division's being disbanded.

Now the judge's suspicions are confirmed. He knows for sure this is a bad group, and he starts throwing the festival cases out one after another. "Is this an SEB case? The Renaissance Pleasure Faire? Case dismissed."

It's very rare when a judge is willing to accept how pervasive the lying by cops is. To accept that means you have no foundation for prosecuting anybody because so much depends on police credibility. The judges usually take the opposite position: "The cops are telling the truth— prove me wrong." This time it was easy. What we had were cops behaving like a street gang, cops with their own set of laws. A bunch of bad guys.

My rookie days in Malibu were an especially fine time for thinking about the nature of crime and criminals. One case in particular was important that way. At prelim, I represented a sixty-two-year-old guy who lived in South Central and who decided, in the way that some miserable alcoholics will, to take a scenic drive up the Pacific Coast Highway, even though his mind was numb. The PCH, in the days before the bumper-to-bumper traffic, was always a lure on a beautiful Sunday. The beach wasn't the main attraction; the road itself was. You wanted to look at the ocean, the crashing waves at the edge of the cliffs as you drove along. But it's a treacherous road. And those drivers who are not sightseeing but actually trying to get somewhere often drive too fast.

My client puts away a quart of rum before he leaves the house. You know, one for the road. And he heads west on the 10 and then north on PCH. He reaches a point above Malibu where the road is split by a cement divider. He's on the wrong side of the road and now he's trapped there by the divider. The inevitable ensues: a couple of split seconds of chaos on the PCH. Cars are just barely avoiding each other and others are crashing. Four people die: a couple in one car and also a woman and her child in a second car.

As it happens my client is a very sweet old guy. But of all the criminals around, drunk drivers are always among the ones for whom I have the least tolerance. Want to go home and get loaded? Fine with me. But there is simply no excuse for indulging some whim and getting in a car and allowing that self-indulgence to end in the death of people. At the time, my guy already has five previous DUI arrests so he knows very well that this is a nasty, dangerous habit.

I do the preliminary hearing in Malibu. I don't think I ever communicated to the guy how totally disgusted with him I was. The couple he killed were immigrants, as I remember it, and nobody knew much about them. He also killed one of the most beloved real estate people in Malibu, a woman who was active in civic organizations and who had three children, one now dead. The mayhem on PCH caused by my client left the other two without a mother.

After I handled the prelim and the case was, of course, deemed appropriate for trial, some other attorney took it over in Superior Court in Santa Monica and my client was convicted of both felony drunk driving and vehicular manslaughter. Ultimately the little old man went to prison for eight years. I didn't shed a tear.

I was a young lawyer, making distinctions. I was forming values. This guy knew he had an alcohol problem, and he had been busted before. He did nothing to stop himself from drinking and driving—and this driving, mind you, was for the fun of it, rather than because he had no choice.

To me his actions were far more reprehensible against that background than some of the other clients I was representing who would get into terrible emotional situations and shoot somebody. They were the ones society and the system seemed to hate most; they were the ones called murderers.

In those days, more than now, a lot of judges and lawyers felt that drug addiction and drug intoxication were mitigating factors in sentencing people.

"Oh, they only drove recklessly because they were in the trap of an addiction, their minds were not normal." They were supposed to be entitled to mercy. But I didn't buy it then and don't now. I never thought being a drug addict was a particularly persuasive reason to go out and commit burglaries and robberies.

It's an interesting state-of-mind issue. Intoxication diminishes normal judgment, it's true. But an aspect of the state-of-mind factor is that these people know that they're addicts and they know the addiction is going to lead them to commit crimes. It's a matter of personal liability. There's a lot of will as well as helplessness here.

These issues came up repeatedly in the West L.A. court that handled the cases coming out of heroin central, the Oakwood section of Venice. I was glad that the normal rotation had landed me in West L.A., a court with six judges and a greater variety of cases, especially serious felonies, than I had encountered in the "run." It was also a renewed opportunity to learn from my more experienced colleagues.

In the busier West L.A. court I'd often have twenty-odd cases on the calendar each day. Some of them were junk, meaning they were obviously bad cases that should not be taken seriously—the evidence was weak, the defendant was actually a fine citizen, the crime was very minor. There would be soft deals on these, for sure. I'd say to the Court, "Judge, I'm ready to have a conference on 1,2,3,4,5,6 and 7. And I think we can get it over with in about fifteen minutes." Those were my good cases. I was bringing them up early in the morning, to impress upon him the prosecution's tendency to make a big deal out of nothing. These piddling violations, I tell him, shouldn't even be in court.

By the time we get to the tough ones, the judge has been dealing out slap-on-the-wrist sentences and dismissing cases all morning. Because he's been in the "two days in jail" and probation mode for the past few hours, he isn't likely to switch into a harsh punitive mode (according to my way of thinking) now that he's dealing with the more serious cases. If you bring up the difficult cases first, the clients get slammed. Now, thirty days in jail seems like a lot to him so we may be able to strike bargains that I can be comfortable with and sell to my clients. In this scheme, I'd save the worst one for last:

"This is a real bad one, Judge. None of this three-, four-day stuff. I realize you're going to have to give this guy at least thirty days or maybe even six months, it's a DUI with two priors and he hit a light post. The city wants to be paid for the post." And, after all that's gone before, when the judge says sternly, "Well, I got to teach this guy a lesson, you're looking at at least forty-five, maybe sixty days in jail on this one." I look glum, but it will be the toughest sentence of the day.

Another reason to take control has to do with an acceptance of responsibility.

"What's this case about?" the judge asks.

Either side can respond, but here's my immutable rule: The defense attorney should be the one to answer. I've been in courts where the PD completely blew it, sat there like a lump of wood. The judge says, "I've got a probation violation report here that maintains your client didn't report to the probation officer." And the defense lawyer is just sitting there, while the client is tugging on his sleeve, "But I did, I did, he just didn't write it down!"

The DA is standing up, screaming, in effect, "Throw the bastard away!"

That's an unprepared defense—and it presents a great potential for injustice. In my approach, I'm the first one to speak: "Judge, we have a probation violation on the calendar. The report says my client didn't report, but he did, in fact, report, so I'm going to request a few more days in order to bring in the proof I need."

It's the prosecutor who's left in the dust.

And, with the same ends in mind, I also make sure I know the judge well, gain his respect and incline him to go my way. (There were times, in later life, when I discovered that some judges could never be won over —and then, what the hell, it didn't matter what I did.)

•

This control of the court suited me very well. It's not that I had that much self-confidence to draw on. I was just very aggressive, domineering, naturally controlling. No one had to teach me how to take over a court-room. I always wanted to control every environment I was in. So I enjoyed this work, and despite a certain degree of self-doubt, I don't think I ever seemed nervous in court. Once I stepped into the ring, I was swinging away, throwing my best punches, and I felt fine.

8

Juvenile Hall

When you start out in criminal law you envision yourself acting on behalf of innocent people accused of crime. You imagine a lifetime in Perry Mason Land, getting those wonderful innocent folks off. About a minute after you get into it for real, you realize that what you're really doing is dealing with the fallout from a screwed-up society. What you mostly find—in the lower echelons of crime, at least—are losers, people who can't figure out much of anything. And so you fight for those people since no one else has. They're at the bottom of the barrel, most will never rise any higher, and as long as they're down there the bullies among us— who aren't all that clever, either—will keep slamming them.

And then as you go on with criminal defense work, you realize that a lot of the tragedy you see among these down-and-out people has a beginning. It's as if someone were writing a script in an intentionally predictable fashion. It starts with the littlest losers, the kids—the clearly deprived kids who, at the earliest stages of life, already show signs that they are going to be incompetent in the greater society, and they are already adrift. A lot of them have been abused. They aren't going to make it through school, they aren't going to get jobs. But they are going to get high on drugs and alcohol, and they will have little respect for the law or its enforcers.

Some of them might have been sweet, good kids in other environments (and a few do manage to escape to the larger society). But too many of them are lost before they're fourteen.

There is family abuse, of course, but there's also cultural abuse, the wrath of a culture that hammers the humanity out of them before they even get started. They're raised amid crime and violence; they're raised in constant disruption and instability. A survivalist's mentality takes hold. And by the time the gangs get their hands on these kids, there's no resisting the allure of the group. Success, prestige, power and accomplishment: that's what the gangs offer. Plus thrills.

Unfortunately we now have a culture where thrill-seeking kids can do it with a 9mm. Our cowardly leaders have made that easy by bowing to the gun lobby.

After the small-potatoes misdemeanors and the prelims of Malibu and West L.A., the day I arrived for work at my next assignment, Eastlake Juvenile Court in East L.A. (we called it "Kiddy Court"), was the day I got into the crime business big time. This was the last stop on the public defender's training rotation before being assigned to adult Superior Court and felony jury trials. (To accommodate this transfer across the county I had enrolled Laine in public school and an after-school program at the Jewish Community Center near my house and twenty miles from Eastlake.)

Juvenile Hall, in those days, was more modern than the Hall of Justice but dingy and drab, with crowded offices. One positive force was a kick-ass supervisor named John Gibbons, who expected the best from us and never took any guff from the courts. The original rehabilitative theory of the juvenile justice system was under constant political attack because of the rising violence of teenagers. The court was shifting into a more punitive mode and it was our job to resist that.

A defense attorney's life among the littlest felons is so grim you wind up pulling back. You don't get close to the kids in Juvenile Court. It's all too awful, mostly going nowhere. You do what you always do—you try to win, achieve some fairness, find some source for rehabilitative "treatment" if you can. But you know that, in general, the authorities are just going to bat these kids from one inadequate, brutal institution to another inadequate, brutal institution.

Then, in the blink of an eye, the kids will be grown-ups. The juvenile authorities can wash their hands of them, and these new adults can commit their next crime and graduate to prison.

When you represent these kids, part of the job is supposed to be helping them shape their future. You try to decide where they are going to live and with whom, try to find the kind of programs that might suit them best. This turns the lawyer into a social worker, and that's an uncomfortable posture for many of us.

In other ways, too, the job is quite distinct from the one with grown-ups. With adults, it's ethically appropriate to do whatever your client wants, so long as it's legal. If my client says to me, "I want to go to trial," even if he's facing sixty years and I tell him I can plea-bargain for six months, there's no ethical problem in my saying, "Okay, we're going to trial." But when it's a kid who's being wrongheaded, you have to recognize that the child doesn't necessarily have the maturity to make wise choices. You overrule him when necessary. And you try to do something that will make his life better, even if he doesn't see the logic.

But it's only in a very few cases that you find you can effect some kind of benign result and rescue a child. Those of us who have worked in the juvenile courts had some mentally ill kids, for instance, that the prosecutors wanted to incarcerate. We steered them into kinder hospital programs instead. But even that was no cause for celebration. Mainly, it avoided a prison environment for a little bit longer.

More often than not, I saw my job as this: If it was a reasonably sensible and a lawful thing to do, I wanted to keep these kids out of the system altogether. I wanted to remove an opportunity for the system to hurt them. And then I'd hope for the best.

The most important thing the move to Juvenile offered was the opportunity to do murder trials. Although minors (the official title for defendants in Juvenile Court) are not entitled to a jury trial (here the old paternalistic model still prevailed), those trials still involved me in the most important criminal justice issues. And it brought my education along in a very direct way. Intellectually, it was forensic evidence in particular, the science of criminalistics, that engaged me. To defend in homicides, you have to learn anatomy, for instance. You have to learn how to read autopsy reports and to understand the various causes of death. It's the emergency room of the legal profession. And to get up to speed you avail yourself of some of the best tutors on earth: the job allows the lawyer to retain experts not just to testify but also to consult. I hired my own forensic pathologists, my own toxicologists. I was dealing with finding scientific solutions to legal puzzles, something that ordinarily didn't come into play in minor cases. And I had to learn enough about physical and medical evidence to know how to question experts, theirs and mine, on the witness stand.

Examining expert witnesses is not as simple as questioning an eyewitness to an event. It's not hard to bring out someone's observations at, say, the scene of an accident: "What did you see? What did you hear? Where were you standing?" But the purpose in calling experts is to get their opinion about events they haven't witnessed. You're calling upon their specialized knowledge and training to tell you something about the evidence that you, as a layman, can't see or understand. So, before experts can offer their conclusions, you must first demonstrate that they have the credentials to evaluate the specific type of evidence in your case. Then you can get into their analysis of the case. With luck—and some skillful preparation—it will be in English and not technical gibberish.

My technique was and is to get them to make *me* understand it and then refine it down one notch for the trier of fact—the judge, in Juvenile Court, and, in an adult trial, usually the jury. For example, when I hire a pathologist to analyze a cause of death issue I say to him, "Okay, I want you to describe a mechanical model of the body to me—translate the biological functions into the simpler language of cause and effect. And if there's something that can be accurately described only by using medical terminology, let's make sure we state and define those terms clearly and repeat them often, or the judge or jury won't understand what we're talking about."

Why do bodies exude blood even after the heart stops beating? Gravity, basically. If the hole is big enough—depending on the position of the body—blood seeps out.

Why, if you're shot, do you die? Usually it's the massive loss of blood, which leads to a blood-pressure drop. The automatic part of the brain can't function at that point, and, deprived of their link to the brain, the heart and lungs won't function. (The volitional part of the brain, the mind, is irrelevant for mere life—that's why people live so long in comas.)

I'm also spending a fair amount of time at the county law library, reading the leading reference books on physical evidence; learning about such things as fingerprints and blood typing and tool marks. It's like being back in school. But the stuff isn't hard to get. This isn't DNA. We're talking Sherlock Holmes, not Henry Lee.

In addition to working with experts, I'm learning to put on all aspects of a defense, although it's difficult to win trials here because kids don't have a right to a jury and judges are a harder sell. In my misdemeanor trials, I rarely put on much of a defense, usually just the client, maybe supported by one or two character witnesses. And, although I had become an effective cross-examiner of the prosecution's witnesses, I was still pretty lame at the different and more difficult task of direct examination.

You can ask leading questions in cross-examination and so control the answers. But with your own witnesses you can't lead. The questions have to be more open-ended, making the resulting answers more unpredictable.

Now, in my juvenile trials, direct examination is unavoidable. The experts and the grown-ups are rarely a problem. But most of my witnesses and all of my clients are graduates of the grunt-and-shrug school of communication. It is a daunting task to teach these kids, many functionally illiterate, to tell their stories coherently. "Yeah" and "Not really" represent the apex of their vocabularies.

Apart from teaching them how to talk in court, you also have to be sure that all the witnesses you call tell consistent and truthful versions of the events. You don't want to get caught in some crossfire of your own making. It's so much more dangerous for the defense to put on a witness who lies than for the prosecution to do it. Never mind the presumption of innocence, the case collapses if the trier of fact thinks the defense is lying. It will be the excuse to convict, because no matter what the rules say, the impulse is to convict.

It's best to start practicing asking nonleading questions in your initial interview with the witness. That way you become familiar with the language the witness uses and can be expected to use again on the stand in explaining the events. Armed with that interview you go over the questions you're going to ask in court with the witness to see if your questions trigger his answers. More often than I care to remember they didn't.

"Why are you telling me that Paco was standing by the car? Last month you told me he was in Cuato's yard. Which is it?"

"Well, yeah, I guess he was in the yard, if that's what I said."

"Guessing isn't going to cut it. Don't you know where he was?"

"Yeah, I know but I disremembered. He was in the yard."

He damn well better have been in that yard. If he was by the car, he's the shooter. But I don't tell the witness that. The less the witness knows about the significance of his testimony, the less likely he will be accused of making up an important fact.

Of course, prosecutors like to pretend that defense lawyers write scripts for their clients and witnesses. Projection on their part, I'm afraid. I'm only the stage manager of these productions, not the playwright. I can and do tell them what the rules are, what they can't say in court. "How do you know the homies were at the Burger King earlier that night, did you see them there?"

"No, Paco's sister told me."

"Don't tell me what someone else told you, that's hearsay. You can't mention them being at Burger King."

"So I don't say I saw the cup?"

"What cup?"

"The Burger King cup?"

"When did you see it?"

"When they threw it out of the car before they started shooting."

"That you can say."

Sometimes, the obstinate nature of kidspeak in general (the rule: never give a straight answer to adults) can drive you crazy. And the vagaries of popular usages of words could be utterly defeating in a search for the truth. I'd ask, "Did Johnny push the guy?"

"Not really."

"Well, what do you mean, 'Not really'? Did he push him or didn't he push him?"

"I will say he didn't push him."

"You will say what happened, you got that? Now did he push him or didn't he, yes or no?"

"No, he didn't push him."

"Then when you say 'Not really,' do you mean 'No'?"

"Yeah, no. He didn't push him."

"Then say 'No,' for chrissake. Because if you say 'Not really,' it can mean 'Yes, sort of.' "

A case in Juvenile that honed some of my skills and crystallized still further my thinking about some of the inequities in the law of homicide involved a trigger-happy, ruthless kid murderer.

The incident begins with a burglary in an initially empty house. The sixteen-year-old girl who lives there comes home from school with her boyfriend. She notices a screen is missing from the bathroom window. She's afraid to enter the house. The boyfriend takes her key and opens the front door. Directly in front of him, down the dimly lit hallway, stands a skinny little seventeen-year-old with a large .45 automatic pistol in his hand. The intruder raises the gun, fires once, and hits the boyfriend right between the eyes. No warning. Nothing.

There was never any question about the identity of the shooter, but evidence pointing to an accomplice—another kid's palm print—is found in the house. And two back windows are ajar, which suggests to the prosecution that two burglars bailed out right after the shooting.

The alleged accomplice, not the shooter, is my client. Although his print is on the living room wall of the house, nobody ever saw him at the scene. But if the prosecution can prove he was in that house participating in a burglary at the time of the shooting, he's as guilty of murder as the kid who actually pulled the trigger. And it's first-degree murder by law. This is called the felony murder rule. It's meant to deter thieves from using weapons during their heists. Not only does it relieve the prosecution from proving premeditation and deliberation, but even an accidental discharge of a weapon resulting in death during the commission of another felony becomes a first-degree murder under this rule. Unlike what I was taught in law school, mens rea doesn't figure into the felony murder rule and I hate it. Most defense lawyers hate it. It doesn't reflect the moral code that weighs punishment against intention.

Those of us who know the impulsive nature of most crimes know how hollow a concept deterrence is. It also strikes me as immoral to punish one person in an unreasonably harsh way in order to send a warning message to someone else who might be inclined to do wrong. Each person, each life should be judged on its own.

My client, however, is not in possession of much of a life at the time. He is pretty typical of the kids you see in Juvenile. Black, fifteen years old, doing badly in school. Definitely a follower. He's pudgy, slow-witted and slow-moving. But I find him to be a nice enough kid. He doesn't send out the hostile vibes of the real troublemakers.

That palm print forces me to learn about what we call the science of fingerprints, which isn't limited to the raised patterns of lines on the tips of our fingers but includes the creases and crevices in the skin of our hands and feet. Although I find it interesting to learn that fingerprints fall into several distinct types (whorls versus loops, for example) and thus can be classified to aid in identifying unknown suspects, that's not the type of information I need for this case. I'm not going to challenge the source of the palm print but rather its age. One of the first things you learn about fingerprints is their durability, illustrated by the fact that scientists found them in King Tut's tomb. Those tomb prints weren't those of latter-day grave robbers because the tomb was never robbed. They belonged to the people who built it and stocked it for the boy king's spiritual journey. Prints can last forever.

In this case I didn't need forever, just two years. Because in a perverse way we had gotten lucky. We learned that this house had been burglarized two years before. And my little angel readily admitted to me that he had been periodically entering and taking things from his neighbors' houses for a number of years. But he vigorously denied being there this time, and I believed him.

So I'm out to establish the basics:

What is a latent fingerprint? (Basically a grease transfer.)

How do they get put in places? (You perspire, even a little, and you touch a smooth surface.)

How long can they endure on a wall? (How long have you got?)

Dusting will not get rid of a fingerprint. Washing might (but no one washes their living room walls unless they're about to paint). Of course painting will, but this wall hadn't been painted for at least six years before the homicide.

So much for the palm print. And as for the two windows, I point out that dust disturbances on the sill of one look more like a point of entry than exit. It's totally logical to assume that a lone burglar/killer entered one way and left the other. Happily, there's no need to put my boy on the witness stand. That's always the riskiest decision the defense can make and utterly unnecessary when, as here, there is plenty of room for doubt. The judge, a thoughtful and compassionate man, announces that he has a reasonable doubt of my client's guilt and dismisses the petition, the Juvenile Court version of a not-guilty verdict.

In my opinion, it wasn't a hard call legally or morally, since the kid wasn't the killer. But I remember how nervous the judge was, how even dismissing a weak case against a nonviolent fifteen-year-old in the privacy of the Juvenile Court (where proceedings are not open to the public) was considered an act of courage. It told me how fragile justice could be. How any shift to the right in the political climate could influence the way judges decided cases, by making the price of courage too high.

For the moment, though, I am tremendously pleased and would have been even if my kid had actually been in the house—and I never did know for sure whether he was or wasn't. What if he had been in the house, say rifling through the wastepaper basket in the back room at the time of the killing? Should he be punished the same as the little killer who in the space of a heartbeat raised a gun and blew away the boyfriend at the front door? Not in my book.

Some of these kids bring you to the very brink of despair. There was one kid who the cops believed was a Crips hitman. He wasn't a typical youngster, in this environment or any other. At fourteen, he radiated poise. His nickname was Kool Aid. He looked like butter wouldn't melt in his mouth. He was a handsome African-American kid who wore glasses and had an IQ of about 140. He had innate charismatic leadership abilities. But in addition to inducing others to do his bidding, he had on occasion acted independently, killing several people himself. At least that's what the cops thought.

I never represented him. A friend did; so I was close to the case but not in it. Here was a kid with extraordinary potential. In another world, he might have been the leader of his fraternity or his school, or the captain of his baseball team. But he was in this world. So he rose to the top of his gang, by fourteen. The gang leaders are always the smart ones. That's how they get to the top. All that intelligence and all that charisma going nowhere.

A problem, as Paul Fitzgerald might say, with Kool Aid was that he wasn't just charming and smart, he was a dyed-in-the-wool sociopath. And not just the transitory kind, typical of many adolescents. The teen years are after all, a rebellious time, a time to defy rules, to take risks. But Kool Aid's psychiatric evaluation made it clear: this was where he was going to stay. Reluctant as the psychiatrist was to write off one so young, there was no doubt that this kid was not going to outgrow the diagnosis: he had no conscience, no remorse, not a moral bone in his body. As I recall, he was a fire-setter and an animal torturer from the age of six. Not so charming. He hated the cops and they hated him. What happened to shape him exactly, I don't know. I'm sure it didn't help that his father was killed by the LAPD and so was his uncle.

I thought this kid was on his way to hell. The cops were going to get him on something big. If they could catch him in the act, the cops were going to take this kid out on the spot, just like they did with the rest of his family. And if they didn't kill him right there, they would see to it that he was thrown away forever. My friend, his lawyer, wanted to save this kid. She tried to find a placement for him short of kid's prison (he wasn't actually charged with murder). But with his LAPD jacket no one would take him. I don't know the outcome. But everything about Kool Aid and his life scared and saddened me.

A few kids like Kool Aid are, in fact, lost. The majority aren't. The problem today isn't really with the Kool Aids; it's with society's refusal to distinguish between him and all the rest who fall into the hands of the system. A great many of these kids really could benefit from therapeutic and educational help.

Even the Kool Aids aren't as simple a problem as the system would like to pretend. I don't think they ever got the chance to do what the criminal law assumes: choose a path, exercise free will. From birth—before their personalities could grow toward that magical level where abstractions like conscience and morality have meaning—they were squeezed into this little chute toward violence, criminality and sociopathy.

In Juvenile, where we just about never made any lives better, I didn't want to sit there crying about it, but I had a growing, gnawing bad feeling about the world around me.

I had always thought the civil rights movement was really going to make a difference. Affirmative action was going to make a difference. The War on Poverty was going to make a difference.

But I saw the culture of the streets now. And that was more powerful. At the time, I felt everything we were doing was wrong.

We're not reaching the root of the problem, I told myself. We have this entire class of people being raised in a different culture with a different set of rules that are dangerous and violent and ugly. And what we're going to do about it is to stomp these people, I'm sure of it. Harder and harder and harder. That's what we know how to do. That makes us feel better.

Sometimes the misery of it all got to even those who didn't share the impulse to stomp.

I'm standing in the public defender's office and Dr. Mike Coburn, a psychiatrist who often works for the defense, comes striding in and he's screaming.

"I've had it! I'm not going to talk to that little asshole anymore. I don't want to talk to any of these little assholes anymore. I can't stand it!"

"Mike. Mike. What is it?"

And he starts to tell me. He's been interviewing a fourteen-year-old kid charged with shooting to death a seventy-year-old man in an alley in South Central. With great excitement the kid has told Mike of his luck in acquiring a sawed-off shotgun. He's riding his bike around the hood with the gun under his jacket. He decides to rob someone and approaches the old man. The guy hands over his wallet. The kid blows him away.

Mike says to him, "Why did you shoot him?"

"What you mean? To find out if the piece worked," the kid says, like Mike is some kind of moron. "What the fuck good is it if it don't work?"

That did it. Mike took himself off the juvenile psychiatric panel. I asked him, "What happened to that kid? What made him so hard?" But Mike had been at it too long.

"You know what?" he shouts. "I don't know and I don't give a shit. What makes any of them this way?"

I do think that my time in Juvenile came too early, in some sense, in my life's education. I didn't yet fully appreciate the power of neglect, rejection and other sorts of abuse to twist the development of children.

Certainly I had been unhappy much of my own childhood and had a difficult mother and an abandoning father. But I also had so many good things, the blessing of my grandmother among them. These kids had nothing.

My days in Juvenile were more than twenty years ago. In the ensuing period, the culture of violence has gotten worse and the official response more harsh. Even the goal of rehabilitation, what was left of it back then, has been supplanted by punishment. I saw it happening. I saw that increasingly the state institutions were simply taking these kids into custody to punish them, period. And it's a totally botched job. Today, by the time they make it into their twenties, one in three black males in the United States is incarcerated, on probation or on parole. In California four out of ten African Americans in their twenties are under the supervision of the criminal justice system one way or another. We really aren't doing anything right and we get more wrong all the time.

By working for a year in Juvenile, I'd stayed twice as long as the assignment usually lasted, partly because I enjoyed working with John Gibbons, the supervisor. But after the year, I was ready for my next rotation: central felony trials. I had had enough. I could do so little to rescue these ruined young lives. Sure it had helped me hone my skills. But I was ready to do the honing somewhere else.

9

Baby Killers

So here I was, back representing adults, where I'm not responsible for their whole future life, just the cases at hand. Good old crime and punishment, not the hypocritical rant of the juvenile system—we're here to straighten out your life, kid, so we'll lock you up for your own good.

I wanted to stop thinking about the wasted lives of children for a while. But I ran smack into the ones that didn't have a chance to be wasted, the ones who were killed as kids.

In my career I encountered three of them. And for me there was a lesson there. Taken together they bring home the truth that while killings look alike, each of them is unique.

If you listen to all the carrying-on these days about the need for mandatory punishment and about so-called victims' rights, you get the sense that what many people want to do is deal with criminals in a uniform way. They want to be firm. They want the punishment to be a clean-cut result of a particular act. You do the crime, you do the time. And you don't get any more compassion, buddy, than you offered the people you hurt.

Doesn't sound bad, at first blush.

The problem is, it doesn't have anything to do with the ways crimes really happen. Let me make my argument with the three child-death cases.

•

The first one involved me only through preliminary hearing while I was still assigned to Municipal Court. But on the other two I was the trial lawyer downtown in central felonies.

I'm in Municipal Court and the paperwork shows up on my desk. There's a murder involving a father who's evidently beaten his child to death. On autopsy, the kid has contusions everywhere, bone fractures of every possible age. And, clearly, she had been beautiful, with perfect little features, a little nose. Freckles. Blond-red hair. She looked like an angel. She must have been beaten constantly.

It's my job to represent the father. A private lawyer has been appointed to represent the wife. (The public defender's office always takes the heavy, whenever possible, and the wife is clearly not the heavy. It was she who told the cops that her husband had beaten the kid.) The couple had two girls, both gorgeous. The dead girl was eight, the survivor about four. In a flophouse in the area known as Palms, the older girl was killed, evidently, with fists and feet after some minor infraction. I think she spilled her milk again.

The mother and father are both poor and pathetic and young, in their mid-twenties. They look like they just stumbled out of the Dust Bowl. Both are missing teeth. The wife, who might once have been pretty, is emaciated and haggard, with stringy, greasy hair. Inexplicably, even though she is skinny, she has a huge loose, flabby, overhanging stomach. Wretched.

The husband, the apparent killer, is a slow-witted Caspar Milquetoast, with thinning, sandy hair. Initially, I've got only a police report. So I go into the tank and interview him for arraignment purposes. He cries all the time and tells me how bad he feels about his poor dead child. Later, I talk to him often at the Hall of Justice jail where he is chained to the table, an oddly familiar situation for him as it turns out: he has this sad story to tell me about his childhood.

Often, he was chained to his bed, but by his cruel father rather than by a law-enforcement officer. Sometimes, he was taken to the outhouse and whipped. His family was dirt-poor, in Oklahoma, I think.

"That was the way I was raised," he says, weeping, and then, about his own child: "I didn't think I was killing her."

As he talks, I try to look sympathetic. But I am not. I can't stand what he's done. I just keep thinking he is a piece of garbage. Intellectually, of course, I understand how his life led him to this moment, but I'm having a hard time listening to him. I'm sure he's been haunted by demons all his life. I know I'm not supposed to be judgmental. But I'm feeling, To hell with him! He is grown now. He fathered children. And children need to be loved and nurtured. At the least they need to not be brutalized by the people they trust the most. For kids, particularly, there's no one else to turn to for help. So he keeps talking and weeping. But I have no feelings for this guy at all. He could tell me about his childhood until he was blue in the face. At that moment, I want to strangle him. I want to do to him what he did to that little girl. That little girl's brief life had been filled with terror.

It is true that what I am witnessing in this instance—and will see time and again in my practice—is the fallout of intergenerational abuse. I will come to understand it better in the years ahead, as I see how patterns of child rearing get repeated in each succeeding generation. The beaten become the beaters. The neglected abandon their kids. And the psychologically abused turn their self-loathing on their children, and so it goes. Philip Larkin got it right:

Man hands on misery to man.
It deepens like a coastal shelf . . .

I don't see the rare success stories, the people who grow up determined to be the opposite kind of parents from what they had.

This particular guy could not control his irrational, angry impulses. But when I see the kind of killing that occurred here—or any abuse of a child—my heart is always with the little one.

Often in my career I've run across the harsh reality that many people in this society are utterly ignorant about what a child is. They think infants are trying to upset them when they cry, that they are demanding, that they are ill-tempered, that they are mean-spirited. They brutalize them because they think they are dealing with just a miniature version of an adult with grown-up motives and abilities and capacities.

I try to educate my abusive clients. I explain that a small child does not think or feel or act the way an adult does. An infant is not malicious or spiteful. The parents complain about how "willfull" their children are.

"Well, when you don't give a little one what they need, they get desperate," I tell them. "But they still need what they need and they learn to manipulate to get it. You reduce this child to being manipulative and contrary because you make the child's life so difficult."

"Well, I don't know about that" is the reply. "I just know I was the same way as a child and my momma hit me upside the head, so I don't see the harm in it. I turned out all right."

Sure you did.

In an absolute biological sense, abusing the young is unnatural. After all, the evolutionary reason that children are cute is that it draws the love and nurturing to them that their vulnerable state requires for survival: the big eyes and the early smile. Responding to that is instinctive. Or it should be. But it's frightening how a few years of bad parenting can undo eons of evolution.

When I finally get the coroner's report, and read about each and every bruise on the child's body, it hardens my heart so against this client that I consider handing the case off to another PD.

"But wait a minute," I tell myself. You weren't appointed this guy's lawyer because you're somebody's mother. You're a public defender. You're supposed to be an advocate for the poor. This guy qualifies, like it or not. So let's leave Earth Mother Rampant at home and get back to work."

I talk to my own pathologist just to make sure we don't have a cause-of-death issue: sometimes even battered children die of other causes. I need to hear everything my client has to say. The mother, for all I know, could have been the actual killer. But he doesn't blame her. I do what I can to challenge the evidence at prelim, just as I would in any case I handled.

This child didn't die due to her father's actions alone. She had a mother, too. And part of my job is to show that the mother shares responsibility for what happened. She may have made a deal with the prosecution to testify against my client, and they may act as if she was an innocent bystander, but I'm not buying it. I want to pin her down on her failure to protect, to intervene, to save her child, lest she paint too sympathetic a picture of herself. She isn't claiming she was afraid of her husband or abused by him. So even though it's not my job to win here, it's important to paint an accurate picture of who this woman is so that the lawyer in the Superior Court who will be assigned this client after me can properly assess the strength of the prosecution's case.

The husband is ultimately tried in Santa Monica Superior Court— defended there by a male lawyer who has more empathy for him than I did. But even with the unlikable mother's testifying under a grant of immunity (which juries often resent), the case is still a slam dunk for the prosecution. The client is convicted and sent to prison. Mother retains custody of the younger child, God help her.

During the case I tell the trial lawyer how much I dislike this sad sack of a killer and he lectures me on it.

"You know the day is going to come when you're going to have to represent one of these guys all the way through trial. You'd better learn how to be less judgmental."

And I respond, "Maybe."

Fast-forward a couple of years. I am trying felony cases for the public defender's office now and run smack into two more dead-baby cases. But I've grown some in the interim and my approach to them contrasts starkly with the first case back in West L.A.

The first is the story of a young mother, a nineteen-year-old, very unattractive, overweight, borderline-retarded African-American girl, with a horrendous background of abuse. The childhood she suffered was a good deal worse than the pathetic father in the first case.

Oddly, she expresses very little self-pity. When I ask her about her own childhood I get just the facts. She'd been sexually molested by her stepfather, beaten unmercifully, rejected by her mother, brutalized by a grandmother. And she was hated by her brothers and sisters because she was dull. She was the butt of jokes. Eventually, she was put out on the street by her family—like so much refuse—and picked up by a black Muslim, twenty years her senior. He was an authoritarian, abusive imprisoner of this girl.

He kept her barefoot and pregnant in a one-bedroom apartment in South Central. She had two children by him.

At about the time that the outside world gets its peek into the continuing tragedy of her life, she had a six-week-old infant son, and her daughter had turned thirteen months old. The little girl's name was Kaneesha.

This mother, with her very limited abilities and her brutalized past— less capable than many a child, really—is left alone all the time to care for these two babies. And the six-week-old is colicky. He doesn't seem to ever sleep. One afternoon when the mother is home alone with them, after another sleepless night, she has finally gotten the infant to sleep. Then little Kaneesha runs over and shakes her brother's crib. He immediately starts wailing.

Whack! Without thinking, the frustrated young mother lashes out, giving Kaneesha the back of her hand. Kaneesha tumbles into the radiator, slamming her head, and falls unconscious to the floor. Three hours later she dies. One hit. No other bruises.

Even though she has just killed her child, I feel nothing but sympathy for this woman. Just learning about her, I am moved by her rejected, painful life, her enslavement by a bastard of a husband. And then the loss of a child. The mother may be dim but she can feel, and she is haunted by the death.

Now, whenever I meet with her, she is in jail, at Sybil Brand, the women's facility. I talk to her in one of the little roomlike interview areas. The walls are waist-high, and then there is a glass partition. But there's a door and I walk through it to sit with her, across a table. Much of the time it is quiet. We don't talk at all. Tears run down her face but she does not sob. When she does speak, she tells me she dreams about her child. Every night: *Whack!* and Kaneesha is dead. But the little girl doesn't stay dead. What she sees in the darkness of her unconscious is a huge creature, a giant Kaneesha, coming at her to kill her. Every night that's what she sees. For months.

The ensuing investigation shows that she was not, typically, an abusing mother. Some family members testify that she was a very good mother, in fact. Others say she never laid a hand on the kid but she did sometimes yell at her. They also say that the husband refused to help out. He was too busy being a man, going off in his suit and tie to who knows what. He had a criminal past, but the Muslims had saved him, helped him transcend his transgressions. Great.

He never came to see his wife in jail. His newfound sense of moral rectitude apparently prevented him from sullying himself by visiting a place of incarceration. Moreover, Mr. Saved was unforgiving. No one else came to see her either. This girl was abandoned once again.

At that time in the downtown felony courts we were operating with what was officially called the "mini master calendar system." All cases sent up to the Superior Court from the prelim muni courts were set in one of three Superior Court departments. Each day there would be forty or so cases in each of the three courts. The cases would stay in its master calendar court until all efforts at plea bargaining had failed and the case had to be sent out to one of the individual courts for trial.

The defense attorneys called the mini masters the "delicatessens." You take your ticket, your turn comes up, you say what you want to deal the case and most times, your order is filled. This was before plea bargaining became a political football and a dirty word. A typical stupid political trick. Plea bargaining in criminal cases was and is no different than settling any case in litigation. Both sides face risks in going to trial. By settling a case, both sides get the certainty of an acceptable resolution.

I knew this case was manslaughter at the most. The deal we struck was a year in the county jail, where she already had resided for several months by the time the case was resolved. So that was counted as part of her time. Nevertheless, her suffering was great. And certainly her future remained bleak. I don't know if she ever got to see her baby boy again.

The next one also involves a teenager, an eighteen-year-old Chicana.

I go to see her after her arrest. She doesn't speak English. I have some Spanish but, in interviews, I speak to her through an interpreter. She's four feet ten inches tall, a sweet little thing. Bright, pretty, shy and sad.

She's been living in L.A. with an aunt and uncle, having come up from Mexico to earn some money. She is engaged to be married to a boy from a good family back home. Her cousins in L.A. encourage her to go out with one of their friends, despite the engagement to someone else. She accedes, goes on the date and the man rapes her. She was a virgin at the time, a hugely important fact because of her impending marriage. Like many victims of date rape, she's too embarrassed to tell anybody about it. She's also ashamed, guilty because she was disloyal to her fiancé in Mexico. Worse yet, the cousin's friend keeps trying to see her again. She rebuffs him, until, finally, he leaves her alone.

Unfortunately, in that one moment of violence, she became pregnant. She doesn't even realize it (talk about denial) until she's five months along, but never sees a doctor. She continues to work. She's getting fat but nobody in the family notices that she's pregnant. They have no reason to suspect this good girl. The girl tells her aunt and uncle nothing.

When she is nine months pregnant, incredibly, they still don't notice. When she goes into labor, she locks herself in the bedroom. She's all by herself.

It is a difficult, painful birth. The relatives are in the house. No one hears a thing. She's utterly silent in her pain. No episiotomy, no anesthesia, no Lamaze. After an excruciating period, this tiny girl gives birth to a nine-pound boy. She cuts the umbilical cord with scissors and proceeds to tie a piece of toweling around the baby's neck. She intends to strangle it.

She tells herself that no one knows she was pregnant and no one ever needs to know. The baby will remain a secret and so will the rape.

Luckily for her the law doesn't punish intentions alone. The baby did not die of strangulation; it never took a breath. She has a perfect technical defense. You can't kill a stillborn child.

Most newborn babies start breathing as soon as their chests clear the birth canal. Some don't. This baby didn't. He was so big and had so much difficulty making it into the world that the force of the birth probably compressed that part of his brain that controls respiration. It was one of those situations where a doctor might have cleared the mucus from his throat and successfully encouraged him to breathe. But this tormented teenage girl didn't know how, even if she had wanted to, which she didn't.

She tells me she thought he might have been dead at the moment of birth. When I ask her why she tied the towel around his neck, she says to make sure he stayed that way. That tells me a lot about her mental state.

The interesting thing is this: the towel around his neck couldn't have strangled him. It wasn't tight enough, as we ascertain later.

But she takes this baby she believes she strangled and places him under the bed. She's in agony, bleeding heavily. Eventually one of her cousins comes looking for her. What a scene! Blood everywhere.

The cousin bends down, sees a towel on the floor, and she goes to pick it up. There's a baby under the bed. The family calls the paramedics, who try to revive the child, to no avail.

The mother is hauled off to the county jail, but to a hospital ward there because she's hemorrhaging. So they sew her up.

The family posts bail for her, still believing, despite everything, that she's a good girl. And they know she's tortured with guilt. She feels that God has cursed her, that she can never make up to God for having killed this baby.

It's my task to persuade her, and everyone else, that she didn't do it.

To that end, I hire a pathologist who helps me learn about alveoli, the air sacs in the lungs. I spend a lot of time reading books on respiration.

As for the trial, I decide to waive a jury and try the case before a judge: it's a volatile case—my client is charged with strangling her baby to death, after all—and a very technical medical defense. I need to prove that her actions did not cause the death of this baby.

The case is sent to a Superior Court commissioner for trial. A commissioner is selected by the regular judges to perform judicial functions in courts where there are more courtrooms than appointed judges to fill them. This one is crotchety old Sam Bubrick.

Sam is smart. But a pain to work with. He has a terrible temper. But, I tell myself, he'll understand the science, even if he doesn't like the case.

My opposition in this case is someone who later became a friend and a client in a civil case: Steve Barshop. He's still a DA, in the Santa Monica office, these days considered one of the mellower ones. At that time, he was a notorious wild man and hothead. There were a lot of hotheads on this case. All three of us—Sam, Steve and I—were pretty emotionally charged.

The coroner was a woman doctor from the Philippines, and I had spoken to her before she took the stand and presented her with my expert's opinion, which initially differed from hers. Her conclusion was that the baby had breathed because there were some open air sacs in the baby's lungs. My expert pointed out that the number and distribution of open sacs were inconsistent with breathing and were caused by the oxygen that was forced into the baby's lungs by the paramedics.

In midtrial, because my expert educated me so well, I had the poise and the confidence to stride up to a board and draw a series of diagrams of infant lungs. I drew one version in which the alveoli (represented by a bunch of circles) were open in a way that would be caused by breathing, another where they appeared uniformly tightly closed and a third, which represented the partial and uneven pattern caused by artificial respiration. The coroner is testifying on cross-examination:

"Which of these three drawings, Doctor, represents the true condition of the baby's lungs you examined?"

She is an open-minded woman and far less defensive than many coroners I have met. She concedes that the closest representation is the third one. She agrees that this pattern is more consistent with the administration of oxygen under pressure than by normal breathing. That concession is the whole ballgame.

As my expert demonstrates with slides, the air sacs are closed in the womb, tightly shut like little sea anemones, and then, only with the first breath, do they spring open. His tissue slides clearly show the difference between air sacs opened by normal breathing and the condition of this baby's lungs. There is no doubt in his opinion that this baby never breathed. Nor could anyone viewing those slides disagree with him.

Since the coroner had determined that the ligature wasn't tight enough to strangle the baby, the fight now was over whether or not it had been smothered in some fashion. But since you can't smother a stillborn baby either, the testimony about the condition of his lungs settled the only real issue in the case.

This was a peculiar case. Go back to what I learned in criminal law at UCLA: you have to have mens rea, the criminal state of mind, and actus rea, the criminal act. Well, that ligature around the baby's neck indicated that my client might well have had the mens rea to kill the baby but in fact didn't kill him. So the actus rea wasn't there.

Usually the argument is the other way. They do the act. But what were they thinking at the time? In fact, I was prepared to go with a state-of-mind defense if the finding was that she did kill the baby. My thinking was inspired by English law. In England, I discovered in the course of preparing for this case, there was a special law that a mother who self-delivers a baby cannot be held criminally responsible for killing it, a recognition of the pain and the hormonal insanity that ensues immediately upon childbirth. Although it's an old English law, it's astonishingly modern in its understanding. One of the things you find out when you're a pregnant woman or when you're waiting for the arrival of a baby and reading all those baby books again is that immediately after birth there is a hormone bath that sloshes through your brain. Everything changes in your body within a matter of minutes. And there is a kind of temporary insanity. Especially when you've been through hours of labor by yourself. It might have been a persuasive defense.

In any event, I didn't have to get to that if I could prove that she never killed the baby because you can't kill a person who was never alive.

So when it was all over, in spite of Steve Barshop's jumping up and down, Commissioner Bubrick asserts most reluctantly, "The baby never breathed."

He looks at Steve. "And you can't prove to me, Mr. Barshop, that the baby breathed."

He acquits the mother, although he definitely would have preferred to convict her. On setting her free, he launches into a tongue lashing of this quivering eighteen-year-old wreck.

"I notice you wear a cross," he says. "You probably consider yourself a good Catholic. What kind of Catholic religion do you believe in that tells you it's okay to kill a baby?"

I can't believe this is going on. I say, "Judge, that is the most offensive thing I've ever heard a judge say. How dare you chide her on her religion? Did you ever give birth by yourself to a nine-pound baby? Has any man ever suffered those pains?" And I storm out of his court.

Outside, I talk to the girl: "This judge is a bigoted man," I tell her. "You don't have to listen to what he says. You did not kill that baby." But she's a wreck nevertheless.

A year later, I'm sitting in the public defender's office downtown, and I get a phone call from the front desk: "There's a girl here, a former client of yours. She wants to see you, says she has a surprise for you." I thought, "Oh, how sweet; someone brought me flowers."

"Well, okay. Can you bring her back here?"

She walks in holding a baby in her arms. Her newly born son. She and her boyfriend in Mexico did marry, in spite of everything, and she'd been living there. She'd just come back to the United States for a visit, and the baby whom she's holding is about two months old and adorable. He looks, chillingly, just like the dead baby I recall from the autopsy photos.

She says, "This is to make up to God for my other baby." She is smiling. But, you know, behind those eyes there's this permanent grief. I can see it.

Still, do we think this baby is about to be the most spoiled little boy ever? Yes, we do.

10

Moving On

Now I'm a central felony trials deputy back downtown at Crime Central, the new Criminal Courts Building, which had replaced the Hall of Justice as public defender headquarters. New, however, did not mean sumptuous. I was assigned a tiny interior office in this sterile building with its endless corridors. The senior lawyers got the windows. I wasn't far enough up the promotional ladder for that, and I didn't really care about the accommodations or that I was only a grade III deputy, not a top-level grade IV. What mattered was that they entrusted me with the defense of felony cases, burglaries, robberies, car thefts, drugs, serious assaults, kidnappings—and especially murders. (I used to beg for the murder cases, which led my supervisor then, Stuart Rappaport, to observe, "Most people run from them, but you don't. I like that.") Among the most significant observations I made during that time in dealing with the most violent acts people commit against each other is that justice, such as it is, always asks who the victim is. Some victims are worth more than others, evidently.

The bias is pervasive. Most of the time the players are too aware to reveal the discrimination that underlies their behavior. The judges are all too smart, if they're bigots, ever to use racial epithets in public or to make antiblack or anti-Chicano remarks anywhere they might be heard and recorded. But at the time, the mid-seventies, it was still okay to disparage women and gays.

In general, to see bigotry you had to look at the patterns. Statistics always tell the story, but they are bloodless. I lived through the experience those stats record. I could see, over time, a pattern of poor, black defendants getting longer sentences than more affluent white ones. A white guy with a job, with an education, was assumed not to be as great a risk to society, so you didn't punish him as hard. Never mind that his crime was just the same as a person from the ghetto with no job and no prospects who would get slammed, because the expectation was that he's just going to screw up again and again. When you think about the morality of it, you start reading *A Clockwork Orange* again.

The race and status of the victim also matter in the outcome of a case. Blacks who kill whites are sentenced most severely of all. They get the death penalty more often than blacks who kill blacks, more often than whites who kill whites, or than whites who kill blacks. In fact, any time a white is killed, the sentence is likely to be harsher. Whites who kill whites are sentenced more severely than whites who kill blacks.

Who's the victim? That will tell you a lot about how the case is going to go.

I had a client during this period, a twenty-two-year-old African-American man, who looked like a girl, not pretty, but light-skinned, slender, with long, reddish dyed hair in plaits. He was a homosexual prostitute who stabbed and killed his boyfriend.

In this case, the victim and the defendant got into an argument in their sleazy hotel room over something trivial. My client tells me that the boyfriend came after him with a hammer and my client thereupon stabbed him in self-defense.

As the case begins, I'm going through the police reports. They don't say anything about a hammer, nothing about it in the property reports, which list everything the police took from the scene. And so the speculation is that maybe the guy is lying to me.

But I don't want to give up on it. I tend to believe my clients (the truth, either way, is crucial to a capable defense and I hate it when they lie to me). As part of my preparation for this case—preparation and not all the more obvious skills is what really distinguishes the successful lawyers from the failures—I go over the scene photographs, many times. This obsessive examination of police evidence is by now habitual with me, anyway. Something always shows up that went unnoticed before. All the criticism that was leveled at the cops during the O. J. Simpson case because of shoddy handling of the crime scene is valid. The crime scene must be handled scrupulously. Photographs in particular—taken diligently at a scene that has not been trashed—can be the central evidence in a case, a tool for the solution of mysteries.

I go to my office and reach for my little magnifying glass (I use it even though my eyesight is still perfect) and I just keep staring at these pictures, as if I were trying to see through them, behind them. In one of them, I actually do. I can see, under magnification, that there is the head of a hammer, barely visible, protruding from beneath the bed in the room.

The cops never saw it, so they never seized it, never noted it. But it is, indisputably, in the photograph. I meet with the DA and the judge, who happens to be a guy I really like, a funny guy, one of the old pros on the court. But he is a male American with a WASP mentality, which, of course, he brings to the table. I go in there to deal the case; all around me there is a buzz of gay jokes. I cut through the joshing, whip out my trusty magnifying glass and make them look through it.

"My guy has always told me this is a self-defense case and that the victim attacked him with a hammer. Here is the hammer! Right?"

Without any apparent thought—the hammer didn't prove anything, just made the defendant's story more plausible—the judge says, dismissively, "Okay. Three months." Just like that.

The DA says, "Involuntary manslaughter. Fine."

They want to get rid of the case even though this guy's got a record as long as your arm, mainly prostitution. Sure, I could go to trial on a self-defense theory. It would take me more than three months just to get through it. In the end, I'd probably win, but maybe not.

With the plea agreement I achieve what is known as a washout. This case is being flushed down the toilet.

I go back to my client and tell him what the deal is: three months.

He bursts into bitter tears. He is deeply, tragically offended.

"Wasn't he worth more than that?" he says of his dead boyfriend. "He was to me. They don't give a shit because he was just a faggot."

He understood the bias well.

"Just a dead faggot," he says, "but I loved him."

Frankly I think the bargain is a fair one. The victim was the aggressor. But the ease with which the case is settled says more about who was involved than what happened. One black gay man kills another, and the system can't wait to wash its hands of it.

As is often true in cases of domestic violence, the only person on earth who cared about this victim was the person who killed him.

•

In my last years as a public defender I also began to learn something else
that I would eventually carry with me into private practice: to respect the
client. That may seem a patently obvious requirement. But the truth is
that public defenders are dealing with people who, in a societal sense,
are beneath their station—the poor, the uneducated, the screwups. And
the tendency is to be patronizing, parental. Forgotten is the fact that it's
the client's case, his life, his future in jeopardy. Clients have a right to
contribute. But a lot of public defenders (and private lawyers as well)
don't ask for input or listen to it when it's offered. They treat every
suggestion on how to handle the case as if it were stupid (generally it is,
but sometimes it isn't). "That's only going to get you in deeper shit," they
say with a wave of the hand, instead of, "Well, that's an interesting point
you're making, Duane. But here's how I think it will play out. What do
you think?"

Most of the time, the client—having been poor and incapable most of
his life—does just what you tell him to do. A plea bargain for fifteen to
life, take it. Sure thing. A few clients aren't so easy, making demands,
asking questions. Since you have sixty-five other cases to worry about at
the same time, this is a pain.

There were, at times, total breakdowns in communication between
public defenders and their clients. The most severe of them played out
in court with the client trying to fire his appointed lawyer. We called it
"client-control problems." There were even episodes where some of the
more paranoid and more violent clients would punch out their lawyers
in court. Fortunately, I had very few client-control problems. I was too
small to hit and I was so zealous that my clients never doubted that I was
on their side. "This lawyer, she fights for me," you'd hear them say. "She
don't take no shit from the DA or judge. She knows how to get those
guys." They knew I wasn't afraid to be aggressive. I wasn't afraid of being
thrown in jail. And I wouldn't "dump" them by pressuring them to take
bad deals.

I'd go to clients and say, "They offered you seven years. I'll break
your arm if you take it. It's not worth seven years. Let's go to trial, let's
fight it."

But once in a while there's that one who wants to ask questions. I'd be
dismissive, impatient, defensive. It was a sign of my insecurity. I didn't
really know all the answers. I couldn't predict with certainty how we'd
come out in trial. And some clients, however unrealistically, wanted cer-

tainty. When you couldn't give it and wouldn't listen, you'd lose control over them. Until I learned better. Until I learned that my need to control them *was* the problem.

This message wasn't delivered at any of the numerous seminars on lawyering that I attended. Learning to respect people wasn't considered a necessary subject in continuing legal educational programs. Where I learned it was in therapy.

My feeling about clients was related to my feelings about relationships with people in general. The lesson: if you really want to have people in your life, you do have to learn to respect their feelings, even if those feelings could result in your suffering pain or rejection. I was always very manipulative, a control freak. One of the most important things I learned in therapy was nobody's going to change anybody. Trying to manipulate people to get what you want doesn't work. Either you get it or you don't get it. You can then decide what you want to do. You can even decide how you are going to feel. But you can't decide how they should feel.

So respect was something I was determined to show clients, to the best of my ability, no matter who they were or what they may have done. With some clients this was very difficult.

So, you fake it.

I had a client, a Ritalin junkie, who was accused of killing someone in a fight in a flophouse. They were both unemployed, with long criminal records, getting money from God knows where and turning it into cheap wine and pills.

The cops had a witness who claimed to have seen the murder. It was not hard to believe that my client had done the deed; he was one of the nastiest men I ever met.

We'd be sitting there in court and he'd object to my questioning of a witness. "I don't think you should ask that question," he'd insist. "You shouldn't ask that question."

I'd smile and say, "Really, Willy, good man."

He'd threaten me. "If you don't win this case, bitch, I'm gonna kill you."

I'd say, "Yeah, but you've got to get out first. And you ain't gonna get out unless I do win the case. And I can't win the case if I'm dead. So stop threatening me!"

I ran to Stuart Rappaport for some advice here. "Help me! I hate this client, Stuart."

"Never show him that you're frightened," Stuart says. But the problem wasn't that I was scared. The problem was that I hated this guy. This was a bad guy on trial for his life. Maybe in his perverse way he was manipulating me because I wound up working twice as hard for him just to be sure that I wasn't letting my dislike for him affect my performance.

His behavior almost undid us more than the evidence. Sometimes, we were in danger of having the jury actually hear what he was saying.

With clenched teeth, I'm smiling back and saying, "If you don't shut up, the jury will hear you."

I ask him, "You think they like you more than me? I don't think so. If you keep this up they will see what a stinker you really are. That can't help you. So, be *qui-et.*"

We tried this case in front of Judge Stan Malone, a smart, capable but often cranky man, with a good heart.

In the course of the trial, we took the jury to view the scene of the crime, this rattrap hotel across the street from Parker Center, LAPD headquarters. It was my theory that the purported eyewitness could not have seen what he claimed he saw from the staircase, looking through the open door of the victim's hotel room. The demonstration at the hotel was persuasive enough. The jury hung ten to two for not guilty. Judge Malone dismissed the case.

Several months later, I throw a party for my best friend, Gerry Chaleff, on the occasion of his leaving the PD's office. Judge Malone is invited and he attends. He sidles up to me and says, "You know, you almost lost that case."

"Oh, really, Judge? Why is that?"

"Because there were some white jurors on that jury who were probably offended by the obvious affection you had for that client."

I say, "The obvious affection, eh? Well, then it worked."

He says, "What worked?"

I say, "That man was threatening to kill me every day."

A few years later I'm in the lockup at the federal courthouse. Guess who's in the tank for a bank robbery? True to form, he calls out to me from the back of the cell, "You know, I still think I should kill you."

"That you, Willy?" I say. "Always a delight to see you, pal."

Why does he disrespect, even hate me? Who knows. As for my part, I tried.

I was fortunate in judges in those days, less so in DAs. I wasn't going to trial all the time because, by now, I had become a very persuasive plea-bargainer. I could persuade judges to give sentences I thought were right, and I could usually reason with prosecutors.

Plea bargaining was and is a crucial part of the system, the only way to move most of the cases along without paralyzing the courts. There was a guy we all knew in private practice who was so eager to get the case over with and collect his fee that he was ready to bargain at the drop of a hat. His opening line, we always said, was: "My client pleads guilty, Your Honor. What's the charge?" But plea bargaining can also be a great tool for fairness. Prosecutors, forever trying to look tough, are likely to overcharge on a crime, go for the maximum, see how much punishment they can exact. Fairness usually dictates that the sentence be somewhere in between acquittal and the maximum. Most of my clients have been guilty of something, but very often not guilty as charged. Moreover, not every defendant is the worst criminal charged with a particular crime. Often the evidence isn't nearly as solid as it appears at first blush. Not every time is the act as egregious as it sounds. And so it makes sense to seek a moral equilibrium. That's what you settle for. And only if you can't find it do you go to trial.

Usually a deal is a deal. But I had one judge who'd accept a plea bargain and then, three weeks later, have buyer's remorse. He was always trying to undo the deal. Sometimes, even the very next day, he'd say, "Boy, you really talked me into one yesterday. I'm not so sure about this." I'd prop him up again. Give him courage. But he never really did back off from a deal, although one time he got close. So in chambers I threw a fit. "I can't move cases in this court if I can't rely on your word." That got him.

I was in the civil courthouse just recently, and I saw him in the hallway, and he said, "Boy, I've been seeing you on TV [doing ABC commentary on the Simpson trial]. Boy, I've got to tell you, you really look good."

And I say, "Everybody tells me I look good. How do I sound?"

"Oh, that was good, too."

The next day I get a letter from him, "Dear Leslie, I hope you don't think I was insulting you by not referring to . . ." He hadn't changed a bit!

My final assignment in the public defender's office, which lasted for two years, was to the Superior Court that everyone considered the best in the county. Presiding over this little bit of heaven was Judge Gordon Ringer. He's notably intelligent. An excellent legal scholar, unlike a lot of the other judges, and remarkably friendly and pleasant to everyone. Best of all, he had what we called a good gut: he knew what a case was worth. This strong sense of equity, of basic fairness, was what distinguished the good judges from the bad. Some of the toughest sentencers, some of the most politically conservative judges, share this sense. It isn't a soft heart that recommended a judge to us; it is street smarts, pragmatism and the courage to do what's right.

Gordon Ringer routinely did the right thing. So much so that after a while I felt there wasn't that much for me to do. I thought, I don't make much of a difference here. We've got a great judge, a fair judge. Of course, I was inclined to feel that way in that I won just about all the court trials of my cases before him. (Given today's political climate, there isn't a judge in L.A. County I'd trust enough to waive jury and try a case to.)

But the fact is that during my last two years as a public defender, it seemed I couldn't lose. I won a few jury trials outright with not guiltys. But I also had a string of hung juries. At the end it seemed like every case was hanging up. And ultimately they'd be disposed of—either dismissed or I'd get a terrific plea bargain. There was a lot of wasted effort here, attributable to a single troublesome DA.

One of the aggravating factors of the last year of my being a PD is that I was stuck trying all my cases against a total bozo of a DA. Not a hardnose, a nut. Although (despite my railing about the breed in general) there were some very good DAs, the higher they were in ranking, the easier they were to deal with. (Some just got lazy, which was also fine for us.) However, this guy was a middle-level trial deputy. Preparation was not his strong suit. He never knew what cases were worth so there was no way of dealing them out.

Time and again, I found myself going to trial on cases that should have been settled because "my" DA didn't understand the case and had a zealot's belief in the prosecution's mandate to win. He was not nasty, he was not uncivil. He was just stubborn, burdened by tunnel vision and totally lacking in common and legal sense.

The worst thing about having a DA like that is that they don't know the rules so they're always trying to do illegal things.

When everybody knows the rules and more or less plays within them, there's a lot less contention in a trial. But when you combine a dumb DA who doesn't know the rules, who makes a perfectly ridiculous argument with a perfectly straight face with an equally unenlightened judge, it can make you crazy. There you are fighting over everything, even the most basic rules ("There is no blanket exception to the hearsay rule for the statements of children, Judge, why are we arguing over this?"). It's like reinventing the wheel every minute. "Uh, Judge, he's not entitled to bring out my client's prior arrest. The charges were dismissed. It's not a prior *conviction.*" "Oh, right, objection sustained." Besides being extremely annoying this type of prosecutorial approach can do real harm. Judges don't like to be seen as being too hard on the prosecution. They get nervous sustaining too many of the defense's objections. (Some DA may label them "soft on crime" and decide to run against them next time their seat is up.) Applying the law of averages, sooner or later the judge is going to overrule even the most righteous objection and allow some truly crappy piece of evidence in, just to look fair.

I wanted to strangle "my" DA. I told him he was an idiot. He'd smile. I told him we were wasting our time in these stupid trials. He'd smile.

"Well, you know, Leslie, that's what the county pays us to do."

"But you can't win, you don't win, you're wasting the taxpayer's money."

"But look at all the experience I'm getting."

"Yeah, but look how you never learn from your mistakes, Dodo."

Anyway, I regarded it as a winning streak of sorts.

Clearly, I had gone about as far as I needed to go in the public defender's office. There were very few openings for grade IV. Deputy public defenders typically languished for years on the promotion list. I didn't think I'd get one in the coming year. And I had some reason to expect that there would be enough lucrative and interesting work in private practice. (It helped a lot that I was on good terms with a number of the better judges, like Leetham, Fredericks and Ringer, and could assume there would be court-appointed cases coming my way.) After seven years as a county employee it was time to try to make it on my own.

11

Private Practice

November 1976. I left the public defender's office with the expectation that private cases would come my way in short order. In the days and months that followed, optimism evaporated quickly. Like lots of other lawyers I was scratching to get what I could. People think lawyers are rolling in dough; in reality, just about every lawyer in private practice is always worrying about the overhead and the next dollar.

A major turning point arrives when I take on a federal court bank robbery case. The defendant is Bobby Crane, a leader in the Aryan Brotherhood gang. This case, in turn, sets in motion a string of events that help define who I am as a defense lawyer for many years to come.

Bobby is by far the most fascinating client I have had up to that moment. He and his associates are my guides into the world of prison gangs, but particularly the Aryan Brotherhood, which, despite what many people initially think, is not a bunch of Nazis. The gang undoubtedly has a racist foundation, though, organized originally as a white inmates' mutual protection society, a sort of gangster pressure group. Also, with its own prison power structure, the gang carries with it the ability to impose a certain amount of order on prison life. The political agenda of the Aryan Brotherhood is about the politics of prison (not some overarching worldview). These guys can't take over the world since most of them aren't ever going to get out into the world again.

There's another prison gang, with the same *raison d'être,* that I ulti-mately get to know well, the Mexican Mafia, whose name is also a bit misleading, a bit grandiose. As much as its members may admire Don Corleone, the Mexican Mafia is not, like the real Mafia, an imposing business enterprise. It's made up of a bunch of cons who boss one another around and physically assault each other in prison in puny power struggles. When the lucky ones get back out on the street, they mostly screw up in short order. They don't have the savvy to make a living, most of them, much less run a drug cartel.

The prison gangs were once encouraged by the prison authorities because they kept order in the joint and kept the inmates busy (knocking each other off, often as not). Now the authorities, in a hysterical overreac-tion, are afraid that the gangs have taken on too much power and need to be crushed.

A bizarre sideshow in prisonland is that some women find many of these caged guys irresistibly attractive. (I've seen it over and over again throughout my years.) The men are often very good looking. They're big, well developed, thanks in part to the very real need to work out and become physically strong in an atmosphere heavy with the odor of vio-lence. They're full of tattoos, too, which seems to have some kind of appeal. They revel in their image: the whole nine yards—death-defying, reckless, brave.

And, from the women's point of view, nothing is sexier than not being able to screw somebody, but wanting to. The bars do it. Bars between skin, evidently, are sexier than anything else.

If you marry them while they're in prison, it's a secure relationship, isn't it? These men don't usually leave you for another woman. They don't get the chance to hang out much at the corner pub or spend some intimate time at happy hour. They're grateful to have you, thrilled when you come to visit.

The women, I've noticed, start to think of themselves as prisoners, too: "We're being transferred to Chino," they'll say.

There's also a code, theoretically, that the gang members live by. I mean, they revere their code like it was the Constitution. It involves tremendous loyalty issues. Number one: you're never supposed to snitch (although half of them end up doing just that). And: "We take care of our women." Another, which relates to men who left women and children behind before they entered prison: "The guys on the outside help out with the spouses and kids of the ones on the inside."

This pride is, of course, a pitiable thing. They want to be gunslingers out of the West. Unfortunately for them, however, this is no longer the frontier; law and order did come to the West, even all the way to California. In the end, hard as the realization may be when it hits them, they're all losers. I find myself thinking about that a lot. All this wasted talent, especially among the leaders. Smart young men. Agile, strong, nice looking, capable of learning. And imprisoned for life by the time I see them.

Bobby Crane is very intelligent, even scholarly, totally self-taught, an enormous reader with unexpected charisma—not surprising for a guy who's climbed to a leadership position. He smiles, he's helpful, he's grateful. Like all the other Aryan Brotherhood guys, he adheres to the rebel iconography of America. Because they have chosen the life of outlaws, career criminals, they correctly conclude that they should treat defense lawyers courteously and gratefully. They appreciate good work. I find working with them a piece of cake. They're not like my previous clients. They're not the poor saps, the pathetic, the drugged-out that I'm so used to.

One perverse benefit in representing them is you don't worry too much about losing, because these guys really have chosen crime as their life. Moreover, Bobby, for example, was already sentenced to life without parole when I met him. He had a murder conviction that would accomplish that. The bank robbery, my assignment, turned out to be a side issue having no impact on his future. (I get a hung jury and then a dismissal.) These Feds, they have some kind of crazy compulsion to throw away taxpayer money by prosecuting a guy who's already in prison for life. Bobby will never get out. So, from the lawyer's point of view, there's no true loss even if you lose. But it's not just an exercise. You still want to make sure the case comes out right. Just because they're cons doesn't mean they're always guilty.

One of my most important jailhouse acquaintances who pops up as a player of one kind or another in a number of my cases is John Stinson, another Aryan Brotherhood leader, although he isn't a power in the gang when I first meet him. At the time he's twenty-one, buck-toothed but handsome and smart. A tough kid from New Jersey who still has that accent. And he has a peculiar laugh—"Eh, eh, eh"—that I find strangely endearing.

When we first met, he was facing trial in a death-penalty case, a drug-involved killing, and acting as his own attorney in court. He asked me for a recommendation for an attorney and I set him up—in more ways than one, as it turned out—with a friend of mine.

Five years later, I walk into the huge visiting room at San Quentin, a place that allows a certain degree of physical contact between the men and the women visiting them, and the first thing I see in the crowd of people visiting each other is my friend, the attorney for the defense, and Stinson. She is on his lap. They are making out. (I already knew they were in love. I had argued with her that it was inappropriate, self-destructive for her to have this relationship with her client. And there she was, carrying on just like the other girls, those losers who throw themselves away on a caged lover. I was embarrassed for her but she was too far gone to notice.)

Although I like John, my involvement with him throughout the years is strictly professional. (I, in fact, fail to see the romantic side of the self-destructive lives any of these guys choose to lead.) I talk to him often. He knows what's going on. I learn about the system and about him. He tells me he's been a heroin addict from the time he was eleven or twelve. He talks about his background and how the world appeared to him as a kid. This is a guy who believes life is a survival struggle. He is the first one of this group actually to use the word "outlaw" in describing himself to me.

I say, "The gunslingers? The Billy the Kids?"

He says, "That's right. That's exactly what it is. There's no desire to lead a straight life. There's no guilt over the things that we do."

No guilt? No conscience?

Well, he says, "Yeah, if you kill the wrong kind of person, but it's hard to feel bad about killing dope dealers and snitches. Nobody kills kids or women or stuff like that. You don't even really talk about killing strangers." (As the years go on, this code is going to become very familiar to me.)

I want to know enough but not too much. I don't want anybody confiding criminality to me. Knowing too much is dangerous from a professional as well as a physical standpoint. At the same time, I'm not going to be like lots of other lawyers who don't know a damn thing about prison life.

The reason I meet John Stinson in the first place is because of a woman he calls "Flower," Bobby Crane's wife.

Her real name is Shirelle, a willowy, doe-eyed, good-looking woman with long dark hair that she likes to wear so that it cascades over her shoulders. She is dedicated to Bobby. Her life revolves around his needs, most specifically his tortuous efforts to gain eventual freedom. Until one day she, too, is facing a life behind bars. She is charged with murder. And I, because of my now-established credentials as a vigorous advocate among the gangsters, defend her.

The hardest cases for the defense lawyer are not when you're representing the psychopathic guilty but when you've got an innocent client, falsely accused.

The case of Shirelle Crane is that kind of case. Innocent woman. Wrongly accused. My primary investigator on this one, as in so many cases, is Cynthia Erdelyi—a blond, big-boned ex-cop with a laid-back California style—who will do yeoman work in establishing Shirelle's innocence.

As Bob Crane's wife, Shirelle is obsessed with his imprisonment and his various cases—futile though her efforts may have been—until, out of the blue, she is charged with the killing of Jack Mahone, a former boyfriend and a gangster being paid back, evidently, for snitching on some of his brethren. She is placed front and center in this case because of the cock-and-bull story told by a man named Frank Ruopoli, the actual killer.

Ruopoli had been arrested on a parole violation (linked to an unrelated crime) and now was looking to make a deal.

He explains his plight to one cop, an Officer Gillissie, and, as it is recorded in a transcribed interview, Ruopoli says the cop "talked to me for a few minutes or so, and told me that uh, if I would cooperate with him, uh, on a matter, if I could, uh, tell him about a crime or so, that he would, uh, see about getting me released."

He knows a lot about the Mahone murder, in light of the fact that he did it. He has to choose somebody else to be the murderer in the story, though. He decides to drop the dime on Shirelle—an obvious choice, given that ex-boyfriend Mahone was staying at her house and was killed there. Ruopoli is also aware that the brotherhood has a contract out on Mahone—who better to accuse than the wife of the chief? His story to the cops is that Shirelle lured Mahone to her house and then shot him to collect on the contract. Shirelle Crane, hit woman.

Ruopoli tells the cops that Shirelle picked up Mahone at the airport. "And when he arrived she took him home. And, uh, once he was in the house after he was comfortable, she asked him to change some music on her stereo and as he bent down to change the music on the stereo, with his head turned, she shot him in the back of the head, with a .38."

Ruopoli takes the cops north on the Pacific Coast Highway toward Malibu and up into Topanga Canyon, a rugged and rural area where you find affluent retreats alongside little stretches of Dogpatch in the woods —used tires and junked cars on a lawn overlooking God's country. That, he says, was where he (helpful guy that he is) buried the dead man after Shirelle killed him. The cops dig up the skeletal remains of Mahone. The only evidence of homicide is the bullet fragments in his skull.

They arrest Shirelle Crane at the Orange County Courthouse as she is chaining up her Schwinn. At the time she's engaged in her everyday routine, being a legal runner and general helpmate (she's filing court papers) for Bobby.

"Why am I being arrested? What's happening?" She is truly stunned.

They search her house, find bloodstains but no gun.

By the time Cynthia and I meet her at the Sybil Brand Institute, the women's county jail, she is a pathetic sight. Shirelle is in one of those mortifying smocks they make women wear, too short, too revealing—you can't even bend over. No bra. No makeup. But she does wear little white socks to complete her infantilization by the system. She seems desperate. She's supposed to be working to help her husband and instead she's got her own immense problem to deal with now. She tells us that she was sick the night of the shooting and not even home. Recovering from a recent hospitalization, she spent the night at her mother's house. That turns out to be the truth.

So I have an alibi on our side, even the hospital records, but I need to buttress all that with firmer, physical evidence if I can. (Who's going to believe a defendant's mother?)

Cynthia, in her comfortable way with cons, does some nosing around with known Aryan Brothers in the prison system. So do I. It turns out that felons in droves are willing to talk about Frank Ruopoli. One of them tells us Ruopoli was bragging about doing the killing. Ruopoli had boasted that he'd "sent the General [Mahone's nickname] to the country," meaning he killed him.

Now John Stinson enters the picture. He tells me that he witnessed Mahone's murder. He saw Ruopoli do it. But following the outlaw code, he won't testify to what he saw, even against a rat like Ruopoli, even for his leader's wife. But he will lead us to the evidence we need. He knew the guy who had loaned Ruopoli the gun that killed Mahone. It's a man named Malcolm Jack Griffin, who had been involved with Ruopoli in a

robbery in San Juan Capistrano. So now Cynthia and I have to go interview Griffin, who's at Chino.

We rendezvous in the parking lot and the guards escort us deep into
the bowels of the prison. The guards are wary. "I'm not sure we can put
you in the same room with this guy," one of them says.

I say—incredulously, given the amount of experience I've had by then
—"Why's that?"

"Well, females don't usually . . ."

"Wait a minute. You got it wrong. I'm a lawyer and this is a private
investigator and I don't want to hear this female stuff. We're not girls on
a picnic. We're here to interview that man and you're going to let us into
that room."

The meeting room itself is strange, cell-like but not an actual cell—no
sink, no toilet, just the familiar Formica table—and there are bars on one
side.

Griffin is brought in. He sits with his back to the bars. He is friendly,
clearly wants to tell us everything to help the wife of an Aryan Brother
(Frank Ruopoli probably should have picked someone else to finger).

As we start the interview, all we know is that he is going to confirm
that once he loaned a gun to Ruopoli of the same caliber that killed
Mahone.

"Look, this is ridiculous, what Frank is saying," Griffin says, scornful
of his Shirelle Crane story. And we talk awhile about the robbery he and
Ruopoli pulled. He tells us about the provenance of the gun (Cynthia
writes all this up in her neat block lettering):

"In the fall of 1978, Frank Ruopoli and I pulled a robbery in San Juan
Capistrano. Frank beat one of the victims, a Mexican lady. We obtained
a gun in the robbery, which was a cheap .38 caliber revolver, blue steel
with a 4½ inch barrel, which I kept. I took the plastic grips off of it, put
wooden grips on it and bound it with black electrical tape. Frank wanted
to borrow it and called me several weeks later, trying to get the gun from
me. He said he had trouble with bikers once and on another occasion he
said he had to kill a toad [a black man]. I finally gave in."

Griffin tells Ruopoli that if he ever uses the gun that he should "snub
off the barrel afterwards" so that any bullets shot from it can't be traced.

The following March, Griffin goes to visit Ruopoli at his house in
Long Beach (Stinson, in one of those rare moments when he wasn't
incarcerated, is living there at the time, too) and is told the gun is gone,
that he got rid of it after he used it in a murder.

Griffin tells us, "We were getting loaded on heroin, and Frank started
bragging: 'The cops don't have the gun, body or bullets.' " (That was

before the moron Ruopoli actually led them to the body and named Shirelle as the killer.)

I interrupt to ask Griffin, "When you loaned him the gun, was it loaded?"

He says, "I loaded it for him."

"Where did you get the bullets from?"

"I had a box," he says.

"You had a whole box of bullets?"

"Yeah."

"And you loaded the gun from that box?"

"Yeah."

"Did you give the box to Ruopoli?"

"No," he says, "I kept it."

The reason he was so protective of the ammunition is that guns can be easier to come by than bullets, and these jokers always figure that when they get out of prison, they're going to want to do another crime, so they'd better keep their bullets someplace safe.

He says he still has the box, in fact, "unless somebody found it."

"Found it where?" I say, my breath coming quick.

He had hidden the bullets in a Styrofoam container under the front shelf in the garage of his parents' house. And he tells us where.

I shove my lined yellow pad across the table and say, "Draw." He does, meticulously rendering a map of the garage, with an arrow pointing to the spot. He authorizes us, in writing, to contact his family and search the garage.

Cynthia drives to Laguna Hills, meets his folks there, and they're cheerful and accommodating. They help her poke around for the box of bullets. And then, there it is, exactly where Griffin said it would be.

"Eureka! Thank you," Cynthia says, and she speeds on back.

Although bullets do distinctly vary in their exact composition, it turns out that those manufactured at the same time (and packaged at the same time) tend to be nearly identical in the makeup of the slug. In nature, whenever you find lead deposits, they contain, besides the lead, other metals in trace amounts. But that combination of lead and trace metals is purely arbitrary and differs from all other lead deposits. If you melt a clump of lead in a vat, any sample from that one vat will have the same percentages of the trace metals, because the processing has made it uniform. The mixture of metals—the specific combination in precisely quantified amounts—becomes the signature of one vat of lead and of the bullets that come from it.

Now it remained for us to show that the slugs of these bullets on

Griffin's garage shelf were from the same vat of lead as the slug in Mahone's head.

The technique that quantifies these trace metals is called neutron activation analysis. I know a scientist at UC Irvine who analyzes bullet fragments this way; he did it in the John F. Kennedy assassination, among other cases. Cynthia brings the box to him and the scientist, Dr. Vincent Guinn, concludes that the makeup of the bullets and the Mahone fragments is "consistent with their having come from a very similar melt, made by the same manufacturer."

We've got the goods.

At trial, I've got Shirelle all dolled up as my own little Barbie. Remembering how pathetic she seemed in jail garb, I go shopping for this tall girl who probably never wore anything but jeans and I buy dressy stuff and nice shoes, but they have to be flats—I don't want her any taller than she already is. (At one point, she and I show up wearing the same shoes, which my husband, Tim, thought was a subtle, very subtle, declaration of solidarity, but it wasn't—I just can't help buying cute shoes.)

We are two days into the prosecution's case, with that murderous fabulist, Ruopoli, on the stand when I get the call from Vince Guinn and decide to bring the proceedings to a screeching halt. Rather than go through a trial I now can't lose, I decide to approach the prosecutor and tell him what I've got. Not just a mother alibi. Not just a prison informant who says Ruopoli did it. But a totally provable story about the gun that was the murder weapon, the actual box of bullets from which the fatal slug was drawn—and the credibility of a nuclear reactor. The DA, Richard Jenkins, is aghast. He asks for a two-day recess in the trial so he can check out our information. Courtroom-shy John Stinson even agrees to talk to the DA "off the record." Two days later Jenkins knows it's all over and he moves to dismiss the charge "in the interest of justice."

The judge is stunned, too. Judge Ronald George—who later becomes chief justice of the California Supreme Court—says, "This is very unusual. In my nine years on the bench, I have not seen such a dramatic or unusual turn of events. It is a tribute to the quality of our legal system." (Less of a tribute, perhaps, is that Ruopoli was never charged. Law enforcement always buries its mistakes.)

Shirelle Crane goes free. The press rushes after her as she leaves the courthouse. They want to know how she feels, what she's going to do now. She thinks on it for a while and she says she has no special plans for the future except "I plan to stick by Bobby because he is my whole life." Of course.

The headline on the front page of the next morning's *Los Angeles*

Times reads "Just Like Perry Mason." And, for once, it was. (Conveniently, all of Perry Mason's clients are innocent and the guilty party is always in the courtroom.)

Shirelle was out. I had learned a lot along the way. My appreciation for the role of science in the courtroom had grown tremendously. I had also gained the respect of some tough customers in prison, which suggested that some other very difficult cases would be funneled my way: the kinds of cases I've always liked the most.

Sometimes, this job is worth all the angst.

12

Bob's Big Boy

Four years into my private practice, I've handled a fair number of homicides, innumerable robberies, burglaries and drug busts, and even a smattering of divorce cases. Only the dramatic and complete exculpation of Shirelle Crane (my Perry Mason case) had brought me any outside attention. My one death-penalty case to date—the defense of a teenage drifter named Jack Denzer—like most murder cases at the time, drew no notice from the public. Now I was about to find myself thrust unwillingly into the destructive glare of the press's intensified spotlight on crime.

It's the end of 1980. My husband, Tim, my fifteen-year-old daughter, Laine, and I are living in a tidy Spanish-style house in the mid-Wilshire area. In the breakfast room of that house one morning, sipping coffee, I open the paper and the banner headline is reporting an all-too-typical but still horrifying crime.

At 2:00 A.M. the previous day, two armed black men, bent on robbing one of the Bob's Big Boy restaurants in West L.A., had herded the eleven people still in the restaurant at that late hour—a store manager and other late-shift employees, some customers—into a walk-in freezer.

The robbers proceed to take their valuables and then begin shooting wildly. Three people are killed immediately and one is mortally shot; those who survive barely do, damaged for life. The manager loses an eye, a waitress loses part of her brain. Others are wounded in lesser ways or emotionally traumatized. The chaos—the wailing and pleading amid the blood in that freezer as the murders proceeded—is difficult to think about. There is something particularly grotesque about the juxtaposition of burgers and fries with blood and shotgun pellets. Not only is the brutality of the attack profoundly shocking; its purpose, to eliminate witnesses, makes it seem all the more like the work of some truly scary, cold killers. I'm thinking (in my layman's mode) dumb-assed, gang-banging, asocialized morons. (I'm wrong, at least with respect to the suspects that are arrested for this, as events will later prove.) The shock value of the shooting is exacerbated by the fact that it happens practically in the American dining room: this is a Bob's Big Boy, after all. Everybody in L.A. has been to one Bob's or another.

So it is the universal nightmare of a terrible crime. It is not part of a drug dispute; it isn't a bunch of warring gang members in a drive-by shooting. It's two killers pouncing, like mountain lions from a ledge, into the lives of a group of seemingly ordinary people who happen to be in a chain restaurant late at night.

For me, it hits home, too, even more literally than it might for many others. What leaps through my mind is: "That's my Bob's!"

Before my divorce from my first husband, when I was pregnant with Laine, we lived in a new apartment building with a little terrace a stone's throw from La Cienega Boulevard where this Bob's is located. La Cienega, lined with small businesses, is one of L.A.'s major north-south arteries and congested most times of the day, as the traffic winds its way toward the Santa Monica Freeway and then on to who knows where. The neighborhood just behind the main drag is quiet, lots of modest, neat houses, many in stucco with Spanish-tile roofs and little lawns shaded by palm trees.

Throughout the neighborhood there are small apartment complexes. A few blocks north of my apartment was our Bob's, which functioned as the local coffee shop. It was airy, high-ceilinged and clean, with the familiar counter for people who are there alone or in a hurry, and booths for everybody else. In those days, I spent quite a bit of time at Bob's, especially during the months when I was home with the baby before beginning law school. Sometimes I'd go with other young mothers from the neighborhood—we'd plant our kids in high chairs; some would order burgers. I preferred the chopped steak with shoestring fries. We sipped our Cokes. Gossiped. It's a family place, a benign place.

As I read about this crime at Bob's, even before the thoughts completely coalesced and before ensuing developments started to bear me out, I was overwhelmed by a bad feeling. Beyond the simple, horrendous facts themselves, I already saw that this particular crime, this one event —murders in a family restaurant—was what the politicians and the press needed.

Even before the Bob's murders, anybody could see that politicians had lost heart in their efforts to solve society's problems; they were turning away from what little remained of the optimism fostered by the Great Society and instead were sowing fear, an amorphous foreboding, to get themselves elected. They struck a defiant posture against crime (as if anybody was for it) and hoped the pose would propel them to public office. The savagery at Bob's handed them their enough-is-enough incident. The last straw. (Consider my own first reaction.)

Now they had a beauty. The press reveled in it, like cheerleaders for fear.

Not only is the coverage of the Bob's murders extravagant in the newspapers and on television. But immediately there are a series of stories in the *Los Angeles Times,* one about black kids leaving the ghetto to victimize the white people in rich neighborhoods.

"One by one and in small bands, young men desperate for money are marauding out of the heart of Los Angeles in a growing wave to prey upon the suburban middle and upper classes, sometimes with senseless savagery," the story says. Illustrating the piece, one map shows shaded areas where the richer neighborhoods of L.A. County are and another shows where the "concentrations of felons" live. It takes little imagination to see killers leaping from one shaded area to the other, shotguns blasting, and then back into their own shaded areas where they hide out in the dark. (Of course, there were such crimes, but their number was minuscule compared to the thousands of black-on-black killings, robberies and burglaries in the ghetto.)

Daryl Gates, the demagogic police chief, helps matters out, in his fashion: "I'm afraid," he says. "Everyone is afraid. And they have a right to be." Great, the police chief is scared.

Before the Bob's murders, the *Times* hardly did any crime stories and now the paper is into them big time. From that day to this, if you buy the *Times,* it's like reading the police blotter, which is why we started calling it the "Police Gazette." It's almost as if the city would be bereft of news if the criminals left town.

•

The politicians fed off the press-driven hysteria and pushed for stiffer sentencing laws, gradually eroding the ability of the criminal justice system to behave wisely, to assess individual factors in individual crimes. The required penalties kept getting harsher. The defendant's rights, in this climate, were going to slide away fast now. This is the kind of climate where people don't even blink when members of victims' families are appointed to parole boards just to be sure that nobody actually gets paroled, just to be sure that the thrust toward vengeance is certain to overwhelm any inclination toward rehabilitation.

All of us in the defense bar knew soon after the marauders article that our side was going to be kicked around now and for some time to come. This was a turning point. We knew that public support for the individual confronted by the powers of government, for the Constitution itself, was ebbing fast and that what we saw as a noble calling was going to be denigrated in the public mind. We were becoming the nurturers of a scourge. In despair—and the state of black humor that usually accompanies it—we joked about printing up some T-shirts: "Counsel for the Marauders." Bob's was going to have bounce. I knew that. Many of us knew it. And it keeps bouncing, even now.

Mostly, I worried about the terrible turn in public sentiment. But in the back of my mind, I also wondered if I would get a piece of this case somehow. I always wanted bigger and bigger cases to keep pushing myself.

I felt ready for a big and complex capital case. I didn't really expect one to come just then. I had a growing reputation as a murder lawyer, but it was mostly among insiders. From the standpoint of notoriety, the Bob's case was one of the biggest to hit town in recent memory. L.A. always loves its "crime of the century" and is happy to have one every decade or so. Bob's was it, for then.

Early the next year, 1981, after the case has already made its highly publicized way through preliminary hearings, I get a call from the clerk of a judge I've known for many years, Nancy Brown. Am I available? "It's a high-publicity death-penalty case." (I've already figured out which one.) My client will be the heavy, twenty-three-year-old Ricky Sanders, a man who has been in trouble with the law for a long time and only recently finished serving time for a burglary.

I definitely want in. It's the lure of the difficult, the big time. Gerry Chaleff and I used to say we wouldn't take death-penalty cases. We didn't want the responsibility, the aggravation, the pressure. But how can you

consider yourself an accomplished and dedicated defense lawyer if you
don't take the hardest cases? Eventually, we each took one and once they
started coming they kept coming.

On the face of it, the Bob's incident is a dead-bang loser. The incredible publicity—in addition to the severity of the crime—is going to put
judge and jury in an even more pro-prosecution mood than otherwise.
The deputy district attorney assigned the case is a man named Harvey
Giss, a dapper lawyer with a full head of hair then. Giss eschews the
usual law-enforcement polyester and dresses well (his cop friends called
him "Hollywood Harve"). And he's into this case, big time. All you have
to do is watch him for ten minutes as he wallows in histrionics about the
"holocaust" in the Bob's freezer and you know he is already feeling the
heat of the spotlight. He is going to perform for the press, obsess about
its judgment—that's what always happens in these horrible media-hyped
situations, these one-out-of-a-thousand cases that draw the piranhas. (Little did I know that before it was all over, Giss, this seemingly smart and
capable man, would be driven into a kind of frenzy about this case from
which he has never emerged.)

In this kind of situation, the brutality of the incident almost always
overwhelms a defense, unless its refutation is tremendously strong. And
the case at hand is a complex one. Much of the evidence implicating
Sanders and the other alleged shooter, Frank Freeman, comes not from
the incident itself but from what was depicted by the prosecution as a
dry-run months earlier, in September. Then Carlitha Stewart, a nineteen-
year-old former waitress at the restaurant who'd been fired, was said to
have schemed to rob the place. In her scheming, she set about enlisting
people to carry out her plan. Over time, after the actual robbery in
December, a number of characters, some of them less than stellar, come
out of the woodwork to say that they heard one way or another that it
was Sanders and Freeman who were drafted to do the dirty work.

These less-than-credible witnesses on the conspiracy, some in and
some out of jail for their own reasons at various times during the trial,
would not be hard to deal with on the stand. But the defense here was
faced with the much more compelling testimony of those truly tragic
survivors, the march of the eyewitnesses. There was no substantial circumstantial evidence, no ballistics evidence pointing to Sanders or Freeman. There were no fingerprints belonging to either of them, even though
the freezer was full of prints, many of them never linked to anybody.

It was a pure eyewitness case.

I know that from the public's point of view, that's often regarded as
the most powerful kind. Circumstantial evidence is deemed weak in

the popular mind. You always hear people say, "Yeah, but it was all circumstantial." Just the opposite is the fact. Under ordinary, sane circumstances, it is circumstantial evidence (How else did all three types of blood get into that Bronco, sir?) that usually wins the day, and circumstantial evidence was absent here. Eyewitness testimony, on the other hand, is inherently unreliable, the human mind being what it is.

Nevertheless, this wasn't one fight I harbored much hope of winning: maybe a hung jury and then a plea bargain, but not much more than that. What I did expect to do was fight ferociously to make this a fair trial for my client. Contrary to my layman's snap judgment my client, Ricky Sanders, is not a gang-banging, unfeeling moron. He is a very handsome, artistic, reticent, hip, intelligent man with a typically deprived and more than usually tragic childhood. When Ricky was eleven, the mother he adored, a God-fearing, hardworking woman, died of leukemia, and his family and his life fell apart. And whatever the snitches and eyewitnesses might say, Ricky never admitted, even in confidence to me, that he took part in the killing. Even if he had, my job was clear—to keep plugging away at the evidence and save his life if I could. I was now going to war for Sanders in a difficult case, where the politicians and the media had made the uphill battle a virtually vertical climb.

Before starting the Sanders trial I thought I was a relatively hardworking lawyer. After starting my private practice I had spent many long nights in the law library trying to prepare my cases to the max—a luxury I never had as a public defender. Moreover, I had taken on some civil and divorce cases and needed to get up to speed in areas of the law I hadn't even thought about since law school.

But trying a high-profile death-penalty case really taught me the meaning of hard work. Although the law in California provides for two attorneys for a death-penalty defendant, I was going it largely alone, with only some help in writing motions from my then–law partner. Weekends were pretty much like weekdays: you just work in sweats instead of suits. I knew I was ready for workaholics anonymous when Laine—now a teenager and someone rarely known to emerge from her bedroom to say hello when I'd crawl home from the office at nine-ish—started cooking dinner for me. "You just look so pitiful, Mom, I thought you needed some help."

Compassion was not, however, what I was getting in my few social encounters during this time. Even among fellow lawyers (though not of the criminal bar), after introductions and before so much as a civil "nice to meet you," I was getting hit with The Question: "How can you represent *those* people." *Ahhh.* What, I wondered, was the perfect comeback to that? I like murder? Death is good for you? I'm rotten to the core? Like a fool I'd usually try some serious answer—talk about the Constitution, presumption of innocence, the evils of the death penalty. Then I realized this was not a question but just a criticism, a bit of self-righteous prejudgment that made the speaker feel oh-so-moral.

I soon learned to turn the question around on them. What do you do for a living? I'd ask. "Heart surgeon, eh? Do you make the patients go to confession before you open them up? Would you let one die if you knew he had killed someone?" Or: "Sell life insurance, do you? Only to people bound for heaven, or can sinners apply?" It shut them up but I doubt that it changed their attitudes.

Eventually, the only socializing Tim and I did was with Gerry Chaleff and his then-girlfriend. Gerry was defending one of the suspects in the Hillside Strangler case at the time and was getting the same leper treatment I was.

Gerry's case was the classic urban nightmare: for weeks the bodies of dead nude women and girls were turning up dumped along the freeways, in the hills and empty lots of Los Angeles. Although most of the victims were known prostitutes, every woman was afraid to leave her house until the killers were caught. The two men accused of the crimes were cousins, Kenneth Bianchi and Angelo Buono, Gerry's client.

So, equally despised, the only place we were safe from snide remarks was in each other's company. We, at least, knew how we could defend them; we even knew why.

As Sanders gets under way, I become certain that my opponent, the deputy district attorney, is the sort of prosecutor who can't be counted on to do a single fair thing. I will watch his every move. I want to fight him inch by inch and make his life miserable. I want to force him to lose his temper, rise to the bait (and he does that very easily, I soon learn). And I like this feeling of antagonism. All the hostility I am building toward this guy isn't counterproductive; it really helps. It keeps both sides punching. You don't win if you don't fight. If you put down your gun and run, you're shot in the back every time.

Sometimes, I think these courtroom battles come across to observers as a game—people see all the jockeying and the strategy. But the Ricky Sanders case was about a brutal crime and about a man who could receive the death penalty for it. That's the *death* penalty. What was playing out, day by day and week by week, was the decision on whether or not the government ought to kill this man. I half expected the court to be draped in black bunting as we proceeded.

The judge in this conflict is James Ideman, a chunky man with close-set, dark eyes and a mechanical smile. Ideman is typically garrulous in chambers but restrained on the bench. He comports himself often like the Marine colonel he once was (his nickname in the back corridors of the courthouse was "The Colonel"). I had always figured him to be a good judge and still do. This case was a low point in our relationship. He made some terrible decisions. Perhaps the spotlight got to him, too.

From the outset there is never much argument about what happened, in broad outline, at the Bob's Big Boy that night.

But do the cops have the right guys? All of the people who experienced this nightmare were, of course, interrogated many times about what they saw by the police, during preliminary hearings and in the separate trials of Sanders and Freeman. There were discrepancies on everything. And I don't mean minor problems. The "taller" killer—that was supposed to be Sanders—was described as being anywhere from five feet seven to six feet three, and his age from nineteen to thirty. Michael Malloy, the store manager and star witness, thought the tall man had a medium build at one point in his recollection and thin build at another. And it went on like that, about everything. When they looked directly at Sanders, some of the witnesses identified him as having been there and some did not. Some grew more sure only as time went on.

People tend to think that memory is like a video camera, that you see things and the image is imprinted in the mind to be played back later. But that's nothing like what memory really is, even when people sound sure of themselves, the way Michael Malloy sometimes did.

As the attorney for the defense, I had a tactical problem with Malloy because he had been so grievously injured: his head was turned to the side when the firing began, which is how he lost an eye. I knew people wanted to believe him. Also, in his training to be a manager of the restaurant, he had been given a manual to read on how to deal with robberies, how to make a mental note about the criminals. It tells you, among other things, to look the assailant in the eye and judge where his eye level is in relationship to your own so you can make an estimate about height. His reading the manual made Malloy seem more credible, as if he were formally trained. But wait a minute. Was this manual any good? One of the things that interferes with recording the images of events that can become memory is fear and the distractions of survival thinking under stress. How could reading a manual make you less fearful when facing the barrel of a gun? Did it make sense to think that Malloy actually benefited from reading it in such a way as to make him a better or more credible witness?

What was this manual doing in the trial anyhow?

I fought like crazy to keep it out—I said it was "bootstrapping" Malloy's testimony, that is, making it appear better than it was. But Ideman, his lips pursed in thought, sided with the prosecutor, and the damned manual came in during Malloy's testimony.

It's my job to attack the testimony of people like this—not the person, who may have suffered terribly, but the testimony—and I whittled away at it for days.

"Did you ever try to do what was suggested in that policy manual, you know, look at his eye level to figure out how many inches taller than you he was?" I asked.

He said he did just that. He said his own height was five feet five and by the use of this little trick he deduced that the assailant was five feet nine.

"At any time since this incident, in your efforts to recollect what this person looked like, did you ever think maybe he was shorter than five feet nine, like maybe between five seven and five nine?"

Yes, that was possible—five seven to five eight was actually possible. So where did that leave us? Since he thought the short assailant was five six to five seven? Short and tall began to mean nothing; everything was merging into a blur. But when he looked at Sanders, he identified him anyway. Positively identified him.

What I really wanted to do was bring in a memory expert who knew something about the fallibility of eyewitness testimony. This was the core of the case. Giss knew that as well as I did. If the jury believes the eyewitnesses, you've got a conviction. If the testimony is all screwed up, as it was in this case, well then, Mr. DA, even bootstrapping with that stupid manual won't close the hole through which I can drive the truck of reasonable doubt.

My intention was to use an expert witness, Dr. Elizabeth Loftus, a professor at the University of Washington, experienced in court testimony and the scientist who had done the cutting-edge research on the nature of memory. Over a large number of experiments with college student participants she had found that, contrary to common belief, our memories for people's faces and appearances are highly unreliable and fade quickly with the passage of even a short period of time. I needed her to explain that we do not carry around complete pictures of people in our minds. Faces, especially those we've seen only once or twice, are extremely hard to remember because they're a combination of so many different visual variables. Moreover, most of us don't normally study a face the way an artist does, and then create a visual image.

In an abnormal context, the experience of a brutal crime in a brief period of time, the face is often accompanied by a hand that carries a weapon. Eyes don't kill you. Guns do. A gun sends your mind whirring in a fearful frenzy. It is a moment of emotional overload for those caught up in the terror. Even if you somehow have the presence of mind to say to yourself, "I want to remember this," the extreme terror of the moment is making that extraordinarily difficult. Bells are going off in your head. Your eyes are open, the image is there, but the mind isn't. You see it, but you don't see it. "I'm going to die" is what you're thinking, "I'm going to die. My baby! My mother, my sister, my husband!" You're not saying, "Mustache, gray, three inches . . ." Maybe you're not even seeing the mustache, much less trying to record the words. Maybe all you really see is the gun.

And if the assailant is a member of a different race, that compounds the difficulty. People of different races when they see each other initially tend to register the stereotypical racial features before they notice individual characteristics. It's not racism, just a fact, growing out of a relative lack of familiarity. For instance, Asians have a terrible time distinguishing one Caucasian face from another or, for that matter, the faces of any other non-Asian people. And, of course, they are not alone. Whites have difficulty telling black men apart just as blacks have a hard time distinguishing whites. And so on.

Still another difficulty is that all memory, but particularly this very ephemeral visual memory, starts slipping away half an hour after the event. As it is fading, assuming it existed in the first place, many people try to hold onto it. They make a commitment to the image with words to assist them. But by then the picture is even less complete than before. So what do they do? They fill in the parts that they no longer have in memory.

Few crime victims are ever interviewed just thirty minutes or so after the ordeal. And after several hours or a number of days, it's questionable whether they have any precise memory left. If they've been talking to the cops all along the way, interrogated in the usual fashion, in which they are led to answers about aspects of the crime that they really don't remember, they start filling in the blanks, just to be helpful. Now what they describe as their memory becomes what they said it was out loud, not what it might have been before.

So I needed Dr. Loftus. She had the expertise to explain all this. If nothing else, it could help the jury understand how there could be so much variance in testimony, without having to call all the witnesses liars. She could address the validity of that manual, too, defuse some of the sense of authority it had brought into the case.

Giss knew she was coming, all right. He was terrified and preparing early to refute her and her material. Just how early was apparent during jury selection—the trial hadn't even begun—when I approached him in court to discuss an unrelated issue.

I am leaning over, talking to him so the jury won't hear the conversation, when I notice that on a pad on his table are these words: "Elizabeth Loftus. I will destroy her." I demand to know how he knew I was going to use her. My intention to call her is still confidential.

Suddenly, I am furious. I know this guy. I have to figure he's been snooping somehow. "Where did you get it, Harve?"

He sees that as the accusation it is, that I believe he's been digging in places he shouldn't. He leans over—and we are, mind you, right in front of the jury—and he hisses, "You fucking whore."

That was not as unusual as it sounds. Giss is the kind of person who routinely calls me names. "Self-righteous bitch" was one of them (but that was nowhere near the jury). And anyway, I'm not so very delicate myself.

But at this moment, I've had it with this jerk. He strikes a posture of being deeply offended that I consider him to be the kind of sleaze who would snoop. He maintains the Loftus note to himself is the product of intelligent guessing. I am mostly enraged. Not buying it. He has cursed at me in front of the jury. This has to stop. We go marching toward chambers to get the judge to intervene before we rip each other apart.

We are yelling in the hallway now, pushing on the judge's door, but the door is resisting (the court clerk is, as it turns out, leaning against it, trying to warn Ideman that there's this little problem between counsel). We burst into chambers. Ideman doesn't have time for this.

"Whatever it is that is bothering you, remember it is nine minutes after three o'clock and we have seventy-eight prospective jurors out there," he says.

No, no, Giss says. He wants to ventilate this now, "otherwise we will be on each other out in front of the jury and start wrestling."

We are both yelling in chambers. I say, "Business is business, and I don't have to take personal insults from anyone."

Now Giss really gets into it. "Nobody called her a thief, a violator of the canons of ethics and a criminal. I don't care if someone calls me an asshole or a shit face, a whore or whatever. But no one is going to call me a legal cheat." Ah, the dignity of the law.

Anyway, this is not a particularly important moment in the trial. Just a spitting match. Except it does suggest how nasty things can get.

The next day, the judge, who had been tolerant and attempting to calm us down all through the spat, has evidently given it some thought overnight and decided it was time to lay down the law. He doesn't like our behavior in the courtroom in general, he says. He says that I had been throwing pencils onto the table among other things and he disapproved of that. He doesn't like Giss's frequent outbursts of anger. He particularly doesn't like the fact that just before we came into his chambers the previous day he could hear us shouting outside his door.

"I let you both in chambers, called in the reporter and thereafter a real donnybrook ensued," he says.

He is going to figure something out. He threatens to put us in jail (just on weekends so as not to interrupt the trial). "I have consulted with the sheriff," he tells us in his formal, measured fashion. "And he informs me that they are ready to receive two civilian prisoners, one male, one female, and provide housing and transportation for you during such periods as you are in custody." He suggests maybe one or both of us ought to get out of the case now, or he might arrange for that. Ideman wants to know if perhaps we were exploding for tactical reasons, to intimidate him. He says that won't work.

It is a blistering rebuke. He doesn't end up doing anything in particular. But I'm sure it had some effect, no matter how small. But the truth is, in cases like this, I don't care what the judge thinks or what he threatens. Nobody is going to call me names in court. Period.

From time to time Elizabeth Loftus's name arises again during discussions in chambers. Then comes the day, as I am putting on my defense, when I bring her to town to call her to the stand.

We have a hearing before the judge, with the jury out, as to whether her testimony can be allowed.

Giss, bent on discrediting Loftus and memory research in general, but evidently fearful of taking Loftus on one-on-one, calls for reinforcements and enlists a district attorney whose specialty is attacking defense scientific witnesses. His method is to try to make science sound like gobbledygook when it suits the prosecution's purpose. But the reason I need Loftus seems to me to be fair on the face of it. One thing I need to show, beyond how faulty memory can be, is that what people generally believe about the nature of memory is often false, so a jury has to be taught to put aside its misconceptions. For instance, no matter how much we all might think so, it doesn't matter how positive someone says he is.

Loftus tells Ideman in response to questioning, "It's just as likely in these studies to find somebody who says, 'I'm absolutely positive'—but is wrong—as to find somebody who says, 'I'm absolutely positive,' but is right." And yet, Loftus says, "people in general and jurors specifically put tremendous weight on the confidence level of the eyewitness. In fact, that, almost more than anything else, controls the extent to which they will believe the eyewitness." Whew. That's an important finding from the scientific research. And the jury needs to know it, along with all the other points Loftus can make. (Then, if the prosecution feels it must, it can always bring on its own witness to dispute her conclusions.)

But Ideman, in a gross misunderstanding of the law—even worse than allowing that restaurant manual into the trial in the first place—believes that, because some of Loftus's contentions are open to debate, that absence of complete consensus invalidates her testimony from a legal point of view. (That ruling would not hold up today, given many court assessments of expert testimony on memory since.) In fact, I think he is merely doing what most judges do, complying with the prosecution request whenever possible.

It's a serious setback, but I regroup and go on. I work all day and all night and I gorge myself along the way: I pick up a Sara Lee chocolate cake at the 7-Eleven and start eating it around 10:00 P.M. and keep going in this gluttonous fashion until about 2:00 A.M., when most of the cake is gone. Later in the trial I switch to cheesecake. This is a defense fueled by cake. I gain eight pounds before it's over. (These days, I can gain twenty, easy, under similar circumstances.)

A serious contaminant in the Bob's Big Boy case is the use of jailhouse informants. This was the beginning of a particularly infamous decade in the history of the California judicial system. The system was routinizing the use of jailhouse snitches to work, hand in hand, with L.A. law enforcers. The idea was that if an inmate could just be placed in a cell next to someone on trial, maybe he could coddle him into a confession that would later be recounted in court. Or, if a confession wasn't actually forthcoming from the defendant, maybe the snitch would say the confession existed anyway. Then the snitch could testify to that and, as payback, gain some favor: a dismissal of his case, preferential treatment, help in getting paroled.

In those days, a man named Leslie White was one of the most productive snitches of all. In 1988, years after the Bob's case, it was he who played the primary role in a series of newspaper articles exposing the DA's practices throughout the decade. He demonstrated for the press, for instance, how he could easily obtain confidential information about an ongoing case—just by using the phones at the county jail—and then get himself placed next to the defendant about whom he now knew so much. After that he would use the information to persuade the authorities that he got that information directly from the accused man and, surprise, you had a confession, as told to Les White.

Once Les White came forward, others did, too. Eventually, there was an official investigation and a grand jury found that the DA's office "failed to fulfill the ethical responsibilities required of a public prosecutor by its deliberate and informed declination to take the action necessary to curtail the misuse of informant testimony."

But back in 1982, Les White—already an accomplished snitch—comes into our story because Harvey Giss is facilitating sexual liaisons between White and one of the witnesses, one of the victims, incredibly, in the Bob's case.

Tami Rogoway and her boyfriend, David Burrell, were the last two patrons remaining in the restaurant when the robbery came down. The young couple were on their way home from a Stevie Wonder concert and dropped into the restaurant. David was one of the four who died. Tami, the only white Anglo among the victims or the survivors, was wounded. The cops soon showed her pictures from a gang photo book. She identified, with a high degree of certainty, a black man named David Hall—a man unrelated to the case in any way—as the "tall" suspect. In early testimony she said her mental picture of the killers was "very hazy." But soon, in court, she is identifying Ricky Sanders as the tall killer.

Giss asks her about the tall guy, whether she saw him in court, and she says, "Yes, I do." And Giss says, "The defendant seated at counsel's table?" And she says, simply, "Yes." As if there had never been a doubt in her mind.

Her enhanced ability to make identifications coincides with a love interest. While doing one of her girlfriends a favor—Tami, older than the other girl, agreed to act as an emissary to a boyfriend imprisoned at Chino—she met Les White, a slender, red-haired, unimpressive-looking career criminal with an apparent ability to con just about anybody.

Les White is a piece of work.

I knew him, too. Because so many friends and associates of snitches and conspirators in this case had prison connections, we were frequently talking to inmates. I began to suspect that too many people we contacted seemed involved with Les White one way or another.

Something is wrong here. With the jury absent, I say to Giss, suspiciously, "Didn't you consider it a little peculiar that this guy, Les White, who was Tami Rogoway's boyfriend, all right, is running around suddenly turning witnesses who have been giving apparently useful information to the defense? Next thing you know these people recant and Les White is in the middle of it all."

Giss concedes that Les White is "romantically linked" to Rogoway in a "sordid sort of way." And, you know, he is "shocked," because she seemed to come from a good family. "It just took me totally by surprise," he says. He denies under oath that he had ever used White for his own purposes.

Not likely, given White's cozy relationship with the DAs. They pay him well. He's earned regular furloughs out of prison, money, conjugal visits. In the Bob's case, as he recalls when he testifies in another matter years after the Bob's trial was over, he would relay information to Tami Rogoway that he had picked up in jail about Sanders and Freeman, even if he knew the information was untrue. Clearly, he was manipulating and buttressing her "memory." It was his notion of pillow talk, in the service of Harvey Giss. When Giss learned how White was implicating him in these later years, he told a reporter that White was a "liar," which was true enough. But Giss, free of any oath at the moment, also said, "I never knew anything about a sexual relationship." Oh, really, Harve?

Years later, the defense gets its hands on Giss's original file. There in the handwriting of Mr. Self-Righteous Prosecutor himself is familiarly noted, "Les had a conjugal visit with Tami. One regular visit . . ." This was on February 17, 1982, before Rogoway got her chance to testify in the Sanders trial.

Beyond the bootstrapping and confusion of Michael Malloy and the manipulation and cover-up concerning Tami Rogoway, there were many more eyewitness problems in this trial.

Ismael Luna, the dishwasher, thinks at one point in his testimony that Sanders was the shorter of the two assailants, but, in any case, he concedes that all black people look alike to him. Derwin Logan, the assistant manager, identifies a lot of people in photos and lineups as being similar to the assailants, but at the trial he doesn't pick Ricky Sanders as one of them. At the preliminary hearing poor Rhonda Robinson, a waitress whose emotional distress required continuing psychiatric treatment, did not identify Ricky Sanders. At the later trial, she does. Now she's sure. And it goes on.

In the final argument, I hammer away at the inconsistencies in every witness's identification testimony. They have each described the suspect in so many contradictory ways that he could be four different people. (My graphics guy had constructed a dozen or so elaborate illustrative boards that took the testimony of each of the witnesses and presented a drawing to match the description offered each time they were questioned —all these different heights, and outfits and hairstyles. When all the boards were displayed for the jury the courtroom felt positively crowded with suspects.)

The prosecutor, Giss, points out the contrary evidence, those consistencies that do exist, while more or less continuously attacking me personally as he goes along. ("I don't want anyone here to think that somebody can just prance through with a final argument not founded on fact and with phantom issues and hitting and running with phantom issues and hitting and running unsupported by the transcript, steal thirteen weeks of very carefully laid—" at which point I object and the tirade stops.)

And he doesn't want the jury to feel sorry for our side. Sure his side brought in expert witnesses but so did ours, he says, referring to the physical evidence and ballistics people. "They had experts when they needed them. You saw the experts' testimony," he says in his typically melodramatic, disingenuous fashion.

Right, Harve. Everybody but the memory expert.

In the end the jury finds Sanders guilty on count after count. As the verdict rolls in, I don't think to myself, Oh, my God, I lost. I immediately start thinking about the next segment of this trial, the penalty phase. Here it is, the death part that I've dreaded for so long. There are few tactics available to us in this phase. One thing that works, when it applies, is you appeal to the jury's sense of fairness: if you can show that someone else who seemed equally or more guilty in the same crime didn't get death, the jury won't give your guy death either. But that isn't an issue here. We're not permitted to tell them that Carlitha Stewart, the mastermind and getaway driver, has pleaded guilty and got twenty-five-years-to-life. And the other alleged shooter, Franklin Freeman, had his case severed from Ricky's and his trial hasn't even started yet.

Among the few remaining tools we have is a plea for mercy.

We try to show that the individual convicted of a terrible crime is nevertheless a human being worthy, perhaps, of compassion.

In an effort to learn more about Ricky's childhood in preparation for this phase, I go to interview the woman in whose Spanish-style house in South Central he lived for two years between the ages of thirteen and fifteen. I'm hoping that, like the family, she might say useful things on Ricky's behalf. She once had a group home for delinquent kids. She is still running the place but now she takes in only the developmentally disabled. What I observe when I visit is appalling: six mentally handicapped kids sitting on a vinyl couch in an anteroom in this huge house where every room is roped off.

The little anteroom has linoleum on the floor and there's a black-and-white television on brackets on the wall near the ceiling. The kids are all watching with their little jaws slack. And she gets six hundred or eight hundred bucks a month for each one of these poor little creatures who are receiving no vocational training, no stimulation and utterly no love in that place.

The woman is cold and businesslike. I show her pictures of Ricky at thirteen. "I think I remember this boy," she says, and she calls to her daughter who is working in the kitchen. And she says, "You remember him?"

"I think so, Ma, I'm not sure."

What emptiness there must have been there. Heartless woman. And I debate putting her on the witness stand to show something about the turning point in the life of a quiet, frail kid who spent two years after the death of his mother, deprived of any warmth at all. I think hard about it and conclude it is probably too subtle.

So I bring on family members who testify about how much Ricky Sanders meant to them. I try to show he was a child of at least some promise short-circuited by the early death of his mother. I put someone on to show how well he did in school, before his life fell apart completely.

I plead with the jury to realize what they are being asked to do. Adding one more killing to those that went before isn't going to accomplish anything, I say. Giss, on the other hand, cites an earlier crime by Sanders, a burglary, and declares him to be the "perfect candidate" for the gas chamber.

As the case goes back to the jury, I find myself dwelling on the jurors, trying to understand them. They have a value system that tells them they're good people and decent people—and I think they are, too. Yet each of them, as is the case with all jurors who are allowed to serve in a capital trial, has indicated a willingness to impose the death penalty. So they are perfectly capable of condemning Ricky Sanders to death. That strikes me as incredible. I find myself, in a rare activity, talking to God. "You understand, God, don't you? How can this be? Morally, I'm right. Right?"

Well, the jury in the end does its worst. It sends Ricky Sanders to death row, where, as the result of snafus and incompetence in the appeal process having nothing to do with strategic delays or anything else intentional, he resides even now.

Bob's Big Boy is, to this writing, the only major case I ever completely lost—all the way to the death penalty.

Ricky Sanders writes to me often from San Quentin in a flowing handwriting that kids don't master anymore: "Dear Leslie, I'm hoping that my few words find you and my li'l pal [my son, Aidan] and all the rest of your loved ones in the very best of health. . . ." He sends me paintings, increasingly more complex in the skill they show, and bold in the use of color. One of them, a beautiful landscape of a tropical waterfall, framed with multicolored parrots, is hung in my son's room. When Aidan was just beginning to talk he would point to it and say, "Look, Mama, doodledoos" (roosters and parrots being one when you're eighteen months).

Ricky's ardent appellate lawyer, Verna Wefald (I never do the appeals on my own trials), faults me, in her brief, for having done too little in the penalty phase to show what a truly horrible, debilitating life Ricky led before the Bob's Big Boy killings.

I have never been entirely happy with how I handled the Sanders penalty phase. Although it was my second death-penalty case, the first one, Denzer, resulted in a verdict of first-degree murder without special circumstances. This eliminated any possibility for a death decision. Thus there was no punishment issue for the jury to decide in a penalty phase. Sanders was the first time I had to put on evidence in support of letting someone live. In retrospect, I always wished that I'd done more, had more experience in making the tough tactical decisions. Maybe I should have put the unfeeling group home operator on the stand after all, if only to show how she exploited the kid, as an example of how the system failed him. (After this case my practice was to hire a penalty-phase investigator, like my friend Casey Cohen, a specialist in interviewing family and friends, to get at every single aspect of a life.)

The appellate lawyer also charges Harvey Giss with the crime of suborning the perjury of Tami Rogoway.

Giss is still a deputy district attorney. His career seems to me to be stuck in aspic, like he's never been able to fully free himself of the Bob's murders. He often says that even though he won this case, I personally took years off his life. Why would you ever admit that someone got to you?

Meanwhile, on death row, I do, ironically, see Ricky Sanders grow and mature. If this conviction is in fact ever overturned I hope I can represent him again. After seventeen more death-penalty cases I could assure him a wiser and more confident lawyer than he got the first time around. If it's not overturned, of course, that's that. They're going to kill him.

13

The Lark

Now I know I said that this trial business isn't a game, that it's a war. But I can't deny that trials are sometimes—very rarely, it's true—fun.

The most entertaining case of my life, coming close on the heels of the Sanders trial, was the trial of Salvador Buenrostro, accused of the contract killing of an affluent paint-store owner, a drug user and snitch named Chuck Snodgrass.

Buenrostro—known as "Mon," as in "man," to signify the respect people had for him—was always one of my very favorite clients, bright with an easy sense of humor, warm and caring when he talks about his kids, the kind of guy you'd happily have over for Thanksgiving dinner— Uncle Mon—unless, of course, his criminal past troubled you.

By the time I was appointed by the court to step into this case in 1982, it already had a long, winding history:

Two friends from childhood, one a doctor and the other a paint-store owner, have a falling out. They are both deep into drugs—dealing, snitching . . . everything. The doctor thinks the paint-store owner is cozying up to federal agents and is likely to give him away. So never mind that the doctor owes the other guy a lot—the paint-store owner's father actually financed the doctor's medical education. This professional healer decides he has to knock off his old friend anyway. To that end, he engages an illiterate lowlife—who likes to brag about the number of killings he's done before—and also his associate, another criminal by trade.

Mon stumbles into this murder plot shortly after he is released from federal prison on a bank robbery conviction. He's residing in a halfway house at the time, where, obviously, you're supposed to keep your nose clean so you can reenter society as a respectable citizen. The problem here is that so many of these people, Mon included, have never experienced anything like a respectable life. They know the streets, they know the prisons. They do not know anything about working for a living. In my experience, many of them can be perfectly charming and likable, even have a strong value system in which they worship family ties, but when it comes to earning money, they do it illegally. When it comes to dealing with each other, their opponents especially, they can be ruthless. Mon always says he would never hurt an "innocent" person, and I believe him. It's his definition of innocence that's the problem.

Dope dealing is Mon's business, the Mexican Mafia is his company, and, after bunking there in the halfway house only a couple of days, he concludes that he needs a stake. He turns to a Mexican Mafia leader named Donald Garcia who, astonishingly, has managed to stay out of prison for many years. Garcia tells Mon, "Well, I don't really have any cash I can give you. I can't find you any dope, either, but these guys owe me like $6,000 for coke that I've supplied them." He names the two punks who have accepted the doctor's contract to kill the store owner. One is Jayson Hunter (his real name is Robert Chavez) and the other is Frank Morales.

He tells Mon that if he can collect from Hunter and Morales he can keep the money and return it "when you get your business going and you got profits." Just one caring gang member helping out another.

Mon goes to see these characters and they tell him, "Yeah, we'd like to pay Garcia the money, but the reason we haven't is because we're owed money from this doctor, Dr. Donald Bulpitt" and that Bulpitt will pay them only after they execute his longtime friend, Snodgrass.

Mon, as he tells the story, subsequently says that he and his blond soon-to-be-wife, Terri Wilson, accompany Morales and Hunter to Pasadena, where Snodgrass is ambushed as he is about to get into his Rolls-Royce. He is shot in front of the Pacific Bell Telephone building, just down the street from the quaint shops and restaurants of Pasadena's fashionable Old Town historic district.

Mon says he is not the killer. He's just along to see that he gets the money that's coming to him. At first Terri backs him up on that.

Initially, although the cops know the major players in this killing, the case is weak—no murder weapon, among other problems—and it is dismissed for lack of evidence before trial.

When he learns he is no longer a suspect, Mon flies the coop altogether, leaving his new wife, Terri, behind, too. He goes to Wisconsin, takes up with another woman and manages to obtain more or less legitimate work—as an alcohol and drug counselor, amazingly enough—on an Indian reservation, where he gets to smoke peyote and sweat ritually. (Although Mon is Mexican-American, he fits right in here, because he looks a bit like a Native American, too, with dark skin, deep lines in his face, jet-black hair.)

The case unravels, however, when Terri Wilson, the scorned wife bent on revenge, tells the police that she wants to change her story: Mon is their guy. She didn't actually see the shooting, she says, but she knows Mon did it. Her story is that she and Mon do go with Hunter and Morales to Pasadena. They get out of the car. Terri says that Mon rushes off. And some minutes later she hears sounds like shots fired and Mon comes running back and they jump into the car and speed away from the scene. They race along the 210 freeway and then the 2 freeway, suddenly out of the urban world and into a stark, mountainous landscape. They exit at Mountain Road, make a quick turn up the hill to a cul-de-sac where the homes press right up to a steep dropoff, protected from the mountainside only by a railing. And Mon hurls the gun over the railing.

Mon's version is different. He hears the shot, too, and it's Jayson Hunter who comes running. And all three of them get in the car and Hunter hands him the gun and tells him to dump it. They drop Hunter off and get rid of the gun.

Whatever. Mon is now in deep trouble. Not only is his former wife testifying against him but so is Jayson Hunter, claiming that Mon did the killing.

So eager is law enforcement to get the shooter in this case that they grant Hunter immunity and place him in the witness-protection program. (Supposedly, this bottom-echelon criminal is in some danger for his role in this trial, but I never see any evidence of that.) They even accede to his insistence that he will not deal with the county district attorney's office but only with the state attorney general's office (Hunter is miffed at the way the DA treated him in the earlier hearings). So the two defendants who remain to be judged by a jury of their peers are Mon and Dr. Bulpitt. Two assistant attorneys general are prosecuting.

The prosecutors' reasoning, I imagine, is this: Bulpitt did the actual contracting and Mon did the actual killing, in their opinion. So the two middlemen, Hunter and his buddy Morales (who is never charged at all), will be let off the hook. Not only will Hunter go free but because he is placed in the witness-protection program, he will get an allowance to help support his family, he will be chauffeured around when he needs a ride and he will live, in general, as a big shot.

This is the crazy, the utterly arbitrary, part about so many of these cases. There is a pretense that the public, at trial, will decide guilt or innocence, that justice is in the public's hands. Yet the cops and the prosecutors are making decisions and deals all along the way, often even before anyone is charged. They decide to go for the death penalty against one of the players in this saga and—at the other extreme—decide it's justifiable and even necessary to coddle the other apparently guilty parties. So while the defense attorney is, by virtual mandate, supposed to be the advocate for the accused, you find the prosecutors, in a sense, doing the same thing, defending the patently guilty when it suits their purposes.

I'm sure that the distinguished state prosecutors were patting themselves on the back for the way they had this all figured out.

But their case was going to fall apart in the most outrageous, hilarious fashion, before their very eyes.

As for the defense case, I start out in reasonably good shape, in my view. The main prosecution witness, Jayson Hunter, the star, is so filthy that he will admit on the stand, under protection of immunity, to having been involved in sixteen murders. A spurned wife won't be hard to deal with, clearly consumed by jealousy—and she, everyone has to acknowledge, didn't say anything against Mon for the year before she became incensed about his seeing someone else. Then she decides to get even.

A potential scheduling problem in this trial is that Hunter, it turns out, has terminal stomach cancer, although he's still well enough to get around. He has already testified in a preliminary hearing to Mon's culpability, and that testimony will be used against Mon if Hunter dies before the full-blown trial. I want to be sure we—my partner in this case was a close colleague, Jerry Gordon—give him the full treatment, that I can cross-examine him to the hilt. I don't want him to die on me before I rip his credibility to shreds. So I arrange to use a device like the one much of the country observed in the O. J. Simpson case, when Rosa Lopez testified on videotape—testimony to be shown to the jury later, just in case she can't be summoned back in person at the appropriate time. Well, there was a good chance Jayson Hunter couldn't be summoned in person at the appropriate time. So we conduct a conditional examination of witness Hunter for the video camera.

During the conditional exam, Hunter starts to behave in a peculiar fashion. I don't really see it at first. But Mon says that this *chulo* (he means rat) is making signals at us.

"What kind of signals?"

"He's going like this," Mon says, demonstrating by moving two of his fingers as if they were walking through the Yellow Pages.

"What does it mean?"

Mon says, "It means I walk. He's going to change his testimony, and then I'm going to walk."

I say, "But Mon, when is he thinking about doing this thing? The guy's going to die."

Mon can't say. "I don't know how this guy thinks," he says.

The conditional exam continues along, with Hunter telling the same story he's been telling, about how Mon was the shooter. I rip into him a bit (he's taking a lot of medication, though, and sometimes he's too weak to go on). I elicit that the state has paid him $30,000 so far for his help in this case. He's combative sometimes, silly sometimes, a terrible witness. I can't believe the jury will believe a thing he says and I'm pretty content with that.

Around about that time, I'm in Municipal Court in Van Nuys—the same town where later I have to handle the Menendez trial—on a small misdemeanor case. In the same courthouse, there's a big publicity trial going on involving Alfred Bloomingdale and his mistress. It turns out Jayson Hunter is there, too, popping in on the big trial as an observer.

And then he comes into my courtroom.

"What are you doing here, Jay?"

"Oh, I wanted to see if there was any action off this Bloomingdale thing," he says. I haven't the foggiest idea what he means but these guys are always working something.

I taunt him a bit. "Aren't you afraid to be out in the open, Jay? Where are your witness protectors?"

"Ditched those guys," he says.

Now he wants to talk to me in private. We go outside onto the courthouse terrace and we're leaning against the wall. People are streaming by, but nobody's paying us any mind.

"You know, your guy Mon," he says, "he didn't do it."

"Yeah, that's what I understand, but who did?"

He whispers, "I did it. I took the dude out."

"Uh-huh, then how come you're testifying under oath for three months that you gave Mon the gun, that Mon agreed to do it, that Mon hid in the bushes? All this bullshit? If you did it?"

"Well, I was going to straighten that out," he says.

"You're going to die, Jay. When were you planning to straighten it out?"

He agrees this is a possible problem.

I make a proposal. "If you know you're telling the truth, and you don't want to see an innocent man fall, you come to my office, we'll tape-record your statement."

"I'll do that," he says, "I'll do that. But listen, these boop-boop cops"— many of these guys actually say "boop-boop" as, I think, an alternative to "bleeping"—"these boop-boop cops shadow me all the time, you know. I think they got a tap on my phone."

We decide on a code. I call his house, ask for Elena, and he calls me back from somewhere.

"Hey, Leslie, it's me, it's Jayson. Here's the deal. You pick me up at the California Commerce Club."

The first time we go to get him, Jerry Gordon and I, we realize we're meeting him in one of these cavernous gambling places thick with card tables, gamblers cheek by jowl, and people milling all over the place, and Jayson Hunter is obviously a person of stature here, well known. I think to myself, Yeah, this guy is terrified, he desperately needs the witness-protection program.

Back at the office, with the tape recorder running, we do a lengthy interview in which he pretty much says what Mon has been saying. That Mon was in the park, only there to make sure they earn the money to pay him, and that it's Jayson who does the hit. (I could speculate about his motives for confessing, but the fact is I don't know them.)

Along the way, it dawns on me that this isn't a tape recording I want the jury to hear. For one thing, I have a certain capacity for coarse speech that springs into full bloom when I interview lowlifes. I probably said "fuck" in its various permutations almost as much as Jayson Hunter did. No good. Not for the jury.

So I say, "You know, Jay, I don't want to have to play just a tape of you. You know if you die and you're not there for trial, a tape recording is not as good as, you know, a video. How would you feel about going out to Pasadena and you show me what you did, where you were, where you went and we videotape it?"

"You mean we do like a film," he says. He likes it. "That's fine, that's cool."

As soon as he's gone, I call my graphics man, Bob Seltzer, the same guy who worked up the eyewitness boards I used in the Bob's Big Boy final argument, and tell him what's up. Can we do it at night? Yeah, we can. Bob will handle the sound; he'll hire a cameraman. A wrinkle is that we're supposed to get a filming permit from the city. But there is no way I want to alert the police about what we're up to with their protected witness.

We designate a night, pick Hunter up and go out to dinner first at the Velvet Turtle, a comfortable chain restaurant. My main concern as we make small talk is that somehow we aren't spotted by any cops who might know anything about the case. Seltzer's main concern, as he recalls sometime later, is that he doesn't want to piss this guy off—the nondescript, pasty guy sitting across the table who happens to be a contract killer. Seltzer is smiling a lot.

Then we go to the intersection of Marengo and Colorado, to the Pacific Bell Telephone Company building, the site of the killing. We're real close to the police station. I am acutely aware of how easily we can be caught.

The camera is loaded with infrared film. Jayson crouches down near where the Rolls was parked and where Snodgrass was standing. He goes "boom, boom, boom." And then he flees, like he says he did during the actual killing, running down into the sunken plaza, up some stairs, across the street, through some alleys and to the getaway car.

We're chasing after him, the cameraman, Seltzer with a boom microphone, Jerry Gordon and I. Running. We're dying inside: some patrol car could come rolling around the corner at any time. But it's great. I'm trying not to laugh.

A few days later, I go to see the video at Seltzer's office, and it is gorgeous. But what really is gorgeous is the trap we've laid for the prosecution.

The trial begins two or three months later and Jayson Hunter is still alive and still on our side. In fact, he likes the relationship. He calls me from time to time, under our code system, and makes small talk. "How you doing, Leslie? How's Mon? What's new?" And constantly complaining about the "boop-boop cops."

Finally, we get to the most delicious time in the trial when Jayson Hunter is called as a witness. One of the assistant attorneys general is taking him back through the story he told at the conditional exam. Early on, Hunter is following the familiar earlier script. He tells how the whole group goes out to Pasadena to case the place. He tells about the gun, which was supplied by Bulpitt and wrapped in a red bandanna and put inside a paper bag. But he has not testified that Mon agreed to do this hit, or anything like that. He is being vague, evasive. The prosecutor, Michael Whelan, is a little concerned about that. Hunter tells him the gun was left in the bag in the bushes by the office building.

He's trying to get Hunter to implicate Mon, the way he always had in the past and he asks him, "Who had you talked to about leaving the bag in the bushes?"

Hunter says, "Frank Morales." The prosecutor is baffled.

"Did you talk to defendant Buenrostro about it?"

"No, sir." And before he's pressed further, Hunter does a riff on Morales. "We went up there, Frank Morales and myself and a few other people, and we checked the whole area out, because Frank is very—he's very precise in what he does. You know, he likes everything to be like in Disneyland, everything to be, you know, perfect. That's the only way I can describe it you know. Everything to be perfect."

This is the Twilight Zone as far as Whelan is concerned and he's fighting it, trying to keep Hunter, his protected witness from wandering off. What was supposed to happen to the gun? he wants to know.

"It was supposed to be picked up later on," says Hunter.

"By whom?"

"By myself."

This should have been the tipoff to Whelan that he ought to stop now, call a recess, and figure out what's going on, but he can't seem to help himself and he keeps forging on.

"What was to happen with the gun while it was in the bushes, if anything?" he asks.

Hunter's enjoying himself at this point and answers, "Nothing. It's not a chicken. Doesn't lay eggs. Nothing can happen to it."

"Was there a reason, Mr. Hunter, to put a gun in a bag in bushes and then come back and pick it up later?"

"Yes, sir," he says. What might that be? "Commit a murder."

"Whose murder?" Whelan asks.

"Chuck Snodgrass."

Whelan, still pushing to get the part about Mon out in the open, asks, "How was it going to kill somebody from a position in the bushes?"

"Somebody had to use it."

"Ah," says Whelan. "Who was going to use it?"

"Myself!" says honest Jayson Hunter. Whelan's jaw goes slack. His mouth is hanging open. And still, he moves on.

"Who did you kill?" Whelan asks, and I'm wondering as the hysterical giggling is trying to rise in my body, Doesn't this guy have any brakes on that runaway train?

"Chuck Snodgrass," Hunter says again. I am covering my face now.

Soon we reveal to the prosecution that this is even worse than they thought. The existence of the tape-recorded confession comes out; so does the filmed version.

Bulpitt's lawyer, who is not in on any of this, is looking at me with a "Jesus, what's going on here!" look.

I mouth the word "Later" to him.

It is a gut-bursting great moment in my courtroom life.

But it is a Thursday. The court won't be in session on Friday. That leaves several days for the prosecutors and everybody else to descend on Jayson Hunter and get him to turn his story back around again. After all, he's on their payroll and, also, they have it in their ability to make his coddled life miserable.

By the time he gets back on the stand, he says that the Thursday testimony and the whole story he gave me was because he was warned that horrible things might happen to his family if he testified against Mon. None of that holds much water when I get around to crossing him —it looks like he doesn't want to lose a meal ticket—and many of the jurors don't believe anything he says.

The jury does convict Mon of conspiracy to commit murder because they know he was part of this thing somehow, but they hang six to six on the murder-for-hire charge because some of them believe Jayson Hunter actually did do the shooting. I think they also resent the fact that Hunter isn't on trial, that somehow a sleazeball like that, a man at least as guilty as Mon, could be the star on the righteous prosecution side.

Given the verdict and the hung jury on the murder count, the case could have dragged on for much longer. But evidently the prosecutors just want to bring this thing to a close. They don't want to have to deal with a possible appeal on the conspiracy conviction and they are hoping not to have to go back and try on the murder again. (For my part, if we do appeal, I am not optimistic about our chances.) So we bargain. Conspiracy carries with it twenty-five-to-life. Second-degree murder is fifteen-to-life.

Mon and I talk. He tells me now that, yeah, he really was the one who pulled the trigger. He says he saw it as a duty in service of Donald Garcia, and anyway, the guy was a snitch, and snitches aren't the same thing as human beings. If he hadn't admitted it to me at that point, I wouldn't have allowed him to take a murder plea, even in the second degree.

But that's what he does in the end.

Mon, when he gets the chance to talk to people about how all this happened, likes to tell them what a good job I did for him. "Leslie was so good," he told a friend of mine. "For a while there she even had me believing I didn't do it."

When this one was over, I didn't have any of those awful regrets that I felt after the Bob's Big Boy case, when I thought that I could have done more in the penalty phase. Here, both Jerry and I felt the case had gone as well as it possibly could.

Only later did I start to get the feeling that this was a Pyrrhic victory after all. Maybe the state knew that paroles were getting so hard to come by that anything with the word "life" at the end of the sentence was going to be just fine from their perspective. But the truth is that this lark of a case took a dark turn. Hunter was never charged, of course, but he did die. Morales was never charged. Dr. Bulpitt is in prison to this day. So is Mon, still strong of mind and body, but about fifty years old, theoretically eligible for parole, but I just don't know if we'll ever pull it off. I haven't laughed about this case in a long time.

14

Pelican Bay

I never look forward to going to Pelican Bay, and wouldn't go if it weren't for Mon. At the far northern end of California, just across from Oregon, it is the state prison that I regard as the cruelest of all, a maximum-security facility where the goals go beyond the usual ones. Here, one of the major aims of the institution, although it is not codified anywhere that I know about, is to break the spirit of the men it confines.

It is a thirteen-hour car ride from L.A. to the prison, just outside of Crescent City. Even when you fly it takes most of the day. It's mid-May and I'm on my way up there for the third time, and dreading it. Mon wants me there, to help with his latest parole hearing. As I suspected at the conclusion of his case, second-degree murder would be no sure ticket for parole for Salvador Buenrostro. Mon is still doing his fifteen-to-life for killing Chuck Snodgrass in 1980. He still sees it as a legitimate killing, differentiated from shooting an "innocent" person. To him, this sort of killing remains something like accepting a dangerous assignment in the military. Loyalty, courage, all that. Despite a demonstrated capacity for violence and other crime (when he was younger, that is—I do believe he is no longer the threat he was), I can't help harboring a soft spot for Mon. He's a mensch, really, a stubborn, macho man. He keeps to his principles, self-destructive though they may be. That's a refreshing change from the run-of-the-mill convicts you deal with every day who are for the most part a bunch of wimps and weenies, tough-talking men who would snitch on their sisters if it meant they could get a better pair of shoes.

Life, for Mon, right now is about as low as life can get. At Pelican Bay State Prison, the penal system has created an institution that shouts out the folly, the sadism—and the injustice—that guide today's incarcerative minds. The bureaucrats are determined to break the prison gangs (which do have power inside, but virtually none on the outside, since outside you have to be a bit smarter). They are going to do it through hard punishment and by turning one man against the other. The penal system takes what any knowledgeable, sensible person would recognize immediately as a group of broken-down losers and, like a dominatrix with a whip, it beats them into the ground until they snivel. The approach is basic and brutal: keep these men in virtual solitary confinement for all their remaining lives—or until they break.

They are considered broken, and the jailers have won, when convicts "debrief." That means when they tell what they know about the criminal activities of everybody they ever knew in their group. Most of them eventually line up to debrief. They say things that are true and things they make up. They talk a blue streak, dying to help themselves out so that they can go to an easier prison or maybe set themselves up for eventual parole if they qualify, although these days, contrary to common belief, it's increasingly difficult to achieve parole under any circumstance.

Mon is refusing to debrief. He has watched others use his stature and the respect he has garnered in prison to their advantage and he is scornful of them. "People used to get out of here by saying they know Mon," he tells me. But what stature he has resides in his manliness. If he ever did debrief and somehow got paroled, everyone in prison would know he'd done it. Unlike those who are there on life without parole, he has the possibility, at fifteen-to-life, to go free. "I'm afraid of what I would think of myself if I did it," he says. His catch-22 looks a lot like caught-forever. He can choose to keep his pride, as he has, in an effort to keep his dignity, but in fact it ensures his perpetual dehumanization.

As I travel toward yet another parole board hearing, I am not hopeful, but daydream optimistically anyway. I always nourish myself with this little fantasy about getting Mon out one of these days and hiring him to work around my house, watch after my kid, drive my car, keep out of trouble for a change.

The first leg of the flight is to San Francisco, then there's an hour-and-a-half layover. I get some lunch, a shrimp cocktail at a seafood restaurant in the airport to kill time, and then walk out on the tarmac toward one of those puddle-jumpers that scare the hell out of a lot of people, me included. The little plane taxis and then lurches north toward Eureka and Arcata, or, as they say in one burp, Eureka-Arcata. We are served by a flight attendant who is partial to the funny-stewardess schtick. When we drop out of the sky and bounce onto the runway, she tells us to remain in our seats until the aircraft comes to a complete stop, adding, "If you do stand up earlier it will be my indication that you have agreed to help me clean the plane." There isn't much laughter. Besides, the way this thing bumps and swerves, I'm not eager to move around anyhow.

In Eureka, in the blink of an eye, you know you've left big-time California far behind; you might as well be in Alaska. This is redwood country, deep woods to the east and north, the Pacific to the west. The airport design mimics a redwood lodge. Out there in the forest somewhere reside who knows how many solid-citizen patriots busy fleeing government interference in their lives, except for wanting to be sure they get their Social Security checks on time. For me, it's a creepy place, creepy for the entire stretch along the Redwood Highway.

I usually come in the spring, when the fog wraps around the massive trees and darkens the tortuous coastal road for the whole two hours it takes to get to Crescent City and the Pelican Bay State Prison. You drive about sixty-five slow miles, constantly threatened by the straining, looming logging trucks. A reasonable conclusion would be that they put the prison all the way up here because they fear the convicts might escape. But that's not it at all.

They could put this airtight prison in downtown Santa Monica and not worry about breakouts. The reason they built it here is that, except for some fishing and logging, there is no work, and the community welcomes even this grim business, as many other recession-weary places have. In just the last fifteen years California has built twenty new prisons. Guards are now paid more than some tenured professors at the state university, and the operating and building costs of prisons have gone from $7 billion to $30 billion a year. The guards' union is now the biggest source of political contributions in the state. This is the one segment of the state's economy that has been growing, come recession or high water. Yessir, it was a fine catch for Crescent City.

But the consequences of that economic decision on inmates—the fact that it often becomes a marathon experience for members of their families to ever visit—are not a consideration, apparently. The siting of the prison is one more callous punishment added to the sentences of these people, who come mostly from poor families without the resources to leave the inner city easily. Those prisoners who do get all the way back home one day find their family structure is already shattered. Invariably. You can bet on it. And while they reside at Pelican Bay their loneliness is thus deeper than it necessarily has to be, according to any penal code or even according to the state's intentions.

For this visit to Pelican Bay, the parole board set a May hearing, a bit later in the season than I'm used to, so there is actually some sun streaming through the grand trees from time to time, making the drive bearable, even uplifting, momentarily. I wind through Orick (the rodeo is coming, according to a sign) and past the burl sculptures (made from the knots of trees) that are the art of the highway. But as art they are just a notch or two up from roadkills: wooden bears line up to beg along the roadside for thousands of yards.

At Crescent City there's a rustic commercial marina—I see no pleasure boats at all. The fog is rolling in again. Past Crescent City at Smith River ("Easter Lily Capital of the World") is a hotel, the Ship Ashore Resort, which always amuses me, and I really do like it as a place to stay, if I have to stay here at all. To enter it you drive through a mobile-home park at the front, many of the homes gussied up with neat little gardens, potted flowers, glass-enclosed porches—a retirement community at the edge of the earth. At the motel behind the mobile homes each of the rooms backs onto the mouth of the Smith River as it opens into the Pacific. Gulls wail. Sea otters peek up through the surface of the water, look around and slide under again. Dark-feathered ducks stand off in the distance all in a row, like the supports to a dock that some storm blew away long ago.

The Ship Ashore Resort is as remote a place as anyone could find but awfully convenient, too, in that it's just a stone's throw from the joint.

Next morning the fog is thick and I can't see more than a few feet of water beneath the room's window; I can barely make out a boulder reaching up from the Smith River obscured in a blanket of gauze. But the view doesn't matter anyhow. I have to drive to Pelican Bay just ten minutes away, but the time-consuming entry procedure is always a bitch. I know a lot of the rules, but always seem to miss some of them. Can't wear any shade of blue so that you aren't confused with the prisoners. Can't wear short skirts (might be titillating) or carry an open pack of cigarettes (might contain contraband). I park the car and walk over to the building marked "SHU VISITING."

SHU stands for security housing units. A tall, beefy officer with close-

cropped hair smiles and starts the visitor-admission routine. He goes
through the contents of my purse. As it happens, I'm carrying a lighter
that is not transparent (might contain who knows what) but fortunately I
also carry one that is, so I can leave the first behind. I've got too many
keys on my person (could be used as weapons), so I'm only allowed to
keep the one car key and the others are returned to the car. And then,
after all the searching of my possessions is completed, I can't make it
through the damned metal detector anyway. This detector is a much
more powerful instrument than you experience at airports. I do believe
it is meant to detect metal in bodily orifices. As it happens, I am sure that
what it's detecting is the metal in my sleeve buttons. A female officer is
summoned to do a wand search. The officers have the right to strip-
search me, too—and if I refuse, simply deny me entrance—but that
proves unnecessary. It's the buttons.

The rules, of course, are only marginally directed at lawyers. It's true
that all sorts of people may have reason to visit this prison. Some of the
rules are commonsense necessities when dealing with convicted criminals
and their associates. Some are simply intended to keep girlfriends from
being sexy (even though they conduct their visit from the other side of
glass): "Female visitors," the official pamphlet says, "must wear brassieres
and undergarments."

The pamphlet also lays down the law, just in case. "The Department
of Corrections is prohibited from recognizing hostages for bargaining to
effect an escape by inmates," it says. Okay. Just so we're straight on that.

A particularly warm touch is that a few feet from the metal detector
there's a glass case with souvenirs that you can bring home from Pelican
Bay, T-shirts, sweatshirts and the like. One of the sweatshirts, a black
hooded one, is especially handsome. It depicts the razor-wire fence
around the institution, a lightning bolt and the word "electrified" running
vertically down the front in decorative letters. Department of Corrections
humor, cute. The atmosphere in this building, dedicated to the serious
business of screening visitors, is a bit more jocular than you might expect.
While I'm being searched, I hear a couple of the deputies in the office
getting off on jokes. O. J.'s gloves-don't-fit jokes: "Who do they fit?" one
of them laughs. "Bishop Tutu?" Cute, so cute. So are the uniformed white
guys telling the jokes. Just your cute little racists.

To leave the visitors' building you're accompanied by an officer into a
big outdoor cage. It opens on one side to let you in and then closes
behind you before the other side opens to let you out. The female officer
and I walk toward the units. They are blue-gray and the walls facing us
have no windows. They look like abandoned handball courts. Beneath

our feet is crushed slate that slopes up to the gray units. On this dreary morning, it is also the very same color as the sky, a world in monotone, everything merging into everything else, bound by the fog.

"It's usually raining when I get here," I small-talk to the deputy. "It's summer now," she says, "so we get fog."

The most cheerful color is the light blue of the gun towers that surround the yard just inside the razor wire (which is, in actuality, electrified, just like the sweatshirt says; Mon tells me that in the morning they send a crew out to pick up the dead birds). There are no inmates to be seen in this part of the institution because they are mostly in isolation, provided with private yards behind their units. "Anyone want yard?" a guard calls out in the morning and those who do will get the chance to walk around alone in the small fenced area adjoining their cells. You quickly realize that in its elaborate efforts to keep these men apart and alone, the state lavishes more attention on this handful of losers than it does on its budding scholars, its medical students or its desperately needy. It wants them more miserable than a chicken in a coop—and has achieved its desire for the most part.

I enter the visiting cubicle, about twice the size of a telephone booth, with, in fact, a phone on the wall to the right. One wall is glass. Mon, his hands cuffed behind his back, is brought to a matching cubicle on the other side of the glass. When his door is locked, he extends his hands through a slot at his back and the cuffs are removed by a guard on the outside of his cubicle. Mon looks more wiry and smaller than he did when I first met him thirteen years ago. He was chubbier then, his face fuller. Now his features seem angular and furrowed but, nearing fifty, he is still handsome. His black hair is still full and dense despite some gray. He used to like shaving his head so he could feel the sun on his scalp when he got outside, but now, he says, everybody shaves and he doesn't want to be like everybody. He smiles when he speaks, shrugs often, uses his hands a lot to gesticulate. He's wearing black-rimmed glasses.

The tattoos leap out at you. There's a woman obliterating the skin of most of each heavily muscled forearm. One of them is in fact two tattoos; when the hairstyles of the early sixties went out, he had to have a new tattoo placed over the one that was there to update the thing.

Usually we talk on the wall phone; today they provide us with a speaker that requires pushing a button to be heard. I try it. "Say something, Mon."

"Something," he says. It's a lame joke. He smiles and shrugs.

They have cut the visiting time, limited to weekends only, to a mere one hour a day for family and friends. A fair reward for a thirteen-hour ride from L.A., don't you think? Unsurprisingly, only on rare occasions does anyone visit two weeks, or even two months, in a row. As his lawyer, I can talk to him for as long as I like to prepare for the parole hearing later in the day. So there's no rush and we chat. He's worried about the teenage daughter. She's been getting into trouble lately, and he wants to be sure she writes to him so he knows what's going on. He's still making excuses for his son, currently incarcerated at Chino. ("It's my fault because I spoiled him," Mon says. "In my better days, you know, he was always the first one on the block to get a bike.") He's been reading *USA Today, Health* magazine, *National Geographic* and a daily law journal, and he gets a kick out of the fact that one of the guards is in awe of his erudition. "You read!" the guard said to him incredulously. Mon laughs as he relates the encounter. Lately, he's been "reading the movies." The movies? "You know, John Grisham books."

It is continually astonishing to me that these men almost invariably adjust, no matter how denigrated and confined they are. Why all of them don't just slip into catatonia is beyond me. Mon tells me in his easygoing way that he's making the best of it, reconciling himself. He wakes up every morning at 3:00 A.M., he believes (they don't allow clocks or watches in the cells), rolls up his mattress and works out—push-ups, sit-ups—until 6:00 A.M., taking occasional breaks. "Lots of kids in their twenties can't keep up with me," he says, without seeming boastful.

He goes nowhere unless escorted by a guard; his food is brought to his cell. He is never physically touched by another human being except for dentists, barbers and the like. When he goes to the dentist he is cuffed, shackled and strip-searched first. But he does get in some socializing, despite all that. When the guard escorts him downstairs to shower and shave, Mon talks quickly and cryptically to men as he passes their cells. There's hollering all over the unit as the men try to reach each other with their voices. A legendary way of communicating is by "kite," a written note that is secretly passed from one inmate to another. This is how they learn news about one another and enforce the rules of the prison culture, sometimes ordering violence done to one or another of their associates.

But Mon thinks the kites have an inflated reputation. "Fifty-five percent of the time a kite never gets anywhere. The guards get it and it goes to the state. Kites are stupid, period," he says. It is a world, he says, "where everybody is spying on everybody else," no matter how great the isolation. And what seems to sadden Mon particularly—this guy who once thought that the most beautiful thing in the world was to be part of the Mexican Mafia where "one man could call another man brother from his heart"—is that "now we spend our lives telling on each other."

Sometimes it sounds like he's actually afraid to leave the prison. Mon, in his half century on earth, has been incarcerated more than not, like most of his friends. "Lots of people grew up in the jails together," he says. "We were in Juvenile together."

There is a routine reliability about life here, no matter how oppressive. The institution gives him an allowance of thirty-five dollars a month; on the outside, he isn't sure he knows where to find thirty-five dollars, short of crime. "Here our needs are low," he says. "You got your color TV in the cell, draw thirty-five dollars a month and get a package from home once every year.

"But when you go out," he says, "it's a shock. There's new cars out there, you're far behind, and what I always said before was, 'Mon, you gotta catch up.' "

Has he changed? Could he make it on the outside? Maybe. He thinks so. "I realize now I can't catch up right away. Every time I think like that I stumble and end up back here. I have to get in line and wait," he says. Sounds good. A hopeful sign.

Paradoxically, as long as he is in prison, he is somebody, a big shot. He is Mon, the guy whom snitches love to rat on, even if they have nothing to say, the guy whom Mexican Mafiosi admire even if he doesn't want anything to do with them anymore. Mon, the man they tried to assassinate because they thought he was a threat to their pathetic power structure, because he just naturally conveys a sense of stature. They saw him as a stop sign. What he was trying to do was stop them from knocking each other off every time they managed to get the opportunity. "That's just too dumb," he says. "You stab somebody and it's supposed to be an ego feather—it's not even a chicken feather."

Assassins attacked him one day when he was shackled in the attorney's visiting room at the Los Angeles County Jail. He was transported there on some flimsy excuse that he might be useful in a case unrelated to his own. Two cons—mysteriously in possession of handcuff keys—got free, wielding their homemade knives, and stabbed him over and over again while he could not move. He can forgive the attack, because, rightly or wrongly, a hit may seem necessary according to the mores of his crowd, but "it's the way they did it," he says, still shaken by the assault after three years. "I was cuffed; I couldn't fight."

He says, and I think it could be at least in part a macho pose, that he holds no resentment for the attackers. He doesn't like to be overtly angry at all. ("That's the past," he says. "I got tomorrow to live for.") He isn't angry about the fact that his wife, Terri, turned on him for the benefit of the police and is a major reason that he is in prison now. He doesn't even want to say anything harsh about the guards at Pelican Bay.

He loves the idea of family, his family as well as anybody else's, and talking about the guards he says, "I know the guard is here to support his family. I'm here because I got caught. Neither one of us wants to be here. I don't want to make his job harder." This sounds weird to me since I know the SHU unit has the toughest guards in the system. Hello, Stockholm Syndrome.

The one thing he's furious about is his TV, which has been on the fritz lately. "That piece of shit," he says, making a spitting gesture without actually spitting. He needs his TV to pass the time and substitute for human association. In fact—although you'll hear some sadistic prison authority talk about how these guys shouldn't be here enjoying themselves watching TV all the time—the penal institution needs television as much as the inmates do. It pacifies them. The one thing the guards and the officials of the institution want is for these discarded people to remain quiet, cause no trouble, until one day they leave or die.

At about fifty, Mon has reached an age when, before they became so politicized, parole boards used to lighten up a bit. They know that men well along in middle age have seen their testosterone seep away. The storm that raged in their brains when they were in their twenties has finally subsided. Men in their fifties and sixties, once violent, are usually no longer much of a threat, and, from the point of view of the institution, as the prisoners' health inevitably declines they become an especially expensive burden. But these days the parole boards are in no mood to be reasonable or trusting.

Mon is realistic as we get ready. "I guess the best we can hope for is they don't yell at me, huh, Leslie?" I laugh. He laughs. In fact the hearing is a disaster. He is not sufficiently remorseful about his crime. ("They want me to grow a little mustache and go around slouching and hanging my head," is how he sees it.) He tries to tell them for the hundredth time why he can't debrief. It's not just pride, he says, but if a member of his family got hurt in retaliation for something Mon might have said, he couldn't live with himself. He starts to choke up as he says this to the board. They are not moved by the sight.

They set his next hearing not for one year or two—but for three years. Years mean nothing to these people. And the applicant is dismissed.

He has tomorrow to live for, Mon says, but I'm afraid as I drive away from Pelican Bay State Prison that all his tomorrows are going to be exactly alike. He's trapped, between merciless pride and a hard place.

It's his own doing, I know that. But I keep thinking, We're spending $35,000 a year to keep him locked up in this place. What would have happened if we had spent a third of that on him when he was growing up? He sure as hell wouldn't be here.

I've seen so many lawyers over the years who stand up in court and let their clients plead guilty to twenty and thirty years and they haven't a clue to what that means. They haven't spent a day inside those places. And if they think twenty or thirty years there is nothing (see how easy it is to say "twenty or thirty" as if they were almost the same number?) then they are stupid, venal people who ought to get out of the defense game.

I am a defense attorney. I have clients to protect: "What do all these numbers mean, Judge? Twenty years . . . fifteen years . . . ten years." The numbers are just thrown around as if prison were a temporary dropoff in life, a meaningless blip. That isn't the reality of it. Reality is you're in this hideous, ugly place where everybody is out to get you. The guards can be vicious. They deprive you of normal human comforts. And depending on what ethnic group you belong to, it is very likely that a lot of guys from other ethnic groups may want to kill you.

People ask how I can defend known criminals. I've been inside prisons, I answer. That's why. Nobody should have to live that way. We've got to find other ways to protect society from people who commit crimes. Except those for whom there absolutely is no hope. Hannibal Lecters have to be locked up and isolated. But most of the people in prison haven't even committed violent crimes. What galls me is that we've never really tried alternatives, let alone prevention. All our resources are directed into punishment. Makes the politicians sound so macho—lock 'em up and throw away the key. But those are *people* we're throwing away—people.

15

Chinatown

When the rains come to sunny Los Angeles, as in most years they do in the winter, it is always as if they take the folks in LaLa Land by surprise. People here don't know how to handle rain. Drivers slow to a crawl. And, slow as they're going, they still crash into each other on the freeways. The airwaves are full of calamity-filled chatter about this crash and that one. If you are on the road during these wet, surreal periods what you want to do is get where you're going and be done with it until the sun comes out again.

During one of those periods, on December 19, 1984, with Christmas shopping in full swing and rain just relentless for days, I am making my way out of downtown and toward the west, toward my office on Wilshire. Abruptly, the traffic obsessions on the radio give way to a breaking story.

On the radio, KFWB, an all-news station, an anchor named Jim Burson comes on to report that "two robbery suspects have been killed in an exchange of fire with police officers" in Chinatown. The reporter on the scene, Dan Abey, picks up the story to say that "two policemen were shot" and now, "as far as we know, five people were shot. . . . Two suspects killed." And he throws it back to Jim.

"All right, Dan, and we'll look forward to your next report on this breaking story."

Cops shot! That's all I need to hear. I'm on the freeway trying to get away from downtown anyway—Chinatown is practically in the shadows of the courthouses—and now I know the roads already moving slowly are going to be a total nightmare. Cops are going to be converging from everywhere. Chinatown, and who knows how much of the rest of downtown, will be cordoned off. I can hear sirens even now.

"Here is a KFWB news bulletin. The Los Angeles Police Department says the police officer shot in Chinatown earlier this afternoon has died. I repeat: the Los Angeles Police Department says the police officer shot in Chinatown earlier this afternoon has died. . . . KFWB's Dan Abey is in downtown Los Angeles and has more from the scene of the shooting. Dan . . ."

Dan observes, in a lame effort to capture the terrible pall the crime is already throwing over the city, "There are no smiles in Chinatown."

But Jesus. This is going to be bad. They are describing the suspects on the radio. I figure those guys don't have a chance. If the cops get the opportunity they may well shoot them virtually on sight. Kill a cop and you're history. When one of their own is killed, the cops always get their man, one way or another. Most of the time, after a cop killing, the LAPD becomes competent all of a sudden. You can tell right at the scene. They get real serious. No banter, not even any tension-breaking gallows humor. It's inappropriate, of course. Compare that to the snuffing of a dope dealer, a comedy routine by comparison.

Despite the gravity of it, this investigation, death of a cop, somehow managed to get off on the wrong foot anyway. Maybe it was the rain.

The attempted robbery and the shooting took place at the Jin Hing Company on Bamboo Lane, a dreary alley (although it looks fine enough, when the sun shines) between Broadway and Hill Street. It is just a few steps from the famous Phoenix Bakery, which specializes in wonderful strawberry shortcakes with almonds pressed around the sides and one of the best places in all of L.A. for birthday cakes and Chinese cookies and novelty cakes. (I've been there often—it's so close to the courts.)

Above the Phoenix at the time is a community police station that is paid for by the merchants and serves more as a public relations gesture than anything else. Two patrol officers man it part-time. As the reports of the shooting come into police headquarters, Bill Gailey is assigned as the investigating officer. He is heartthrob material, one of the smartest, most honest and handsome policemen I was ever lucky enough to meet. (He reminds me a little of Robert Redford.) He is slow getting to the scene, however, even though LAPD headquarters, Parker Center, is just a few blocks away. All the streets are already cordoned off and he practically has to blast his way through. Crowds of cops in yellow slickers are at the scene by the time he arrives. In groups large and small they are huddling in doorways—as well as in the store itself—to get out of the rain. Somehow, the police chief, the never-publicity-shy Daryl Gates, has managed to beat Bill there and has already traipsed through the tiny store. Some evidence has been moved prematurely.

Gailey is horrified; it is the worst mess he's seen except in cases of arson where fire and firemen destroy everything: "You guys have fucked up my crime scene!" he yells into the crowd.

As all of that is going on, I am driving slowly and thinking to myself that this is one I really might get—not just a remote possibility—but something that could very well come to me in light of how I've been working my way up through these ghastly crimes. I know a lot of the judges think highly of my abilities and by this time good judges are looking to appoint good lawyers to the death cases. Coincidentally, I've just been introduced to the judge recently assigned to the felony arraignment court, the judge who makes the court appointments on the big cases. And this is one big case that I really want. I keep learning so much on this job, maneuvering myself into niches of humanity that I never would get to see or understand except for my choice of career, and this one has about it the mystery, the miasma, yes, of Chinatown, a shadowy place that puts on a happy face for the public but where, beneath the surface, there are always deals and power struggles. Even the crimes tend to be different: it's gambling and prostitution that are really big and so is robbery. But, surprisingly perhaps, given our stereotypes about Asians, rarely drugs.

And this huge case comes at a time when crime among Asians—a group about whom, at this point, I understand very little—is expanding rapidly. The second wave of Vietnamese refugees has arrived in town. The first were the ones you always hear about, remarkable stories, kids who seem to arrive here full-blown as class valedictorians and candidates for scholarship to UCLA. But the second wave is poorer, more at loose ends, less able to learn English, succeed in school, find work. So like so many others on the ladder's bottom rung at this far edge of America, they dream "The Dream" without the means to fulfill it.

Even though this crime results in several eyewitnesses, as well as a lot of physical evidence, it is not a classic whodunit like many of the others I've described so far. Within a couple of days it becomes clear who was involved. The problem here is, who's done exactly what? And unlike my experience in many other cases, this is one that allows me, using all the tools I've honed, from the analysis of physical evidence to the conducting of dogged cross-examination, to develop a compelling theory of what really happened. That's the gratifying part about the work: when you can go beyond challenging the mettle of the prosecution's case to provide a truly persuasive alternative explanation. When you do that and a prosecutor—with the state's vastly superior resources—sticks to his own version, he begins to look perverse.

Although I must say that describing this episode to the non-Asian reader poses a cross-ethnic stumbling block. The Asian names can be hard to hang onto at first.

There is Peter Chan, ultimately my client. That isn't his actual Chinese name but, fortunately, it is what he is almost always called. And there is also someone known as Peter Chin but his real name is John Cheong, which was what we came to call him in court, to avoid confusion with Peter Chan. There is Sang Nam Chinh (who, as the robbery unfolds, is shot, if you can believe it, in the chin), but he is often called just Nam. Some of the other names are perhaps simpler—since they have no resemblance to the word "chin"—like Robert Woo and Thong Huynh, who is usually known as Hac Qui (which means "Blacky" or "Black Ghost").

But whatever the names, all the people are interesting.

Take Robert Woo, for instance. He was twenty-six at the time of the shooting and so thin he looked anorexic. He had been in prison in China after trying to escape to freedom in Hong Kong. When he finally did make it to Hong Kong, and then to San Francisco, he took up crime as a means of earning a living and ultimately became a police informant so close to one of the cops that he was virtually adopted into that officer's family. He moved to L.A. and was one of several members of this clique who had a stake in a brothel on South Reno Street, a few blocks from Chinatown (it was also familiarly known as the "chicken house" and was not ever supposed to be mentioned at trial, but somehow got slipped in anyway). When the news of the Chinatown cop killing emerged, Robert Woo's putative adoptive father, the police officer from San Francisco, was obsessed with one plaintive question: "Did my 'son' kill the cop?" he asked.

Peter Chan, twenty-nine, the oldest son in a respectable Chinese-American family, had gotten into trouble in New York with gangs, but in L.A. you could find signs that he was making efforts to go at least somewhat more legit: he owned a noodle business, lived with the same woman for years and had a little son, Calvin Chan. But he also gambled too much for his health, and his "wife" had a big taste for jewelry.

The most pathetic of the group, perhaps, was Nam Chinh, nineteen years old and, though ethnically Chinese, a Vietnam boat refugee, whose mother sent him off from Saigon with the prayer that he would make his family proud. He didn't. He had trouble learning English, did poorly at almost everything and then he fell into the thrall of a streetwise Vietnamese gangster, the wily Hac Qui, twenty-one.

Many of the facts in the case are never in dispute.

At about noon, Leon Lee, seventy, white-haired, dignified and businesslike, still vigorous, arrives at his little store—it's not quite twenty feet wide—the Jin Hing, and unlocks the door. He switches on the lights but they do little to cut through the gloom. As usual he removes some of the more valuable items, jewelry in particular, from the safe and places them in the display cases. On a sunny day, the jade jewelry in the cases to the right, the books on collectibles in the center and the screens, paintings, vases crammed everywhere have an irresistible, glowing charm, and shoppers' eyes move from one to the next, with Leon Lee or his thirty-eight-year-old son Robert hovering over them, offering friendly guidance. On this dark and rainy day, the place is more like a poorly lighted walk-in storage closet, cluttered and dim.

An hour and a half later, Robert Lee arrives. Robert is frequently the one to tend to customers in the display area of the store. He is soft-spoken, wears dark-rimmed heavy glasses, above which loom his heavy, dark eyebrows. His deeply furrowed face and natural attentiveness convey intelligence. He is late, having run errands all morning. And his father has already completed the setup of the store. But it doesn't matter. Not a single customer has come through the rain to the Jin Hing yet.

At two o'clock, when Leon, Robert and a relative, Betty Yip, are having lunch in a little kitchen area behind dividers that cut the public part of the store off from the office and other work areas, somebody finally arrives: two men in dark suits. The double door is locked, as it always is even during business hours, and Robert Lee walks over to it, sees what he thinks are businessmen, unbolts the door and lets them in.

Unfortunately, they are robbers, albeit impeccably dressed and seemingly well-mannered. One is Robert Woo, twenty-six, in a black suit. The other is John Cheong, thirty, in a blue suit. They ask to see gold coins, Indianhead ten-dollar coins worth $300 to $400 apiece (a clever request because the coins are kept in the safe even after the store opens). Once the safe is open, they pull their handguns—Woo has a small automatic and Cheong has a .38-caliber blue steel revolver—and they announce, "This is a holdup." Meanwhile Nam, the youngest of the group, is standing nervously in the rain in Bamboo Lane. He is armed with a stainless-steel revolver and dressed in a multicolored windbreaker (no need to look all that respectable since the robbery is already going down), and one of the men in suits lets him in.

Suddenly, things are getting more complicated. Some customers arrive and John Cheong, still looking so proper, opens the door and lets them in. They are directed to the back where Nam already is guarding the others.

Unknown to Cheong, minutes before, both Leon and Robert Lee had pressed silent alarm remote activators that they carried in their shirt pockets.

That leads to a police radio broadcast picked up by a number of police officers in the area, but the closest are Archie Nagao, twenty-nine, a slightly built Japanese-American who happens to be a crack marksman, and twenty-seven-year-old Duane Johnson, six feet four, 240 pounds, an easygoing Anglo cop who had only recently been assigned to Chinatown. Despite his expertise with a gun, Archie, according to some of his colleagues, was never an especially likely candidate for street work. His temperament is too mild. He is a bit quirky, too: inside his clamshell holster (a holster that pops open) he carries a Japanese flag, the Rising Sun, which he believes will distract an assailant if Archie ever has to draw his gun in a fight.

Johnson, for his part, asked for this job in Chinatown because the hours were good and he wanted to be home with his pregnant wife as much as possible. But shortly after getting the assignment and observing a little about the complex, sometimes violent culture of Chinatown, he told his wife to get his funeral plans in the works, just in case.

On December 19, a few minutes after two o'clock, the police operator calls out on the radio, "Any central unit identify and handle a two-one-one silent, four-one-two Bamboo Lane, that's four-one-two Bamboo Lane at the Jin Hing Company."

Archie Nagao answers the call at the substation over the Phoenix Bakery (officially their two-man team is dubbed 1Z22). But Nagao isn't sure what the operator is saying. He responds, "One Zebra two-two, what's the call on Bamboo Lane?" The description is repeated.

"Central," he says, "we'll handle."

He is already wearing his yellow rain slicker but Johnson has to get his on quickly. They walk rapidly but do not run, because the alley is slick in the rain. Anyway, it takes them less than a minute to get there. They are wary but not extraordinarily so—there have been so many false silent alarms lately—and from that moment on just about everything they do goes wrong.

They look into the store. Although they see a cluster of people at the back they don't recognize them as hostages. They don't see anyone with weapons, no one who looks like a bad guy. A man in a suit lets them in, must be a proprietor. Johnson walks in first, Nagao follows. Their guns are not drawn. Neither one hangs back, a tactic that would allow him to keep the whole place in his view. (When possible, cops are supposed to "diagonally deploy," with one positioned in a near corner and the other in a far corner, so that they can control an area until backup comes.) Instead, they both saunter deeper into the store, Archie moving down the narrow aisle on the left, Duane taking the one on the right. Unwittingly, they have placed themselves in an extraordinarily dangerous situation where there are armed robbers in front of them and in back of them with Cheong still standing at the front door—although at first they don't know it. In the gloom they don't realize how much has already gone wrong here. Johnson tries to find out if everything is all right. "Your alarm went off!" he shouts to the people in the back of the store.

Then all hell breaks loose. John Cheong, moving rapidly up the right aisle, reaches behind his back for the gun in his waistband and takes aim at Archie's head. Archie struggles to unholster his own gun but Cheong fires first, shooting Archie in the neck. Archie, still standing despite the wound, fires back, hitting Cheong. Johnson now is also firing and Cheong is shot dead, left sprawled on the floor, right hand splayed out, his gun, with just one of its five shots expended, lying near him. Nam, who had been guarding the people at the back, makes a run toward the stairs in the middle of the store. Duane Johnson is standing three feet from the stairwell with his back toward Nam and the others, his attention still on Cheong and his partner officer in front of him. As Nam runs for it, he shoots and kills Officer Johnson and races down the stairs. Moments later he is back trying to shoot his way out to the front—and is himself shot by Archie Nagao, who has crawled toward the doorway and reloaded. Nam is shot in the chin—the early pictures show him with an actual hole in his chin—and the buttock. Meanwhile, Leon Lee, the older man, is aware of bullets crackling in the air all around him; he sees Duane Johnson falling, and then, as he recalls it, the "black suit swing the gun to me," and Leon reaches into a little drawer in his workbench, grabs his own gun, and shoots and kills Robert Woo. Something like thirty shots had been fired in eleven seconds.

Archie Nagao ultimately makes it back out to Bamboo Lane, severely injured, bleeding badly.

Alarming calls from civilians on the street and from the store itself start coming into the police emergency system, one of them from Glenwood Wong, a young stockbroker who was one of the customers in the store. He gets the emergency operator:

"Yes, please," he says, courteous even in the whirlwind, "there's been a shooting . . . four-one-two Bamboo Lane . . . in Chinatown. . . ." He says that he thinks that two cops are down. The police radio band comes alive as emergency calls and responses burst through the dreary day.

The two other suspects implicated in this maelstrom are Peter Chan, ultimately my client, and twenty-one-year-old Hac Qui. Peter was involved in planning the robbery from the beginning—it was supposed to net $100,000 and he was in trouble over gambling debts. It was Peter who went to the Jin Hing on the day before the robbery to scope it out. (Robert Lee even approached him in the store, asked if he needed help, felt bad as he was unable to offer any when Peter declined and left.)

I always believed that Hac Qui, like Nam, a Vietnamese of ethnic Chinese extraction and a leader among the street toughs, was as much, if not more, involved in the planning. Both men were getaway drivers. But their fates could not have differed more.

As the case breaks initially, Peter is believed to be one of the killers inside the Jin Hing, the mysterious fourth man. And Hac Qui is believed, erroneously, to be a minor player (who eventually is convicted merely as an accessory after the fact for assisting the wounded Nam in his escape from the scene—but later he reveals much more about his activities, after he gets immunity from the prosecution in return for laying the entire scheme at Peter's feet). It was Hac Qui who waited on nearby Bernard Street in a cruddy old banged-up brown car until the staggering, bleeding Nam made it out of the store, down the back alley, up Hill Street and into Hac Qui's car. It was Hac Qui who drove Nam away from the scene to the suburban house that his coterie of Vietnamese refugee kids used as a sort of dormitory, where the cops finally found Nam cowering in a closet. (At first they nearly missed him, hidden under a pile of clothes—Gailey checked in the closet after the others didn't spot him, pulled away the clothes, saw this wreck of a boy who shouted out in fear, startling Gailey, who leaped backward.)

As an attorney in this mess, my job is going to be to demonstrate that Peter—although certainly guilty of a good deal here—was never in the store, and never anticipated that anyone would be shot, assertions he made unwaveringly through a series of withering interrogations, while admitting his part in planning the robbery and even supplying the others with guns. If it's true that he was not in the store during the holdup, then there's no evidence that Peter shared the intent to kill that the shooters in the store clearly demonstrated. As he is a nonshooter without a personal intent to kill, the special circumstances provisions don't apply. If a jury accepts his story there would be no possibility of either a death sentence or life imprisonment without parole even if they convict him of first-degree murder as an aider and abettor of the robbery felony murder.

Defense lawyers don't get the chance to defend the innocent very often, but commonly—and very important—we have to do just this: defend someone who is less culpable than charged and in peril of unjust punishment.

In demonstrating that Peter was never in the store, I have to overcome the fact that both Robert Lee and Leon Lee, two decent men, said he was there. It turns out that Peter's version is the truth. But it takes three and a half years of labor, including a preliminary hearing and a thirteen-month jury trial, to finally work through all the evidence, sort out the facts and come away feeling that at least the story has been told correctly this time.

Peter, as I recall, was arrested first. It wasn't such a difficult task for the cops, because the dead Robert Woo was carrying one of Peter's business cards with him and also a beeper that linked him to Peter. As soon as they had Peter in a cell he was eager to talk. Bill Gailey and Bennie Lee, a Chinese-American cop, walked into the cell and basically found Peter flipping out, rattling on crazily.

That was fine, from the cops' point of view. Gailey wanted him to just keep talking and motioned to Lee to remain quiet. "Uh-huh, yeah" and the like was about all they said as Peter dug a hole for himself.

At first, like most people, Peter was trying to say he wasn't involved and then, as time went on, it was clear to them that he was in fact very involved. And it seemed obvious to Peter that he ought to tell as much as he could—on the record. He implicated Nam and Hac Qui. He told them he scoped out the store the day before and that he detailed the place to Robert Woo; he admitted that he explained to Robert Woo how to escape to the getaway cars. And that Woo then went to a friend, Ronnie Tong, who was the proud possessor of a credit card and who arranged for a rental car, a Ford LTD, for Woo, who intended to use it in the getaway. Peter told the cops that he was supposed to be a getaway driver and so was Hac Qui. He said two cars were better than one so that the robbers could split up after the crime. He said that he was outside in the Ford LTD and when no one came he drove around and then left—but he never went into the shop itself, never fired a shot, never killed a cop.

As Peter rambles on, Gailey and Bennie Lee aren't buying any of it.

Gailey leads Peter through a horrifying (to Peter) story of what they found. They tell him people in the store have identified him.

Peter is incredulous. "How could, how could they, you know, how could that possibly be possible?"

"Listen, stop," the exasperated Gailey commands. "We're givin' you a chance, right now, to tell your story. If you want to tell it, fine. If you want to sit there and make up bullshit stories, that's fine, too."

He tells him, Bennie Lee "can read you like a book. Every time you go into that act, it means you're lyin' through your teeth."

And then, worse still, he suggests to Peter that his fingerprints were in the store.

"Let me tell you a little story," the smooth Gailey says, "about physical evidence. Do you know what physical evidence is?"

Peter says he does. Gailey tells him how people leave fingerprints on objects, which are then lifted from the objects and placed on cards.

"And then I looked at the card and then I took some ink and put it on your fingers and put your fingerprints on the card. . . . And I took the card with your fingerprints on it and I put it up next to the card with the fingerprints from the table."

Peter takes the bait. "I got fingerprints on the table because I went, I went inside the store," he says, "on the day before—that's the only way it could have happened."

Peter is frantic but sticks to his version of what happened on the day of the shootings, "Nam shot the policeman. I was not inside the store."

Gailey says, "Sure."

The fingerprint lecture was a ploy. The fact is that there never were any of Peter's fingerprints found in that place. But of the two men, Peter and the cop, Gailey was a whole lot smarter.

There was no lawyer there yet.

As I remember it, I got the call early on Christmas Eve. Usually on Christmas Eve Laine, Tim and I went out to his parents' house and we'd stay overnight to celebrate Christmas Day there.

But instead this time I go to the office first. I have a feeling that I might get a call. I know the Chinatown suspects are being brought in to Division 30 that day. I'm hanging around, nothing much to do. It's Christmas Eve Monday and no one's been at work since the Friday before.

*My parents, Sylvia and
Sol Newberger, on their
wedding day, 1938.*

*A rare photo of my mother
and grandmother hugging.*

*My father and me in
Brooklyn, 1944.*

*Me and Grandma,
early 1944.*

*Me, my brother, Ira, and my baby sister,
Robin, spring 1953.*

The ballerina, aged nine.

Jijeey and me at the San Francisco mission, 1965.

Law school graduation day, 1969.

Judge Tom Fredricks,
one of my mentors.

Me and the Weather
Underground
bombers at Frontera
State Prison for
Women. Left to
right, *Leslie Mullins,*
me, Judy Bissell.

Tim's and my wedding, August 13, 1977.

Dr. Donald Bulpitt, who contracted the hit on his boyhood friend Charles Snodgrass.

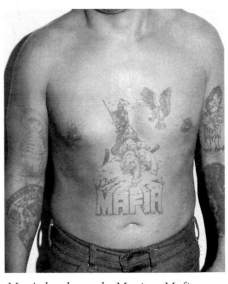

Mon's loyalty to the Mexican Mafia— spelled out on his abdomen.

Mon's first arrest by the Pasadena P.D.

Mon, in a black T-shirt, with wife-turned-witness, Terri Wilson, on his right. His mother and brother, Jesse Infante, are on his left.

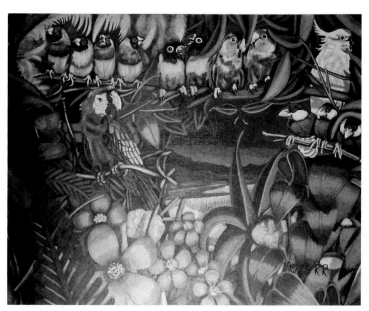

Death row art—Aidan's doodleloos—a painting by Ricky Sanders, my client in the Bob's Big Boy murder case.

The crowd of officers "trashing"
Gailey's crime scene in Chinatown.

The north aisle of the Jin Hing Co.

Officer Duane Johnson, who was
killed during the robbery at Jin Hing
Co., and his wife, Kathleen.

Archie Nagao, the officer who survived the shooting, demonstrating his final firing position for the LAPD investigators.

Sang Nam Chinh as he looked two days before the homicides, without the face injuries.

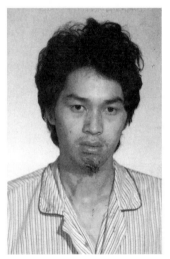

Sang Nam Chinh after his arrest for the Chinatown murders, with the injury to his chin received during his gunfight with Officer Nagao.

My client in the Chinatown case, Hau Cheong (Peter) Chan.

Amtul Parwez, the mother of eleven-year-old murder victim Raheel Parwez.

Sattar Ahmed, Parwez's brother and chief suspect in the killing, who fled the country before Parwez's arrest.

The dumpster where Raheel Parwez's dismembered body was found.

Bonnie Esther's wedding to her second husband, two and a half years after she shot husband number one. On Bonnie's right is daughter Marie, and Marie's young son, with whom she was pregnant at the time of the shooting. On Bonnie's left, her new husband, and to his left, her son John Jr.

Arnel Salvatierra's booking photo.

Oscar Salvatierra, in a white shirt with hands clasped in front of him, at a reception in Washington, D.C., with Ferdinand and Imelda Marcos.

Roberto Lopez with a perm.

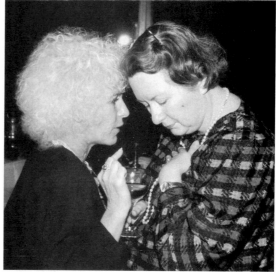

Me and Judge Nancy Brown (who later performed Lyle's wedding) sometime in 1987 or 1988.

Roman Luisi and Isabella, four months before he was killed.

Lyle being big brother to one-month-old Erik.

Erik's high school graduation picture, June 1989, two months before the homicides.

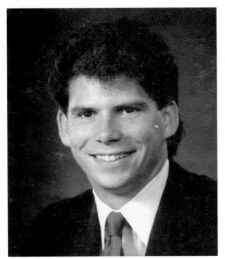

Lyle's high school graduation picture, June 1986.

The Menendez I defense team. Left to right: *Jill Lansing, me, Michael Burt, and Marcia Morrissey.*

Lyle Menendez's lead counsel in the second trial, public defender Charles Gessler, and me celebrating Lyle's wedding.

Menendez I press conference after the hung jury for Erik. Linda Deutch is behind my right shoulder, Marcia Morrissey is on the far right of the picture.

Me and Barbara Walters during the shooting of her "Fascinating People of 1994" show.

Me and Tim in Ireland, 1991.

The house in Ireland we rent (the white one at the end of the road).

Just as I decide it's time to go home and do some last-minute wrapping of Christmas presents, the phone rings. It's the judge of the arraignment court herself, not even her clerk, who would normally place the call.

"Oh, you're there . . . I'm calling you about the Chinatown case."

"I sort of suspected you were."

"I'm holding the heavy for you," she says.

I'm at the court in twenty minutes. Peter, Nam and Hac Qui are in the lockup. The public defender's office will be representing Nam, but the case attorney can't be there that day. Hac Qui got real lucky: he is assigned a sharp-witted prominent Japanese-American lawyer named Michael Yamaki. (Years later, his wife, local TV news anchor Tricia Toyota, conducts the controversial Judge Ito interview that airs just before the Simpson case starts.)

Peter is a nervous wreck but, happily for me, fluent in English, as there is a shortage of Chinese-language interpreters in the courthouse this Christmas Eve afternoon. After two hours of getting acquainted and trying to calm Peter down, I put the case over for arraignment until I can see some police reports. So far the case is in Bill Gailey's notes and mind; no reports have been typed up. Moreover, in the great Paul Fitzgerald tradition it's time to slow the freight train of justice down a bit.

I head to my in-laws' place and that evening get a call from Peter's younger brother, Michael Chan, a Stanford-educated engineer, who isn't sure he really wants a lawyer who's been appointed by the court and paid for by the state. "Don't you work for the government?" he asks. "Aren't you paid by the same people that pay the DA?" And he asks me candidly, "Wouldn't we be better off hiring our own lawyer?"

This case is fascinating, big, complex, exotic, and I want it. I am very uncomfortable laying a sales pitch on appointed clients, although I'll do it with private ones; it feels strange to do it in cases where I'm selected by the judge. Nevertheless, I'm going to. I know this is bound to be an expensive case and no matter how comfortable Michael and his family may think they are (it's the gambling Peter who is broke), they will be financially destroyed by it. Even at the modest, court-appointed rate, I will ultimately be paid over $300,000 to handle it. I also, at this point, am feeling my oats. I don't know any lawyer I'd trust more than I to defend Peter Chan (but I manage to restrain myself from saying that out loud). I tell Michael it's a disastrous mistake to go looking for someone else when they don't have the money to hire the very best. I give him the names of references, lawyers to call and ask about me. I'm sure one of them was my old buddy Gerry Chaleff.

I realize that even when I get the case, as I do, I'm going to have a PR problem with this family in the early stages. They're going to keep wondering if I'm really on their side.

I go down to see Peter to discuss this issue the day after Christmas at the county jail. He is respectful, you might even say demure. He tells me he's an actual businessman who has been trying to go straight, but didn't. He relates the statements he has already made to the police implicating himself thoroughly. He tells me who the players are, which is the beginning of my effort to get the names straight. And, I swear, it takes me just about a year to feel comfortable with all of them, aliases and nicknames included.

It's obvious that he's not a gang member now and he's not a thug, although he has been almost mind-numbingly stupid and greedy, as he concedes. But I remind him that this is more than stupid. A cop is dead, another wounded; his buddies are dead. I tell him this means a murder charge even though he was outside at the time. He is shocked and deeply remorseful. I do believe him as he tells his story. But to the very end he never saw the justice in the felony murder rule. "But I didn't kill anyone, I wouldn't kill anyone," he pleads. "How can I be just as guilty?"

As part of the PR task, Tim and I do something we've never done before and very rarely since—we socialize with his family. They—based on what I believe are Hong Kong cultural notions—seem to believe that if they aren't paying for something it has no value.

To reassure them, Tim and I regularly meet them at one or another of the huge Hong Kong restaurants that are springing up in places like suburban Alhambra. They are always formally attired—suits and dresses. They always insist on paying, which is at least marginally questionable, given the fact that I'm appointed at county expense. The lawyer is not supposed to take gifts from a court-appointed client. But I rationalize it: this isn't the client per se, and I need to know the family as well as possible if this goes to a death-penalty phase and they have to testify in a plea for mercy.

Invariably these restaurants boast huge chandeliers, big banquettes and large tables out in the open. The menus offer dishes about much of which, to this day, I haven't got a clue. They are all in Chinese and the Chans always order—copiously. One thing I do learn: shark's fin soup is good, very, very, good. Peter's mother and father are always there, his girlfriend, Wah, and Calvin, their little boy. Michael Chan is there, having arrived in his immaculate BMW, with his wife, Margo.

At first, Tim and I are apprehensive, "Oh, God, what are we going to talk about." But never mind. These are cordial people who are eager to discuss family matters and tell stories about their lives. There was one relative, a boy named Anthony who had a brain tumor, and much discussion centered on his operation and the miracle of his recovery. We rarely talk about Peter's case.

If I bring away anything from all of this it is a profound gratitude for the chance to get to know people from a culture so different from my own. The distance between us diminishes and the Chans are simply human beings, extremely warm ones. I hope they think as well of us as we do of them.

At the end of each of these banquets, along with the delicious mango pudding, comes the moment I dread: Mrs. Chan, tears welling up, clasps my hand and says, "You save my son, you save my Peter?"

"Yes," I tell her, "yes, I will." (God willing.)

The opposition in this case is a deputy DA named Larry Longo, an amusingly suave guy in the habit of going bonkers—he'd start gesticulating wildly and talking so loudly in private that the whole place could hear him ("Keep your voice down, Larry," I warned him time and again). He had an act out of some movie. He always seemed to arrange it so that he could be casually leaning against the railing as the jury paraded in, like he was Cary Grant. My legal partner on this case, Howard Gillingham, called him "Mr. Casual"—to his face. Larry was impervious. He didn't do his preparation but didn't care. The law, he freely acknowledged, got in the way. He was devious, too. But unlike Harvey Giss in the Bob's Big Boy case, there wasn't much malice in Larry. He was too heavy-handed, too much fun—despite the furious fights we generally engaged in. He'd call me at home a lot to chat, a perfectly okay way for opposing lawyers to sound each other out. Although sometimes I think I talked to Larry more than I did to Gillingham during this case. (I don't believe we ever did learn anything useful from each other over the phone—but that banter helped make the vitriol of the fight more bearable.)

Once, when we took the jury to see the crime scene, Larry and I were standing at the Jin Hing, and remarkably, I suddenly became aware that he had his arm around my shoulder. Purely reflexive on his part, I'm sure.

His partner at the prosecution table was a woman named Terry Adamson, a daughter of a prominent L.A. family. She, like Larry, lived in Malibu, which meant they could carpool. Terry approached me once when she overheard me talking to Peter about the terrible food he's getting during the trial. A young man who is used to eating great Chinese food all his life, he is now reduced to bologna, which happens to be the foundation of the nutritional pyramid in the penal system. She's appalled not because it tastes lousy but because, she says, "Don't they know it's carcinogenic? He shouldn't eat that."

This makes me wheel around. "Well, look at it this way, Terry," I say. "If you're successful in this prosecution, Peter will die in the gas chamber long before the bologna gets the chance to kill him."

Whether by design or chance, whenever Larry Longo pulled one of his sleazy stunts, Terry was nowhere to be found. She kept clean enough, I guess. She's a judge now.

The most outrageous aspect of Longo's conduct centers on discovery issues. These are days when the defense still does not have to show its hand but the prosecution does, a system that makes terrific sense, since the defendant ought to know what the case is against him so he can defend himself. (Only mindless antidefendant hysteria could, and did, ultimately make the defense reveal its hand, too, as if the act of putting on a defense of the accused could possibly be equated with the government bringing a case *against* an individual.)

Longo's prize was Hac Qui. This guy had become Peter's archenemy. That way Hac Qui achieved police protection and immunity—not bad given his implication in this and other crimes—and also got the opportunity to retaliate against Peter, who he believed had turned him in and also doomed Hac Qui's little Vietnamese "brother," Nam.

Hac Qui made his story more elaborate by the minute: beyond simply planning this operation, he said, Peter had even instructed the men in the virtues of using Uzis to kill cops, should any of them arrive while the robbery was going on. This was particularly troubling from a defense point of view, since I meant to show that Peter never had any intention of killing anyone, much less a cop. It was also obvious bull since no one involved had an Uzi or had tried to get one.

As Hac Qui came to testify in trial with information that seemed brand-new about things Peter said or did, Longo always professed as much surprise as I did. Why, he didn't have any idea! But of course he did. He was interviewing Hac Qui in private, no tape recorder, no notes, feeding him information that made the prosecution case richer. I complained often to the judge. "Seems every time Mr. Longo sits down with the witness privately, up pop new statements."

At one point, I got a call from Gailey, who tipped me off that Longo was interviewing Hac Qui and refusing to tape-record him. The cops, Gailey told me, had walked out.

On cross—and increasingly I am seeing the many uses of cross as a weapon against the prosecution—I get Hac Qui to acknowledge this routine.

"On Friday, the two hours you spent with Mr. Longo, you didn't see a tape recorder. Correct?"

"I see a tape recorder, but I don't see it turn on," Hac Qui responds.

And then I say, "On Saturday, in fact, before you spent the two hours with Mr. Longo, hadn't the police brought you over to his office?"

"Yes."

"And then the police left you alone with Mr. Longo for those two hours, right?"

"It can't be said that way," Hac Qui says, trying to help Longo, "because they went out, perhaps got coffee, and they came back later on."

The judge, a usually nonassertive woman named Jean Matusinka, was actually moved to order Longo to use a tape recorder all the time—a very rare order—but he disregarded it anyway.

Later, in trial, we had the dumbfounding moment where Hac Qui is testifying to incriminating things Peter is supposed to have said to him during a secretly taped conversation in a police car. Only none of the really incriminating stuff he claims was said can be heard on the tape (which we had electronically enhanced). Oh, says Hac Qui, that was all said in a whisper. This sent me through the roof. I dubbed the witness "Charlie McCarthy." I could visualize Longo playing Edgar Bergen in his little prep sessions, Hac Qui sitting on his lap, Longo's hand up his back. Ventriloquism or perjury depending on your point of view.

Exasperated, I protest, "We have tapes of the police car. So far virtually everything he testified was said in the police car is not on the tape."

"There's a lot of whispering on the tapes," the sympathetic judge says.

"That's when it happened," says Larry confidently. Sure. Very fortunate.

"Goddamn it!" I shout, Hac Qui is lying. "What does it take to see that this is collusion between the prosecution and this witness. This is a capital case!"

Longo takes umbrage. "Why do I have to put up with her accusations?"

"Because you don't tape-record your interviews, that's why," I say.

In the end, Hac Qui actually contaminated the prosecution case. The jury saw that he was a liar and one coached by the prosecutor.

Another outrageous thing Larry Longo did was that—while rewarding the lying Hac Qui—he tried to punish an honest man. Archie Nagao, the wounded cop, took the stand to testify and refused to identify any of the robbers. He maintained that in all the chaos he simply could not remember who was who. I was so impressed. This was a guy who had every reason to construct memories. He was physically wounded and angry and he was humiliated. I had spent my whole career watching cops lie for no good reason. And this guy, with every reason in the world to lie, refused. If he had said Peter Chan was in the place, I would have had a terrible time on cross; how much could I do with a brutally wounded, traumatized, soft-spoken good man?

Archie's refusal was beyond Longo's comprehension. He questioned him relentlessly. (Meantime, the courtroom seats are filled with uniformed officers, there ostensibly to lend support but actually there to influence the jury—and I protest to some effect, gaining some limitations on their presence.)

At one point Longo is making Archie retrace on the stand every step he and Duane Johnson took right after entering the store. He's being asked to recount everything he did, everything he thought, everything he looked at. Finally, Longo is questioning him about his observation of the jewelry display cases. Archie's answers reveal that he wasn't particularly focused on the displays; he was looking at the people in the back. At first I think, What is Larry's theory? Is he going to argue that Peter was hiding behind the counters (to explain why Archie never saw a fourth man)? But the others in the store would have seen Peter from the back if he was concealed behind the counter Longo is pointing out to Nagao.

Then Longo asks to approach the witness to show him a photograph of the smashed jewelry display cases. All of a sudden it dawns on me what he's trying to do. And I think, "Oh, you stupid shit, you're not going to do that to this poor guy." It's crazy, but this is Larry Longo. He's trying to prove Archie was negligent: by failing to notice the broken glass he failed to recognize a robbery in progress. Nagao, meantime, is practically out of it on the stand. The poster boy for post-traumatic stress. He can barely speak. Longo is whipping him for being a bad cop, for failing his partner and for not telling a useful story. It is a nasty display by a frustrated DA. The judge is getting concerned. I'm beside myself. We need to talk.

Out of the hearing of the jury, I say, "Let me tell the court what I'm horrified at. If Officer Nagao commits suicide because he's . . ."

The judge agrees that might be where we're heading and says, stunningly, "I know Mr. Longo is not very sensitive to these issues, but you have to realize Officer Nagao comes from a different culture than you do, where honor means a great deal."

Larry tries to respond. "Don't say a word, Mr. Longo," the judge says. "You're reinforcing in his mind what he's been thinking already for two years." Larry tries to bluster back but is told to be quiet.

I say, "We don't want this witness committing suicide this week, and this jury holding it against our client. I don't want him dead, period, because he's a nice boy."

Larry is worn-out by this time. "I assure you the prosecution agrees with that," he says formally, bringing to a close one of the more bizarre moments I have ever seen in court. (Archie Nagao was assigned to a desk job, where he remains to this day.)

But in the end, Longo, his witnesses and his behavior, as time-consuming and exasperating as they may have been—were side issues compared to the core of the defense tactic: maneuvering Robert Lee, the wounded prosecution witness, toward—however briefly—turning around on the stand and supporting the case for Peter Chan.

Robert Lee never meant to be a central figure in any of this. When the firing started he scurried to the kitchen, way in the back of the store, to hide. A stairway leads from the back of the store to the rear alley, and Robert hears someone coming up the stairs. He peeks down, sees a figure, although there are no lights on the stairs. He grabs a broom and edges back into the kitchen; the man reaches the top of the stairs. Robert says he sees his face and his gun. The man is holding a silver revolver, he says.

He says, in one version, the man coming up the stairs is Peter Chan. He says he hit him with the broom. Firing is going on all over the place. The man runs back down the stairs. Then, he says, a second man comes running up the stairs—with a different gun. He says this time it is Nam, and Robert Lee strikes him in the upper part of the body. Nam fires his gun, hitting Robert in the chest. Nam then manages to open the heavy steel door at the top of the stairs that leads to the alley. (His stainless-steel revolver is later found on the doorsill when the investigating officers arrive.)

Robert staggers out into the workroom, with a telephone in his hands, and calls the police. He does not know where his father is or that Leon is unharmed. Robert is taken to the hospital and later identifies the two dead robbers, Peter Cheong and Robert Woo, with confidence. But all the way to trial he is always a little vague and confused about Nam and Peter Chan. He believes they are about the same height and age, although there is a seven-year and three-inch difference, and he knows they don't look much like the men in the suits. At one point, he describes them both as dressed the same.

But how could it be that there were two men on the stairway if Peter Chan is telling the truth? The stairway account is critical to the prosecution because it's the only way Peter, if he had been in the store, could have left—Archie Nagao was at the front and nobody fled past him. The prosecution's theory is that after Nam shot Robert Lee, Peter Chan returned up the stairs and fled into the alley as Nam already had. But the trail of blood tells a different story. There are droplets of blood on virtually every step of the staircase leading from the landing across from Duane Johnson's body to the back door. Peter Chan has no injuries when he is arrested two days later. It is determined that all of the blood on the stairs is Nam's. What is significant is that not one drop is disturbed, smudged or stepped on as it would be if someone else was fleeing behind the wounded and bleeding Nam as he made his way up to the back door. I take a lot of time with the criminalist (Doreen Musick, a very impressive witness—no bumbling Dennis Fung of O. J. infamy here), going over every drop of that blood without ever revealing my purpose. (Years later Longo told me that he didn't understand why I was spending so much time on the blood evidence until my final argument about no footprints in the blood caught him completely by surprise. "Boy, I sure didn't see that one coming.")

Clearly, Robert Lee's memory has been contaminated by events. He met Peter Chan the day before the robbery when Peter visited the store, so he was in fact familiar with his face. He saw pictures in the newspapers of the suspects and was shown them by the police. And he was taken through a reenactment by the police and the prosecution, which, of course, reinforced the story of the fourth man in his mind.

In the months before trial, he hears what the other witnesses have to say and that, he concedes, leads him to figure things out, "logically." He asserts, incredibly, that his memory is better now than it was soon after the crime, when he was often confused.

He knows, he says, that the first guy who came up the stairs did not look like the wild-eyed guy who shot him later: not the right face and not the right gun.

But, as for my position, I do believe my own client, number one, and, better still, I know what Nam says about that day, about his frenzied efforts to escape out the back despite the fact that the rear door would not open on the first try.

I tell Robert Lee on cross that I'm going to ask him a question. "I want you to assume something that will be established. All right? And ask you if you knew that, would it change what you think is your memory, your opinion of your memory. Okay? Here's what I want you to consider: This man, Nam Chinh, has told someone that he ran up the staircase twice. First with the silver gun. Then he was shot, badly shot, and picked up the black gun and ran up the stairs with the black gun and shot you."

I am looking directly into Robert Lee's eyes. I see what the jury must surely have seen, that he is saying to himself, Oops, could be.

There is no response. He does not answer the question.

I drive on. It is very important to make sure the jury does get my point (a lot of lawyers like to wait for final argument but I think that's bull because the jury is making up its mind all along the way).

"If you knew that this man has admitted, okay, that he first ran up the stairs with a silver gun. Then he couldn't get past you because of your broomstick, and he went back to the front room where Officer Nagao was guarding the front door and he picked up the black gun and tried to get out past Officer Nagao and couldn't and he was shot by Officer Nagao. So he took the black gun back to the stairs to get past you and your broomstick. And he shot you. If you knew that he had said that, that it was him each time. . . . Does that change your opinion of your memory that it was Peter Chan on the staircase somehow with the silver gun?"

Robert Lee, again, does not respond. But it is as good as a yes.

What happened and what I explain later on is that Robert saw Nam twice, but looking very different each time, once before he acquired a hole in his chin and a wound in his butt and was in extreme agony and once after—with his face contorted and his eyes wild. He saw him once with an unsullied windbreaker and once with a windbreaker covered in blood so that it looked like a different jacket. In addition, he saw him once with a silver gun and once with a black one. (It was one of the lessons from the Bob's Big Boy case: eyewitnesses see guns, not faces.)

He concedes that it was the difference in the guns—the one thing he knew for sure—and the contortions of the second face that firmly persuaded him, for the first time, that there were four men in the store. With that, he gives it away.

Soon, Robert Lee does what most prosecution witnesses do: he tries to take it back, continues to insist that there were in fact four men. But the three-man version is by now well established in the jury. And it makes sense to them.

When I get my chance for final argument, I begin by turning to a black-board.

"I don't want to start out by turning my back to you," I tell the jury, "but I have to do something for me." I write "STAY CALM" on the blackboard. I intend to keep looking over there so I don't blow it. I have to take this thing step by step. "I've been on this case since December 24, 1984"—I tell them on March 9, 1988—"so I've been waiting three and a half years to get the mess straightened out."

The court reporters can point to the sign whenever I start racing too fast.

"So will the judge," says the judge.

And I tell the jury to signal me by just looking over to the blackboard if things get out of hand.

I aided myself another way. I had designed a chart that I set up in front of the jury: "Proof That Peter Chan Was Not in the Store." It summarized the evidence for the jury, of course, but it also did something major for me. It let me see an outline for my final argument without ever having to look at notes. Argument is incalculably more effective if you don't have to look at notes.

The argument lasts more than two days. Along the way, I indulge in a song. I tell the jury I won't try to stick to the melody and I'm not sure I have every word of the late Tim Hardin's lyrics right, but I think it goes this way:

> If I listened long enough to you,
> I'd find a way to believe that it's all true,
> Knowing that you lied straightfaced while I cried
> Still I look for a reason to believe.

Now, you do that with someone you love, I tell them. "You're looking for excuses to believe. But when you're a juror in a criminal case, you're supposed to be looking for reasons to disbelieve."

It's my way of getting at reasonable doubt—and God knows there is every reason to doubt that Peter was in that store.

As the trial draws to a close, we catch a break. A decision comes down from a higher court that seems to indicate that, in instances with some similarity to this one, the judge should instruct the jury on second-degree murder in addition to the felony-murder instruction—which would have meant first degree for a conspirator even if he never actually entered the store. When she decides to instruct on the second, Longo goes nuts. For my part, I think it's an incredible twist, but just peachy.

The day comes when the jury declares it has a verdict. This is always the most horrible time. You believe the worst, no matter how well the trial might have gone. It is three o'clock in the afternoon on a Friday. I'm in a preliminary hearing on a murder case in the Pomona branch court— an hour from the downtown "Chinatown" courtroom. Judge Matusinka always leaves at four o'clock sharp and can't delay because she is the driver for a judicial carpool. She will not change that routine just because we have a verdict and now there isn't time for everybody involved to get to the court before she leaves. We'll have to sweat it out without knowing the result through the weekend.

I am, of course, sure—buttressed by something negative a juror mumbled just earlier—that they've gone for a first. I cannot bear to dwell on it. I get on my knees on the floor of my sixty-year-old bathroom, with its original tile, and I begin to scrub and scrape, with steel wool, a paint scraper, a hard bristle brush. I work all day Saturday, Saturday night and all day Sunday. Every once in a while, the case pierces through my mind, and I think, "Oh, God, help me! Oh, no. Back to the tiles!"

I make progress, congratulating myself along the way. Every square centimeter, one by one, is attacked with my arsenal of weapons and Comet and chlorine bleach. The floor is gradually revealing its original brilliance. My knees ache and they are raw. My hands are swollen and I cannot make them open and close easily. By Monday, the bathroom is sparkling. A different room.

And on Monday, the verdict is announced. "We the jury in the above entitled action find the defendant Peter Chan guilty of the murder of Duane Johnson as alleged in Count 1 and find it to be of the second degree." He was, of course, convicted of the robberies of the jewelry store and the patrons. But the jury acquitted Peter of the murders of John Cheong and Robert Woo (he was charged with their deaths under a doctrine of vicarious liability, which I had argued did not apply to someone who was not present when the violence instigated by the robbers began).

Nam was convicted of first-degree murder by his separate jury. After a penalty trial he got life without parole. (When Archie Nagao heard that in the courtroom—not the death penalty!—he shrieked and ran down the hallway until Gailey caught him.)

I've never known exactly why Peter's jury went for a second. Maybe it was the sense of equity that jurors often feel. They must have reasoned that Peter, who they did believe was outside the store, should get something less than a first.

A second ordinarily carries fifteen-to-life, with, of course, the possibility of parole.

It's a fantastic victory for me, in my way of thinking. I got the story absolutely right—even though it defied telling for so long. And I got a conviction that wasn't as extreme as it might have been.

Elated—there is always that elation, but it does not last long—I call Tim. He asks me how I feel and I tell him something like, "I'm in seventh heaven." This is a dumb remark under the circumstances. A reporter overhears it and publishes it in a way to make me look shallow and insensitive. There I am, elated in a cop killing. But, you know, my guy wasn't the shooter—guilty as hell but not the actual killer—and I don't like the felony murder rule any better than Peter does. So sure I feel good —things came out right for a change. By the same token I don't find that second-degree judgment unfair at all.

Ultimately, the judge manages to pile on so many consecutive penalties that Peter gets thirty-eight years to life, which effectively, I think, means he probably won't be getting out. But that happens, and, while his sentence seems too harsh to me, it was not painfully unjust. He did conspire in the planning and commission of this disastrous robbery and he went with the rest of these heavily armed guys to the scene. What did he imagine? Nobody was going to get hurt? That's denial, not innocence.

16

A Beautiful Boy

A case that came my way during the defense of Peter Chan never offered the satisfaction of Chinatown—because nobody ever figured it out, and I doubt that anybody ever will. It was easily the most gruesome experience of my career. It was so gruesome that even I had moments when the gore got to me.

This is the case of the death by strangulation—and the subsequent grotesque dismemberment—of a beautiful eleven-year-old Pakistani-American boy named Raheel Parwez, who, in life, was by all accounts a sweet and gentle child. He was adjudged above average in behavior at school and capable academically. I have seen pictures of him alive, smiling charmingly, his eyes bright, his hair mussed and falling over his forehead. And I have seen pictures of him dead, but only after the coroners pieced his face back together again. My task was to defend the accused killer, Raheel's father, Khalid Parwez, a mild-mannered obstetrician with the Kaiser HMO in West L.A. (just blocks, as it happens, from the infamous Bob's Big Boy on La Cienega).

I had, at this point in my life, handled several cases involving charges of murder in the context of domestic violence, the killing of one family member by another. These killings (rarely, in fact, first-degree murders) have much less to do with anybody's notion of the criminal mind than they do with the overwrought and unbearable emotions that sometimes infect and destroy families. But this murder of a child wasn't like anything else I had seen. It certainly bore no resemblance to those cases where the evidence showed the kind of abuse and terror that I was familiar with from defending battered wives who killed spouses or abused kids who killed their parents. There was no history of maltreatment by my client toward either of his two sons, although allegations of psychological maltreatment by their mother surfaced in the divorce and custody battle that preceded the homicide. I took this one on with considerable apprehension. It had two ingredients that always made my job more painful and more demanding: a dead child and a totally respectable, utterly panic-stricken client.

As a parent myself, I found it difficult to live with the facts of this murder and mutilation of an innocent child. The only other time I had represented a man accused of killing his child, my client had been a guilty wretch, a chronic child abuser for whom I felt no sympathy. This new client was different, so much easier to relate to. But the facts of this case were so much worse, particularly those that could turn a jury against the accused before even one piece of evidence was presented in court.

It was of some (although small) comfort for me to believe that the act of strangulation that took the life of that winsome boy with the beautiful smile occurred while he was asleep so that he couldn't have known what was happening. Nevertheless, I knew this wasn't going to be an easy assignment no matter how I rationalized the facts of the killing nor how worthy Khalid Parwez was of a vigorous defense.

I had a special reason for taking on this case. My dear friend Valerie Colb was Parwez's divorce lawyer. She had represented him in the hearings that resulted in his gaining physical custody of Raheel. The child's murder and the accusation against Dr. Parwez brought on a crisis of conscience for Valerie. She believed utterly in Parwez's innocence. She had to. She was the instrument by which he got to keep his boy. In vindicating him I would be vindicating her judgment as well. I didn't think she could live with even a shadow of guilt hanging over Parwez. She, too, wouldn't be free unless he was acquitted.

Here was a case that everyone predicted I would lose. It was reeking with prejudice, particularly since it took place in the late eighties when the lingering humiliation inflicted on the American psyche by fundamentalist Muslims in Iran had fomented deep prejudice against Muslims of all national origins. It was being tried in a community—Pomona—where the jury would be white and presumably even less sympathetic than another might be in a growing atmosphere of antagonism toward immigrants. The gruesomeness of the crime had, moreover, played well into the public thirst for vengeance.

The leading rabble-rouser in this instance was none other than the DA du jour, Ira Reiner, who rushed to Pomona, personally filed the charges against Dr. Parwez and called for his death. He said the murder "cries out for the imposition of the death penalty." Unfortunately for his ambition, the law in the state of California at that time provided no legitimate basis for his seeking the death penalty. There were none of the required special circumstances—like multiple murder, or murder in the commission of a felony—that applied to the facts of this case. In desperation, he latched on to one that had already been nullified by the California Supreme Court as unconstitutional—the commission of a killing that is "especially heinous, atrocious and cruel, manifesting exceptional depravity." Not only was this special circumstance unconstitutional at the time (because it was too vague: atrocious is in the eyes of the beholder) but all the descriptives that it lists applied, in this instance, to acts after the killing, not during it. The boy was dead, thank God, when these sick and revolting things were done to his body. He'd been killed, in fact, by your run-of-the-mill ligature around the neck.

Valerie Colb, the divorce lawyer, was not only the catalyst for my involvement in this case but ultimately its star witness at trial. It all started, however, with a routine phone call to the court in which I was trying the Chinatown case.

My office has standing orders not to call me in the middle of the trial day unless there is an emergency. My staff felt this one measured up. The message, handed to me during a morning session of testimony in the Chinatown trial, was that Valerie Colb needed to talk to me, urgent. During the recess I return the call and Valerie tells me that the son of a divorce client of hers has been found murdered and the sheriff's department has been asking her client, the physician father, some very accusatory questions. Do I think he needs the advice of a criminal lawyer? "Get him into my office this evening," I tell her. "He's the suspect."

That night I meet Dr. Parwez; he's grief-stricken, confused, incredulous that the cops suspect him of killing this child, for whose custody he fought so hard and long. For me, it's not difficult to figure why the cops are suspicious. The child disappeared, evidently kidnapped a day before a scheduled hearing in which his mother had been seeking to overturn the custody arrangements by claiming that Raheel expressed a desire to live with her. (Nabeel, the younger son, was so attached to his father that his mother, Amtul, couldn't work on his sympathies the way she had on her older son.) To make matters worse, she has gotten to the police first and is telling them that the child wanted to live with her and that Parwez had him killed to prevent the child from backing up her request for custody. (The absurdity here is that Raheel was never even scheduled to testify at the custody hearing.)

I advise Parwez, who has not yet been arrested, to refer all future requests for interviews by the cops to me. I promise to contact and meet with the homicide investigators the next day (a day off from the Chinatown trial) and to stay in touch with him.

The meeting with the sheriff's homicide investigators is illuminating, in a negative sort of way. They suggest that Parwez's religion, a Muslim sect called Ahmadi, may have played some unspecified role in the murder of the child. I smell racism and it scares me.

Two days later, the bailiff slips me a note, another urgent message from Valerie. Parwez has been arrested. That evening, as Valerie and I drive out to the sheriff's substation where he's being held for booking, Valerie gives me her take on the major players:

Amtul, Parwez's ex-wife, underwent a major transformation in her personality and lifestyle about a year and a half before the divorce. She claims to have messianic visions, delusions that she is the new savior of the Ahmadi faith. She has been known to make dark references to the Abraham and Isaac story (part of the Islamic tradition, too), in which the parent is asked to sacrifice his child. And her obsession with her role as religious leader had manifested itself outwardly with her change from a bikini-clad, thoroughly Westernized past to a form of veiled Islam that even seemed extreme to other members of the sect. Moreover, she has become your last-pound-of-flesh man-hater.

As for Dr. Parwez, whom Valerie has known under the most stressful circumstances, she believes he is a good man, certainly not the kind of maniac who could have strangled and dissected his own son. Moreover, she cannot imagine a motive. It's true a custody hearing was scheduled for the day after Raheel disappeared—giving rise to the argument that Parwez was going to kill his kid rather than let Amtul have him—but Parwez is in fact in zero danger of losing the boy and Valerie has been constantly reassuring him of that. The wife has to demonstrate "a material change in circumstances" resulting in detriment to the child should he stay with Parwez—and there simply are no facts she can present at the hearing to support the claim. There is nothing about this father-son relationship, past or present, that indicates child abuse of any kind. Valerie's reassurances carry weight. Every time she has ever reassured

Parwez about a particular outcome in this case she has always been proven right—so he has every reason to be confident in her judgment this time.

Valerie and I get to the sheriff's station near Pomona around six o'clock and go directly to Parwez's cell. He's still in his suit. His face is ashen. And he is freaking out. He's weeping and his Omar Sharif good looks are contorted by the misery. He is so pathetic. I feel very sorry for him. This is going to be a long haul and he is going to suffer for quite some time. At this point it is still a death-penalty case, so he doesn't even qualify for bail, a fact he cannot grasp. Although the unconstitutional "heinous, atrocious and cruel" special-circumstances allegation is stricken by the judge later in the preliminary hearing, resulting in bail being set, Parwez can never raise the $3 million required by the prelim judge. He remains in jail for two years until the conclusion of the trial.

The police are far more comfortable suspecting Parwez and not Amtul because, among other fallacious assumptions, men are seen as violent and women are not. At first glance, the prospects look as poor as can be from the Parwez point of view: that impending custody hearing provides the conflict and possible motive in the prosecution's view. Parwez is a doctor trained in anatomy; a surgeon, in fact, and one who served a year's residency in pathology, facts that point to skill in dissection. Also, he has been caught presumably lying to the police: he told the cops that he was unaware of any new address for his brother Sattar, yet the apartment where the boy was evidently killed was rented in Sattar's name and Parwez's palm print is found there.

The cops are certain they've got their killer; he appears to them, I'm sure, through that prism of prejudice, like a Muslim fanatic hiding out all this time as a benign obstetrician and concerned parent. Parwez and I have explained to the cops that he was at the hospital delivering babies and monitoring mothers in labor during the time that Raheel was missing and apparently killed. They rejected his alibi without ever checking the patient records or talking to the Kaiser employees. Determined to be ignorant and preserve their preconceptions, they have done a classic job —and this phrase was not invented by Johnnie Cochran specifically for the O. J. Simpson case—of rushing to judgment. And that pressures them to color their reports and their testimony to support a guilt theory to which they now are absolutely wed.

The central string of events begins on November 16, 1987. Raheel and his younger brother, Nabeel, are driven to their respective schools by a neighbor who also has two children to drop off. Raheel never gets to school. He is picked up out front by someone in a blue Oldsmobile, a car that resembles the one Dr. Parwez's brother Sattar drives. (As the facts are revealed, Sattar is quickly and clearly implicated in this murder, but the cops drop the ball; Sattar slips away, probably to Pakistan. Interpol makes some feeble attempt to find him and fails. He never returns.)

Evidently Raheel is taken from school to Sattar's unit at a sprawling, neat condominium development called Hacienda Pines. Inside the unit the sheriff's lab people find small but telling quantities of human hair and blood evidence. The rental records for this unit show that Khalid Parwez only very recently helped the unemployed brother—whom he's been supporting—rent one of the condos so that he can move out of the Parwez house. Parwez, recently remarried, seems to have grown weary of his malingering brother.

It is a functional, small apartment with the standard sort of inexpensive appliances, including a white enamel, four-burner electric stove—with Dr. Parwez's palm print on it. Parwez had in fact been there, of course, to see the apartment with his brother. He had, apparently, leaned on the stove. There are none of his prints elsewhere in the house. Many other prints are found, however, some of which probably belong to Sattar, but there is no record of the brother's prints on file and no way of getting them, since he has vanished. It will not be the existence of Parwez's single palm print on the stove that's the most crucial print evidence in the case, from my point of view. It's the lack of his prints on the gruesome items associated with the dismemberment of the body that seems most telling.

During the entire period when the crime was being committed, Khalid Parwez is on twenty-four-hour duty at Kaiser as the lead doctor in the obstetrics ward. If the ward is busy, both the designated number-one doctor and the second in charge will end up staying awake all night. If the shift is quiet, one or both will try to catch some sleep. On this night there is at least one woman whom Parwez has been monitoring closely and conceivably might present an emergency somewhere along the line. But both doctors feel free enough to go to sleep in the little rooms reserved for them behind the operating theater. Parwez is not seen between 2:00 A.M. and 6:30 A.M.

The second in charge, Dr. Brenda Fabe, tells us that there is no way that a doctor can predict emergencies or when they will occur, because problems develop during labor that cannot be anticipated when the patient is first admitted. When a serious problem does develop, especially one that dictates delivering a baby by caesarean section, both doctors must be in attendance on very short notice. Dr. Fabe seems incredulous at the notion, put forward by the cops, that Dr. Parwez sneaked out to do the crime during those early-morning hours. If he did, she says, and an emergency cropped up, he would "be a dead duck if called to assist his partner."

And even if this cautious man ever did do such a rash thing, was four and a half hours time enough? The Hacienda Pines condos are quite some distance, maybe an hour and a half away from Kaiser depending on the traffic. The mutilation of Raheel was so thorough that, in the opinion of experts, it probably took hours.

We talk to everyone on duty that night at that hospital. We locate the housekeepers who saw Parwez emerging from his sleeping room, hair mussed, eyes puffy with sleep at six-thirty. We learn that there were only two doors that doctors could enter and exit after midnight, and people stationed at those doors didn't see Parwez do either.

Still, of course, the prosecution isn't going to be deterred by any alibi. And confronted by such horror, I can't be sure the jury will listen to reason either.

The remains of the boy are discovered on November 17, the day after he missed school. A maintenance man for the condos, a Polish immigrant named Zenon Kalarus (who, strangely enough, as a teenager was forced to work in a slaughterhouse as a butcher for the Nazis), is on duty and going about his rounds. He needs some cardboard to mix plaster and decides to search for some in a nearby Dumpster. He sees some cartons under a plastic trash bag, reaches for the bag with his left hand but finds it surprisingly heavy; it needs two hands, and he becomes curious about its contents. He takes this bag and some others like it out of the Dumpster; peeking inside the trash bags he sees numerous smaller plastic bags, like the kind they pack groceries in at the supermarket. He puts his finds in a shopping cart he happens to have with him and begins opening the smaller bags. "I see the first was the bones," he says, "and another two bags was the pieces of meat."

He decides, this curious former butcher, "no pork, no beef," but whatever it is, it smells fresh and seems warm to him. Is it edible? (Listening to this testimony, knowing exactly what it is this strange scavenger has found, I am struck, not for the first time, by the fact that even the peripheral players in this already bizarre case are weird.) Ultimately, it is the skull, shorn of skin and most of its flesh, that tips him off. "I was shaking. I started to shake, and then I didn't know what to do," he says.

His heart is pounding. He returns the bags to the Dumpster. He has a cigarette, drinks some coffee in one of the apartments. Now he hears a trash truck off in the distance! And he acts. He hurries to his supervisor.

"I found some meat in the trash, some body," he tells him. "I figure out that's a human body."

"It's what? What is it?"

"I says, 'Come on.' "

Soon, they do the appropriate things. The maintenance man stands watch to ward off the trash truck if it arrives before the cops, whom the supervisor has called.

It takes no spectacular detective work to learn that this is the cut-up body of Raheel Parwez because—and again, this is just so insane—the killer has apparently not only thrown the grim result of his macabre work into the Dumpster right outside the scene of the crime, but included with it Raheel's clothes and his wallet with his picture ID. That's a mind-scrambling fact, if you're trying to figure out what happened here, since the only logical assumption is that the body was cut up to discard it in such a way that it would not be identifiable.

Also found in trash bags in the Dumpster is a length of white rope that is identified by the coroner's criminalist as the ligature causing death. There are also yards of blood-spattered black plastic sheeting containing dozens of hand, palm and footprints of an adult, and the blood-smeared flattened cardboard packing box for a child's basketball hoop and back-stop. In photos taken by the sheriff's office during a search of Parwez's house there is shown, in the children's playroom, a basketball hoop and backstop of the same brand as the bloody box in the Dumpster. The criminalist's theory is that to accomplish the dissection of the body the sheeting was laid down on the carpet in the bedroom of the apartment, the flattened cardboard box on top of it, and on top of that the bread cutting board from the kitchen. Although these items contain dozens of prints clear and detailed enough to use for identification when compared with a known person's prints, none of them match those of Parwez. Since his prints are not on file, there is no way to know whether or not they are Sattar's.

To prepare for this case, I need to do two things. I need to learn something about Islamic life here in L.A. and I need to analyze the evidence, learn as much as I can about how the cutting was done. Was it really the work of a medical professional, as the prosecution will assert, or did it simply require an understanding of anatomy? Brother Sattar studied anatomy in college in Pakistan. Could he have done this on his own? All the pictures of the hundreds of body parts—removed from those supermarket shopping bags, the flesh cut into little chunks, the face after it was lifted off in pieces and then as it was reassembled, the extracted and cut-up organs—need to be studied carefully. I don't know which pictures the prosecution will choose; I don't know which of them offer clues to the expertise, if any, of the cutter. So I must be familiar with them all.

It's a night when Tim is not at home, he's having dinner with a friend as I remember it, and I am in my house alone. I spread the photos out on the dining room table. As I look at them, horror is welling up in me, overcoming me. I can't do this. I can't look at these here alone at night. I begin to repackage them. I wish I could scrunch them together and shove them back in an envelope quickly. But I can't; they have to be packaged neatly, which takes much longer than unpacking them. I have to bind them with rubber bands, place the proper labels on them. I am re-straining myself from cracking up. I keep telling myself, "No. This is okay. This is just biology." But I keep looking up at the windows, imagining the ghouls that will come through and join my nightmare.

Eventually, I look at the photos many times, often with my pathology expert, but never at night and alone at home again.

Parwez, in his capacity as a doctor, tells me he wants to see the pic-tures; he says he might be able to help out. That unsettles me. I know he's a professional who deals with tissues and organs all the time. But I don't need his input. I have my own pathologist. Also, I'm afraid he might look at these things, fail to find that place in his mind where he can be detached, freak out and then have nowhere to go but back to his cell bearing these horrible images. Or he might look at them, deal with them completely unemotionally, clinically—and, if I saw that lack of emotion on examining the tiny cut-up pieces of his own son, it would freak *me* out.

I never do show them to him.

Part of this investigation turns out to be a wonderful experience. Because I need to talk to the Muslim women in Parwez's circle about the family, I get the chance to go into their homes, peek behind the veil in a sense. As a matter of fact they dress much more casually at home than in the street, and also these seemingly cowed women are quite outspoken when you sit around with them and talk the way friends do.

They come from a culture that makes me uncomfortable, it's true. I have always found the notion of arranged marriages repugnant, for instance. But some of these women aren't too pleased with the setup either. One, married to a man who's beneath her, tells me right up front, "It's bad for me and I'm not happy in this marriage, but I love my children." I hardly know these women and they are opening up like that.

I get to go to one of their social gatherings and they seem so free when they're with their own sex. They dance together and have an intense warmth toward one another that you often fail to see in Western women. I feel surprisingly comfortable among them, like we could have a slumber party any old time. Girlfriends.

They gossip a lot, too. Amtul is somebody they're eager to talk about. They don't like her. But their comments are different from those of Parwez, who harps on her readily apparent emotional instability. They're telling me she's a phony, somebody with a superior attitude. They find it ridiculous that she made this leap from Miss Westernized American in a bikini to someone who wears a veil that covers her face so thoroughly. "We don't even dress that way," one of them tells me. "Amtul looks like an Arab woman, like she's from Saudi Arabia. When she did that we all thought, Ah, what craziness is she up to now?"

For her appearances in court, a more evidently pragmatic Amtul undergoes yet another transformation. On the stand, she is lovely in her Western clothes, her dark hair cascading over her shoulders, a cute little flower over her right ear for accent.

When we get to trial, Amtul is not hard to deal with. She is evasive throughout and clearly has been her former husband's worst enemy for a long time. Sattar, the missing participant, is an easy target. Everyone believes he is involved in Raheel's kidnapping and murder. The questions are, did he act alone and, if so, what was his motive? He might have been angry at Parwez for reasons we don't understand; he could have had some arrangement with Amtul, having fallen under her cultish powers (some anecdotal evidence pointed that way). Anything is possible but it is all maddeningly elusive. Sattar, of course, is unavailable for questioning.

A perhaps more difficult problem in dealing with the evidence is to demonstrate that a doctor wasn't required for this dissection. In this grisly work, there are jagged, zigzag incisions that would make no doctor proud, and the effort to remove the scalp was patently clumsy. Also persuasive—in the grim context of my argument—is what was done to the bowel. Here, as in any discussion of physical evidence in a murder case, I have to be very clinical in summarizing the evidence for the jury, to make sure that reason is not obscured by the horror of it all. I remind them of the testimony in which they learned that a trained pathologist (like Parwez) always seals the bowel off with two ties, close together, and then cuts between those ties—each one creating a sealed end—so that the bowel is closed and cannot leak. But this bowel did leak. I tell the jury, "We know that because Dr. Wegner, the coroner, saw loose fecal material among the remains. So this was not done the way pathologists, including Parwez, are taught to do it." I'm taking evidence that could have been potentially damaging, Parwez's early training in pathology, and turning it to his advantage.

Valerie is spectacular as she testifies on the absence of motive. Before she testifies we meet at a Bob's Big Boy near my office (I do not think of the murders at the other one at all as I do this; if I fixated on every crime scene, I'd have to stay home). She is far more nervous than I expect her to be (even lawyers can get stage fright), forgetting what she knows, anxious about whether she'll say it right. But on the stand she is beautiful, looks like a princess in her red dress. She is soft-spoken, which is a change of pace in this case—I'm not soft-spoken even when I try. She looks at the jury occasionally but doesn't stare at them. She smiles, injects some humor into the testimony, offers to be helpful. "Yes, I do have the papers on file; would you like me to get them?"

And this is something you can't prep somebody for: she conveys to the jury without needing to really say it that she is fond of Parwez.

Valerie tells the jury that she never had any doubts about his ability as a father, that his home was the right place for the kids to be, that she was absolutely positive he had nothing to fear from a custody hearing.

In their testimony, the other doctors from the ob-gyn service at Kaiser, and the patients whose babies Dr. Parwez delivered over that crucial twenty-four-hour period, paint the picture of a hardworking, dedicated doctor showing no signs of stress or preoccupation as he went about his duties that day. Not what you would expect from a man actively conspiring to kill his own abducted child. As luck would have it, the two patients who witnessed Parwez's behavior late that fateful night are both Orthodox Jewish women. I was mindful of the subtle message their participation in the defense would convey to the jury. If these Jews were on the side of the Muslim, Parwez, then you, too, dear juror, can overcome the shadow of the Ayatollah.

This is a case, in the end, with virtually no evidence against my client.

There is that palm print in the apartment. But at the other end of the county there are half a dozen healthy newborn babies and their beaming moms to attest to Dr. Parwez's whereabouts. After that, you have speculation and prejudice. The deputy district attorney argues that Sattar is part of the murder plot. As a matter of tactics, and based on Parwez's training, he takes the position that Parwez personally dismembered the child. He makes it an all-or-nothing choice for the jury by refusing to argue that Parwez could be guilty as a co-conspirator even if Sattar did the actual killing. But I argue that the evidence of all those unmatched prints on the murder tools points to Sattar as the actual killer—Sattar who fled while Parwez remained.

The jury has no difficulty in concluding that Sattar was the real killer. They even suspect Amtul in her madness was in cahoots with Sattar. Only one juror stands in the way of acquittal—one of those people who goes into the jury room and, essentially, puts her hands over her ears and refuses to listen to anybody: "He's guilty and I don't want to hear anything else." That's formally called "refusal to deliberate" and is reason for removal. The judge investigates for a day or two, decides this juror is behaving irrationally and exercises the judicial right to replace her with an alternate, a man who, fortunately for my side, is inclined toward a speedy acquittal.

So since he agrees with the eleven others, the verdict is assured very soon after he enters the room. I assume that's the situation and go down to the court the next day. The jury had been instructed that with the introduction of a new member it must start deliberations over from the beginning. They obviously took that rule seriously, and on that day nothing happens. They keep me and Parwez waiting all that day and into the morning of the next, when they figure it's finally safe, that it looks okay. We have a verdict, an acquittal.

Parwez and I go into the jury room to thank them. They applaud as we walk in. They shake his hand. They hug him. They offer the condolences they must have been feeling all along on the loss of his child. And he breaks down in tears.

I would hear from these jurors for years afterward, as they wanted to know how Parwez was doing and how Nabeel was. They were really nice people.

When that acquittal came rolling in, I didn't forget Ira Reiner, the DA who had gone out of his way to inflame public prejudice against my client. I tell the press, "I just want everyone in this county to understand that their district attorney wanted to give the gas chamber to an innocent man."

Reiner had committed the prosecutor's cardinal sin, pronouncing a man yet to face trial as guilty and demanding his punishment. But in this society he is not the only one contributing to this kind of prejudgment. This sort of leaping to conclusions of guilt happens with disgraceful frequency in the media every day.

In spite of nostrums we've all learned as children about there being two sides to every story, the public seems to forget repeatedly that the story that emerges in the beginning is almost always incomplete, misleading or downright wrong. This tendency of the media and the public to form snap judgments of guilt is in direct conflict with the very nature of the judicial process. That process is geared toward methodical, highly regimented, careful contemplation of evidence for the very reason that the truth is not instantly apparent; it takes time and effort to ascertain the real facts. Only one side can go first and in our system that's the prosecution. Unless we are willing to wait until we've heard from the accused before we make up our minds, no innocent citizen is safe. Innocent unless and until proven guilty is the letter of the law. "Where there's smoke there's fire" is the rule of the lynch mob. Unfortunately, the tendency toward presumption of guilt seems most pronounced in cases where the crime is so vile that it excites instant anger and outrage. But these are the same situations in which the penalties are so extreme that we risk executing the innocent.

As it happens, only part of the truth ever did emerge here, of course: we established that Parwez did not leave Kaiser and go and kill and dissect his kid. But it is not a victory to savor, given that the presumed source of all those fingerprints, Sattar Ahmed (who obviously knew what happened), fled into the depths of the subcontinent, presumably, and that we will never know the motive, never really understand what happened in this ghastly crime.

A sidelight in this case is that I came to appreciate the tribulations of divorce lawyers even more than I had before. Under the best of circumstances, they are dealing with people who have not committed a crime, have no reason to feel guilty and can't understand why they have to pay lawyers part of their assets in order to retain the rest of them. It is devastating to these clients to realize, as many must, that the harder they fight the more it costs them and the more they lose. The lawyer, in these cases, starts to look like part of the problem. A divorce lawyer rarely ends up winning anything for a client emotionally; at best the lawyer wins something financially. Money, generally, is the entire issue. Unless of course it is a fight over the kids, and then it gets really nasty and painful. Even without the Solomonic struggles over custody, divorce trials are often very ugly contests: people hide assets, they try to destroy their partners. And then the lawyer, having overseen this domestic train wreck, moves on to another one.

Criminal lawyers, by contrast, are frequently loved by their clients, constantly referred by them to others, but divorce lawyers are not often loved; they are killed more often by clients, their own and those they oppose, than any other type of attorney.

The work takes a tremendous emotional toll. And for Valerie Colb, it was even worse than usual. She had arranged this whole Parwez divorce "in the best interest of the child." And the boy was murdered. She knew that Parwez did not kill his son. But how could she not feel some amorphous guilt? She was a party to this in some vague way. This child came into the ambit of her care. At the same time that she had to deal with the death of Raheel, her life was being threatened by the husband of one of her other clients. Stress on top of stress. Valerie was having a very hard time of it.

Divorce law. You can keep it.

17

Abuse
_____

The internal dialogue with myself goes like this: "What are *you* doing judging this woman? Here you expect a jury to be sympathetic and understanding and *you're* rejecting her?"

The plight of abused women—especially in the early years of private practice when I began to handle a string of such cases—did give me trouble as I tried to avoid turning on them the way so many people do. Often I would just keep my thoughts about a poor wretch to myself, thoughts like: How could you be so weak? How could you be so forgiving? How could you accept so much blame for that animal's sadistic behavior? How could you take that garbage from that sleazebucket and still tell me you *loved* him?

It took me quite awhile, really, to get myself past the prejudice. Men have trouble understanding the victimization of these people because they can't believe the women would put up with it if they didn't actually like it. Women, like me, often have trouble, I think, because the experiences of battered women are psychologically threatening to us. I tend to identify with these people as women, after all. And it makes me recoil: I will never be a victim. Not me. I have rejected that possibility all my life. I won't take crap from anyone. I will always fight back. Why don't they?

I have to get it through my head that these women are not me; so I have to distance myself a bit, understand them better, the brainwashing, the entrapment, the desperation and, almost invariably, the emotionally crippling experiences of their childhoods. I have to realize that, like all living organisms, they are trying to find their own ways to survive, their own ways to evade the pain, no matter how futile and pathetic.

I have never been a knee-jerk feminist who automatically embraces the image of the poor woman-as-victim violated by a universe of evil men. In fact, in the early days of my private practice I joined and then withdrew from one of the more prominent feminist lawyers' organizations because it was infused with the kind of single-minded mentality that made its members utterly unconcerned with the fair trial or due-process rights of any of the accused men who victimized women. I suspected that if they had their way, these feminist lawyers would install castration as a viable form of punishment, although I bet they wouldn't endorse sterilization of abusive mothers.

Although I do not believe feminism should skew the criminal law, I have no personal sympathy for the battering male, the cowardly, brutal, controlling enslavers out there. As far as I'm concerned many of them deserve the slow death by torture that they instead inflict on their wives and children. The criminal law, as it regards a homicide committed by an abused woman, still has something of the caveman mentality about it. One aspect of our criminal codes that is clearly out of whack with the psychological reality of the lives of women—and children—is the notion of self-defense. Self-defense is a concept developed to deal with the assault of one man against another, *mano a mano,* two theoretically equal antagonists. One attacks or threatens and the other responds. But no woman or child ever is going to win that kind of battle against an enraged, domineering, controlling man. A woman, or a child, needs alternative defenses, and one reasonable way to defend yourself, even though your mind is engulfed in terror, is to wait to attack your tormentor when he is unarmed and unsuspecting. That's the only way you can get out of there alive, maybe.

Much of my education about the abuse of women—along with a deep and growing empathy—evolved from three killings. Two of them struck me as offering traditional legal defenses (self-defense and "diminished capacity") that made it unnecessary to rely on the newer concept of battered women's syndrome to explain what happened. But the last was classic, a textbook case of how long-term brutalizing can trigger a violent response.

•

Laura Schindler is about fifty when I first meet her, and obviously she had been gorgeous when she was young. Even now she is an attractive woman, great cheekbones, thick blond hair, big eyes, pouty lips and delicate frame. She's girlish, the pink-ruffle type, even in middle age. But I notice that she is not sexy. And that, I think, is because of the rape. Years earlier, working in a hospital, she was attacked in an alley on the way to her car by a stranger. She was pulled to the ground, never really saw the face of the rapist. She is a victim—and I don't mean that in any sloppy sentimental way—a true victim who never does get over that traumatizing experience.

Rather late in life, she marries Lou Schindler, a man of charm and some money, a good storyteller (it is typical of middle-class and upper-middle-class batterers that they can be so seductively likable; that's why women fall madly in love with them and stay that way even under the most unbearable circumstances). He doesn't tell her right away how an earlier wife died—the mother of his six-year-old daughter; he just says he's a widower. But it doesn't take long. The fact is that he killed that earlier wife, June, shot her while she was on the telephone, in a fit of jealous rage and then got lucky. He was convicted of manslaughter and spent only two years in jail.

Lou Schindler is not what you would call remorseful. He brags about the killing often; it was a high point of his life. Laura, my client, makes the mistake of telling this lout about her lowest point, the rape. So, ever after, Lou thinks it's funny to sneak up behind her from time to time to give her a bit of a jolt. He belittles her continually, calls her names. He is domineering, jealous and sadistic. She is, as so many of these women are, self-loathing anyway, and tries to put up with all of Lou's anger, which seems more justified to her than it might to you or me. She is eager to please, even if that proves damn near impossible.

But one night Lou goes too far. He tells her, "I'm going to kill you the way I killed June." Bingo! She spirals into full-blown terror. Technically, the psychiatrists call what she experiences a fugue state: the term for people who are experiencing extreme dissociation, unaware of their surroundings, their thoughts, their actions, unconscious, but still awake. Next thing she knows, she's holding the gun. He's in bed. There's a bullet in the back of his head. She can't remember any of it. But she knows one thing.

"I shot Daddy, I shot Daddy!" she screams in anguish and horror as she runs down the hallway toward Lou's daughter's room. "I'm calling the police."

She does. And she gets a lawyer, Paul Geragos—the very same one who, as a district attorney years before, prosecuted Lou for killing June. That choice should make sense to just about anybody because she is obviously looking for someone who understands the true lethality of this maniac. But in trial, the choice of lawyer is turned against her. The prosecution argues that she couldn't have been in a fugue state or for that matter genuinely remorseful if she had the presence of mind to hire the very same guy who put her husband away. These kinds of illogical and tortured arguments have put many a sympathetic defendant behind bars. It convicted Laura Schindler and sent her to prison for second-degree murder. She was granted bail on appeal by the appellate court after serving three months of her sentence.

As it happens, a prosecutor is not supposed to use the choice of lawyer as a weapon against a defendant. Technically, it's a violation of the constitutional Sixth Amendment right to counsel of one's choosing. It's also a dirty trick to bring this up in front of a jury when Laura Schindler has no chance to change advocates. But the judge in this case is a notoriously cranky misogynist, Laurence Rittenband, who—by allowing the prosecutor to use this low tactic—commits a stupendous error that will, in the end, undo the unjust verdict. I've never thought "error" was the right word for that sort of ruling; I generally figure that when judges make clearly bad decisions it is to advance their own agenda. That's how a prejudiced judge determines a trial's outcome. This call is so obviously wrong that the conviction is reversed on appeal by the intermediate appellate court, and the Supreme Court refuses to give the prosecution a shot at restoring it. When a defendant's appeal of his conviction is granted it doesn't mean the case is over. What he's won is the right to go through a second trial.

So I get the case next to prepare for the second trial. I'm in the early years of private practice, barely making it, and my immediate concern is getting paid. Laura has resources: half of the community property of her marriage. Her half is hers whether she killed this guy or not. But the old-time, bow-tied arrogant lawyer for the bank serving as executor of the probate estate is not going along with that reasoning. The hell with him. I may be just a lowly criminal lawyer but I can remember what I learned about probate law and community property in law school and I'm not going to be intimidated by this guy's corporate lawyer superiority, his age or his gender. I go storming into his office and lay down the law literally and figuratively. "No more snookering anybody over this money!" This woman needs to be able to live and she needs to be able to pay her legal costs.

And the bank's man shows a little respect, finally, and relents when he realizes I can't be fooled and I won't be nice.

In trying the case, I stay away from the "battered wife syndrome" as a defense because I don't want to fall into a trap where Laura has to fit every one of the characteristics that make up a syndrome, where she has to be compared to every other abused wife who kills. For one thing Lou never laid a hand on her. His abuse was in the nature of psychological battering, which is harder for a jury to accept and, at that time, was not as well studied for syndrome-producing effects as it has been by now. Secondly, Lou was a wife killer who, in threatening Laura, was threatening the meekest of women. I didn't need more than that to explain why she believed that he was capable of killing her, particularly when he just threatened to do so. Rarely do you have a case where you can show that a person who threatens violence has also carried out that threat in the past. Beyond that, Laura was in that mental state called "fugue" at the time of the shooting, giving me a second line of defense, "diminished capacity" or mens rea affected by mental disease, in this case a temporary one.

Beyond the nature of the technical defenses, I realize I have some pretty straightforward stuff to elicit sympathy for my client. Here is a shy, traumatized woman, who's been raped and abused, a woman whose life experience has left her with a heightened sense of fear. And here's this loud-mouthed vulgar bully—a certifiable killer—who torments her throughout the marriage and then finally threatens to murder her. I also figure that when the jury hears that when Lou Schindler killed wife number one his infant daughter lay sleeping ten feet away from the smoking gun, the prosecution is going to lose its usual "we represent the innocent victim" moral advantage.

It does not hurt the defense that Laura can't recall killing her husband because she has nothing to gain by amnesia. She's not denying she did the killing the way other people who claim amnesia often do, but it would be nice to know exactly what happened. For one thing, juries are suspicious of claims of memory loss. If she could remember shooting Lou she'd lose nothing by it and would enhance her credibility with the jury. Beyond that I believe that her memory loss is a product of extreme terror. Better for her to relate that terror, make it real for the jury rather than say she went blank. So I hire a psychiatrist who turns to hypnosis, which, unfortunately, fails to bring forth any additional memory. But the psychiatrist goes on to testify about why Laura was such a fearful person and that her lack of memory is genuine. She is behaving much the way someone with a multiple personality does. She can't confront the terror. Fugue is her coping mechanism.

In any event I have what I believe is a pretty solid "unreasonable self-defense" case that will result in no more than a manslaughter conviction. This kind of self-defense—exactly the same theory that I would argue in the first Menendez trial ten years later—is called "unreasonable" or "imperfect" because the threat may not be as real or as immediate as it seems to you at the time, but you believe you are in mortal danger to the depths of your being. As self-defense, it is legitimate, but flawed. Unlike perfect self-defense, though, a killing under these circumstances does not constitute justifiable homicide and can't result in an acquittal.

There's a fine line with Laura, however. Her fear isn't so unreasonable —is it? This is a threat from a man who killed his previous wife, after all. And the trial judge later instructs the jury to consider perfect self-defense as well.

But Laura, on the stand, starts out doing herself no favors. She is a terrible witness. She is frightened and wants to please, as usual: Little Miss Goody Two-shoes. The person she wants to please in this instance, however, is the prosecutor! She is answering questions in ways that help him out. Saying things that aren't true just to be agreeable. That is suicide.

The prosecutor, a DA named David Wells—a man blessed with the deepest blue eyes imaginable, eyes that seem to jump out of his face as he looks at you—asks her something like, "And then did you argue with him?," trying to demonstrate that she had a combative nature.

And she answers, meekly, "Yes, I did."

I can't believe what I'm hearing. We interviewed everyone who knew this couple and they are unanimous in their observations that Laura never said "boo" to Lou, let alone argued with him.

After that self-destructive performance, I take her out into the hallway and I go ballistic. "What the hell is going on?"

I go over with her, one more time, some of the actual facts about her relationship with her husband and then I get her back on the stand.

"Did you argue with him?" I ask.

"No."

"So why did you answer the DA that way?"

And she says, in that really timid way of hers, almost a whisper, "Because that's what I thought he wanted to hear."

The upshot is the jury hangs. It's so strange: Five for second-degree murder, six for not guilty and one for manslaughter. Although there was enough evidence of Lou's lethality to support a verdict of not guilty on a self-defense theory, he was, after all, asleep when she shot him. So, being a realist, I figured the jury would opt for imperfect self-defense and bring back a manslaughter conviction. But only one juror—the one I thought was especially weak—evaluated the case the way I did.

Now comes the time to do a deal. Certainly we don't want to try this thing a third time.

The DA is a good guy in my book, a man willing to learn and keep his mind open. This same prosecutor who argued so strenuously in the first trial to put Laura in prison now has softened a bit. We eventually agree that she will plead to voluntary manslaughter, as long as I can pick the judge who gets to set the punishment. (We are definitely going to stay away from Judge Rittenband, though not as dramatically as Roman Polanski did a few years before to avoid the prison sentence Rittenband was about to impose on him: we didn't have to leave the country, only change courtrooms to find justice in the Santa Monica branch.)

Laura has already served several months in prison before she made bail on appeal—and she is a patently shattered woman who is no threat whatsoever to anyone. I believe she should remain free and be placed on probation. So she'll have to report once a month to a probation officer. Compared to what they're used to she'll be a treat. Although it's always nerve-racking to have a client make what's known as an "open" guilty plea, one with no agreement on the sentence, as we get closer to the day of sentencing it becomes obvious that the other players in this drama are beginning to understand Laura the way I do.

The probation officer calls me. She tells me she thinks it's a shame that Laura ever had to see the inside of a prison. This is a very good sign. She calls back; she has recommended probation. Judges don't have to follow probation officers' recommendations, but I have every reason to believe that where we are going for sentencing, the judge will.

We are transferred to the courtroom of Judge Charles Woodmansee, one of the most respected jurists in Los Angeles. The opposite in temperament to Rittenband, he is a thoughtful, understated, scholarly and humane judge. Although he is among the most senior of the Santa Monica judges, he is now handling mainly civil matters, no criminal trials. His "courtroom" is in one of the temporary (read "permanent") makeshift trailers set up in the parking lot of the courthouse. It is a tiny, shabby space (no majesty-of-government vibes in here). And it's in that little place that Laura and I are waiting for the judge to bring some closure to this sad ordeal. Laura is sitting at this tacky table. I'm standing. The judge is in his chambers reading the probation report.

Before he emerges, Dave Wells comes over to us and says, "Leslie, do you mind if I say something to your client? I want to talk to her before the judge comes out, before she's sentenced."

I say, "Is that okay with you, Laura?" It is, of course. I step back so they can talk and those deep blues can look into Laura's.

He says, "Mrs. Schindler, I want to apologize to you for having you put in prison last time." (Wow.)

"I never thought, as a prosecutor," he goes on, "that I'd be happy to have a case reversed, but I'm glad this one was. I just didn't understand." What a mensch.

The judge was a mensch, too. He was almost apologetic in placing her on probation.

I heard from Laura for many years after; eventually the contacts stopped. Knowing Laura, I'm sure it's because she didn't want to bother me.

Howard Weitzman calls. You may remember him as the successful defender of John DeLorean and O.J.'s first lawyer, before the Shapiro/ Cochran team took over. He's the guy who couldn't convince Simpson not to talk to the police. We all assumed he quit in disgust. When he calls me he says, "I want to refer a case to you. This is your kind of case," he says, warmly. "It's this woman who killed her husband." And Weitzman seems to genuinely like her: "She's a sweetheart," he says. "She's also the sister-in-law of a city councilman, which may mean we've got some extra clout here, and has been active in community work." I feel pretty flattered that Howard called on me. Until I meet the client and learn she doesn't have any money. And hasn't paid Weitzman anything. (Actually, I'm still flattered, just a bit more suspicious of Howard's motives than I was at first: I'm learning why lawyers like to represent dope dealers. They've always got money.)

I like this woman, Alice Hayes Wallace, a great deal, too, and ultimately settle on taking the case for half my usual fee at the time for noncapital homicides: I charge her $25,000, the amount her family can lend her. There are lots of similarities to the Laura Schindler case—a woman imprisoned in her home by a jealous control freak—but also differences that make it more typical of battered-wife homicide cases. Here the dead husband did not have the unique history of killing a previous wife so we are relying on a more psychological explanation for Alice's actions. Alice, a beautiful African-American woman, fell for your typical abuser, a flamboyant romantic who swept her off her feet with flowers and cards and lovely dates. But when, after she got pregnant, she married him, she still hardly knew him.

As soon as her lover says "I do," he becomes Julian Wallace the despot. He effectively imprisons Alice in their home, a condo in the San Fernando Valley. He calls her constantly and if the phone is busy flies into a rage. He isolates her from friends and family. He is not as physically abusive as a lot of these jerks, but he does choke her once and throws her around from time to time. There's a dent in the wall where her head hit it. In fact, like most bullies, he doesn't require too much physical violence. He can do all the dominating he needs with words alone. (Throughout this case, I keep being reminded of my stepfather, Dave, who scared the hell out of me just with his booming voice. He never raised a hand to me, but intimidated very well just with his voice.)

Alice is miserable. An abusive mother had left her with the typical low view of herself and a sense that she had to be good all the time, no matter how monstrous the people around her might be. She suffers from hormone problems. She is carrying twins, and once they are born, the beautiful Alice plummets into the deepest sort of depression. She is sleep-deprived, exhausted, edgy, easily startled.

Meantime, Julian leaves her to take care of the kids by herself while he goes out with the guys. Half the time he hides the phone so she can't make calls.

It's beyond bearable. She gets up the nerve to complain. But he can't tolerate that. They're at the top of the stairs in this condo, and he lifts her into the air and threatens to hurl her down the stairs. She's screaming, frees herself and flees back into the bedroom where there is a gun.

Now, he's gone downstairs. Or maybe he's left—she doesn't know. And she is feeling panic rise in her. What next? What next? With great stealth, dressed in her nightgown and with her bare feet padding silently on the carpeting, she makes her way down the stairs, armed. It is an enclosed stairway so all she can see is the bottom, nothing to either side. She makes it to the base of the stairs, heart pounding, and he lunges at her from the right just as she clears the wall of the stairway. She pulls the trigger, one shot, through the heart.

I never knew Julian Wallace. The only time I ever saw him was in a picture at the base of the stairs, wearing a blue shirt made especially notable by the bullet hole right in the middle of it.

I can relate the sequence of events with some confidence now, but during the development of the case, in an eerie echo of Schindler, Alice

Hayes Wallace also had memory problems about the fatal moment. She knew she went down the stairs armed but, for the life of her, couldn't remember the details.

So there I am in my office, preparing her for testimony. What I want to do is bring her along stage by stage so that she is absolutely clear on the nature of the questioning, how it builds and where it is all headed. But the problem I have is that she is so vague on the shooting. I tell her we'll try a little reenactment.

"Step up on the chair," I say, and she does. It's a little green chair that clients sit on during interviews.

"Close your eyes," and she does.

And she says, trying to imagine the scene, "Okay, I'm coming down the stairs," and then she gets to the bottom and I lunge at her and she screams and begins crying. She's completely hysterical.

I'm saying it's okay, it's okay (although I don't feel calm at all, since I also freaked myself out in the process). She says she remembers now. She remembers feeling as she pulled away from him that she was clenching her fists and since one of them had the gun in it the clenching action pulled the trigger without her ever actually willing it to happen. This is not acting. It is as genuine a moment as I have ever witnessed, and I believe we now know exactly what happened.

The question that juries and lots of other people always wonder in cases like these is, Why did she go down there at all if she was so frightened? To answer that during the trial I bring in a psychiatrist who explains how sometimes when you're terrified but not sure if the fear is justified (imagine, in ordinary life, you hear a noise in the house and it may be an intruder or it may be the cat), you can't bear not knowing the truth. Is the threat genuine or, God willing, is it a figment of your imagination? You could run. But you have to know. You can't bear not knowing. And so you approach, even as terror constricts your throat and tightens your chest.

Did he leave? Is he there?

Then, he lunges!

I truly felt that this case deserved an acquittal, that it was an excusable homicide, an accident. The jury didn't agree, but they did convict her of only involuntary manslaughter, the least culpable criminal homicide. The judge went easy on her, granting three years of probation with no jail time, in large measure because of the wonderful work Casey Cohen did as my investigator. He solicited comments from prominent people, blacks and whites alike, from all over L.A. who had known Alice before the suffocating marriage to Julian Wallace, when she was active in the community doing church work, as well as other charities.

The mayor wrote a letter on her behalf; so did Johnnie Cochran; so did judges and business people. We got over one hundred of these great letters. She'd left a trail of kindness behind her ten miles wide.

An executive at a talent and literary agency implores, "I can only request that Your Honor consider what Alice means to so many people and her true sense of goodness." A producer describes her "as one of the most talented, energetic, intelligent personalities I have had the pleasure of knowing." And it goes on like that, letter after letter.

After the trial, Alice and I keep in touch. She never marries again. She does go into therapy. But like a lot of people who have been abused one way or another, she persists in needing someone to tell her what to do, run her life for her. In 1991 I find out that Alice is a patient of Dr. Jerome Oziel, the psychologist whose betrayal of the Menendez brothers' confidences had led to their arrest the previous March. Casey Cohen remained good friends with Alice. She told him that although she was aware of the negative publicity about Oziel's ethics she couldn't bring herself to break with him.

I call and tell her, "Look, I just feel I have to warn you about this guy Oziel. He's probably the most evil person I've come across in my whole career. He just exploits people, and uses people and abuses their trust."

One problem is that Oziel and others like him, in the guise of helping damaged people who've been controlled all their lives, just keep on controlling them to satisfy their own needs. The result isn't therapy so much as an affirmation of inadequacy by the patient and the cheap thrill of omnipotence for the manipulative therapist.

Alice does eventually extricate herself from Oziel but I think sometimes that even with the best of therapy, people who've really been broken can only be made better—they can't be fixed. Alice is extraordinarily solicitous of the feelings of her daughters, the twins. When we last spoke about the girls—they were ten at the time—she still hadn't told them the whole story. She was painting the killing as a pure accident at a time when she was ill; she long ago gave them photographs of the father they couldn't possibly remember and has encouraged them to love an idealized version of him.

When they get angry at her for killing Julian Wallace, she accepts their anger. Alice has always been good at accepting blame.

As each of these cases moves along, I get the feeling that there is a growing awareness among some prosecutors and judges that battered women who kill are not killing out of hatred and they're not killing out of revenge, that they are tortured women who are reacting to years of pain inflicted on them by their tormentors. (This, by the way, is an understanding rarely extended to abused children.) In court procedures, the new insights haven't gone far enough, in my opinion, but at least we usually can get all the evidence concerning the relationship between the parties before the jury without having a judge short-circuit the defense.

In Bonnie Esther, another abused woman, I did have that textbook example of a battered spouse. In fact, Lenore Walker, the nation's preeminent expert on the syndrome, told me after a two-and-a-half-day evaluation that if she'd known about Bonnie when she wrote *The Battered Woman,* her definitive book, "Bonnie would have been the model."

As for my own growing empathy, this one really put me to the test. Here was a woman who remained in a dehumanizing relationship for twenty-two years—even though she was smart, educated, capable and actually propping up the whole business of her husband, who was a bastard pure and simple. I think the public image of battered women is that they are poor little Cinderellas in rags on their hands and knees scrubbing. But that is often far from the truth. Many are beaten brutally and still function in the world outside their nightmare.

John Esther was a personal-injury lawyer. He was also a drunken bum incapable of doing any work. While he's semi-stuporous, Bonnie is interviewing clients, she's signing up cases, she's sending clients out for medical treatment, she's making sure the reports come in, she's dealing with the insurance adjusters—everything except going to court. When they do have a court obligation, maybe John will be sober enough, but if he's not Bonnie arranges for another lawyer to go in for them.

She cooks and does the other housework, too. And there's hell to pay if she cooks something he doesn't like. He hits her with a belt, with his hands, with a gun, and kicks her. Once he pistol-whipped her. The cops come occasionally and make their reports, but their intervention does not ameliorate anything. There are scars on Bonnie's body, and friends and relatives see them but do nothing. John Esther, in his cruelty, even brings girlfriends to the house and makes Bonnie watch. I mean, we're talking major-league tormenting here.

Meantime she writes letters to him (it's safer than talking) and tells him how all the troubles between them are her fault. She's going to mend her ways. She's going to make him love her again. Textbook. (And, as much as I know about all this now, I'm thinking, "Oh, God, how could you take this crap, how could you stay with this creep.")

When I meet Bonnie, I notice that she has a truly fine figure but a weary face (not surprising) and a completely unbecoming, strange hairdo, a helmet of yellowy-brown hair, like an old-fashioned pageboy. It turns out, of course, that's the way good ol' John insisted she look. Who knows why.

I am reading a lot about battered women at this point, and talking to Lenore Walker. This case finally gets me past my own inclination to blame the victim. The prison that a demented relationship has created for this woman is simply too real, too awful.

The final, fatal week is a bad one. As I recall it, John beats her during that week. Also, he starts in on their sixteen-year-old daughter, berating her, trying to destroy her relationship with her boyfriend. He hits her. He's never done that before. But he's been drunk and raging for days now.

Their daughter's boyfriend is outside the house and a terrible scene is about to erupt. John, screaming at both mother and daughter upstairs, now runs downstairs to confront the boy on the lawn and harangue the neighbors, who see it all.

Bonnie can't take it. It's not the personal humiliation. She's had years of that. And the neighbors, well, they've known that John Esther is a raging drunk for years, too. But this is different. He's physically assaulted the daughter for the first time and is threatening the boyfriend. And Bonnie knows it's about to get much more dangerous for the young couple. (John is about to discover what Bonnie already knows, that their daughter is pregnant. Bonnie believes he will kill the girl for sure.) Bonnie grabs John's gun, runs down the stairs after him. She has reached that point of irrational desperation that is so often the trigger in these killings. On the way out, she tells her daughter, "Call the police because I'm going to shoot him." And she does. In front of all those horrified neighbors. Shoots him to death. It happens so fast that you can actually hear the shots on the 911 tape.

•

It's strange the way you come to understand the texture of other people's lives. People can tell you the stories about what happened, but it doesn't reach you emotionally until something transports you into their life. That something happened on the day, early on in our relationship, when I visited Bonnie Esther in the house she had shared with John.

My purpose was the same as in any homicide case—the obligatory visit to the scene. I need her to walk through the events of the fateful night, to see where she was when she told her daughter to call the police, where she stood when she fired the gun, where the body fell.

But Bonnie can't tell the story of that night without digressing to her obsession, John, and how she tried to please him, to make it right. She tells me a story about preparing some soup for his dinner. She had already made an elaborate meal, meatloaf, all his favorite trimmings. He snarled that he wasn't hungry (too drunk, no doubt) and that all he wanted was some soup. So she had opened a can of Campbell's vegetable and was heating it on the stove when he stormed into the kitchen, looked in the pot, growled, "I wanted tomato, dumb bitch," and hurled the boiling soup, pot and all, at her face. The splatters are still on the kitchen wall.

The whole house, in fact, bears witness to John Esther's violence, holes punched in walls, broken locks on the bedroom door (she had tried to hide from his wrath). She shows me where he kept the gun, the one she shot him with, the one he pistol-whipped her with.

It is a depressing, sordid story. But the full weight of it doesn't really come home to me until I go to use the bathroom on the second floor. There are years of muck crusted on the sink fixtures, the walls of the shower, the floor around the toilet. The smeared mirror looks like it has never seen a droplet of Windex in fifteen years. I don't get it. Bonnie ran an entire law practice, she is meticulous in her personal grooming, I know she's depressed just now, but why does this house look like it has never been cleaned? As gently as possible I broach the subject.

"You know, Bonnie, you've got a lot on your mind. Why don't you get someone in here to clean the house once a week?" (Or, I'm thinking, cut the weeds in the front and back yards, and pick up the trash that litters both.)

"John," she says, "didn't believe in having anyone come in to clean— it was an invasion of privacy. Anyway, it was my job."

"Doesn't look like you had much time to do that job," I say.

"That's because when John was home I had to spend all my time paying attention to him, what he wanted, what he needed. He wouldn't let me go off into another room. He didn't like it if I ignored him to clean the house. If I tried he would grab the Comet away from me and throw it and demand that I return to the den and do things for him."

"Like what?"

"Like change the channel on the TV, or fix him another drink, or just sit there."

I realize early on that if we go to trial, there is going to be a problem with Bonnie even greater than with the other women: I'm afraid she might end up glorifying this monster, declaring her love, taking the blame. God help us. And she is so frightened besides, a shaky, nervous, quivering, birdlike creature. At times, she seems semi-comatose and can barely speak at all.

The DA, another of the better ones, is amenable to a deal. He knows that Bonnie Esther shot her husband outside the house at a moment when he wasn't actually threatening her, which reduces the argument for self-defense. But he also knows all the corroborating evidence of prior abuse, the cops' records, for instance. The sheriff's deputies who arrested Bonnie were so sympathetic (noting the numerous bruises on her body) that they released her on her own recognizance—no bail necessary for a murder charge! We agree that she will plead guilty to voluntary manslaughter and go to prison for a diagnostic report. But if the diagnostic panel decides to be tough and recommends prison for her and the judge is inclined to go along, then I get to withdraw the plea and we go to trial. The one thing I will never agree to is an actual prison sentence for Bonnie Esther. I tell the DA, "She does not belong there."

Bonnie can't even handle the thirty-two days that she has to stay there during the period when they're doing the report. These days are a torment because, naturally, she is drawn to the companionship of other women who've also killed abusive husbands and boyfriends. Unfortunately most of them are serving long sentences for first- and second-degree murder. Bonnie writes to me every day, sometimes more than once a day. Her letters are full of fear. She begs me to come see her. I go. She is convinced that she will wind up like her new friends, spending years in prison.

"That's not going to happen, Bonnie," I tell her.

"We could go to trial and lose," she says in despair.

"That's not going to happen, either," I tell her.

She keeps referring to the other women there, some, like Brenda Aris, as worthy of sympathy and understanding as she is, women who've killed husbands as bad if not worse than John Esther.

"Bad lawyering," I tell her, "male lawyering, Bonnie. You know those guys, the type who think battered wives are masochistic, that they like getting smacked around. If the lawyer doesn't understand the psychology, the justice of their client's cause, the jury sure won't. But that's them, Bonnie, not me and not you."

While delivering this pep talk to my terrified client I am thinking to myself: "Jesus, that panel better get it right because poor Bonnie will never live through a trial, she'll have a heart attack and die on the witness stand."

While she's at the prison, I keep checking in with one of the institution's officials. We share an interest in some prisoners' rights legislation pending in Sacramento. I make a point of seeing him on my visit. I talk to him several times during Bonnie's stay. I know this guy will have a tie-breaking vote if the people doing the evaluation can't agree on a recommendation. One of the evaluators, in a display of warped wisdom, does ultimately claim that Bonnie is a future threat because she might get into another twenty-two-year relationship with another brutal spouse and do the same thing again. How insane!

The prison psychiatrist sees it the other way. He writes that she's no threat to anybody. I turn to my chatty prison official, my friend, the one I've been coddling. He gets the chance to vote and he goes our way.

Now the judge still has to agree and I'm a bit nervous as we head back into court. I walk into his chambers. This judge is an informal, jolly sort of guy. He's holding a 250-page report (compiled by Casey Cohen) in his hand bearing witness to Bonnie's whole past.

I say, "Judge, do we have a problem?"

He says, "No problem. All we've got here is some jerk who was asking for it lying dead on his lawn with eight shots in his back."

A postscript to the sorry story of Bonnie Esther has to do with her son, who is away at college at the time of the trial and is beginning to sound to me like a carbon copy of his pop. He is abusing his mother verbally, berating her on the phone, blaming her and defending his dad. And she's taking it, of course. So when he's in L.A., I call him into the office, give him a batch of battered-wife literature and I say, "You're going back to school now, you're going to behave yourself and you're going to get good grades because your mother doesn't need any more aggravation. But if you think you're old enough to mouth off to your mother you're also old enough to learn something. So read this stuff I'm giving you and send me a short report. Then I'll know whether you've grown up or not."

Not too much later, he sends me a letter and tells me he understands much more now about the way men ought to behave and he realizes he was in fact beginning to resemble his father. He also apologizes to his mother. He tells her that he is sorry that he wasn't able to come to her aid when she needed him.

I felt awfully good about that. He was a bright kid, just twenty. I'm only too aware of how unforgiving the generational cycle is, how the son becomes the father—but maybe this time we broke the chain. For once.

18

Patricide

Among the many stupid assertions about the 1989 killings of Jose and Kitty Menendez by their sons, none were more ill-informed than the charge that Erik and Lyle did it for money. Homicides only happen in families where things have gone wrong beyond the wildest imaginings of normal people. I doubt that even those of us who come from neurotic or punitive families can begin to truly invent the intense suffering that is commonplace in some of these homes.

The circumstances of these killings are even more baffling when they happen against the backdrop of apparent middle-class ordinariness. Such was the killing of Oscar Salvatierra by his slender, studious-looking seventeen-year-old son, Arnel, a case that lured me still deeper into the sickness of families and, coincidentally, prepared me well for the rigors and revelations of Menendez.

In early 1986, the Salvatierras were a family of seven (the parents, a paternal grandmother and four children) living in a pleasant one-story Glendale house, designed as so many of these homes are, to blend into the arid, hilly surroundings: the façade of the house is stone combined with wood paneling. Usually parked in front of the house was a conversion van, a camper, for family outings. Behind the house, on the steeply rising hillside, wildflowers bloom.

Oscar was a pudgy man of forty-one who for some time had been a mostly unemployed accountant, but now he had a more regular job as marketing director of a Filipino newspaper whose editorials frequently criticized Philippine dictator Ferdinand Marcos. His wife, Lily, like her husband a Filipino by birth, was the main source of income for the family, working unfailingly as a pharmacist. The kids attended local public schools. Arnel, thoroughly Americanized in dress and speech, well-behaved in school and very bright, was doing surprisingly poorly in high school (Chemistry, D; Biology, F; American Government, D. "Attitude and effort are poor, tests scores are low, absences are affecting progress").

At first, the murder looks like a political hit: Oscar Salvatierra, apparently asleep at the time, is shot three times in the head, each shot a mortal wound. He is found on his back, still mostly under his sheets. The blood from the head wounds, coursing down onto the pillowcases, has created great clouds of red over an Asian design of leafy trees. Nothing in the room seems disturbed. It is, on the whole, a very precise killing. And suspicions about why he was killed are quick in coming.

The police know that he has just recently received an ominous letter. "*Philippine News* is a disgrace to the Filipino community in the U.S.," it says. "Through your paper, your unwarranted accusations and lies have attacked your own countrymen. . . . For your crimes you are sentenced to death by execution." The warning is painstakingly composed of letters taken from periodicals. It is an odd threat because Oscar Salvatierra was never in the forefront of the anti-Marcos movement that seems to be the target of the letter.

In Manila, Corazon Aquino, in a tough political fight against Marcos, hails Oscar Salvatierra as a martyr anyway. U.S. Senator Alan Cranston and New York Representative Stephen Solarz decry this political terrorism.

The international furor lasts not much more than twenty-four hours, however. The day after Salvatierra is killed, Arnel's girlfriend, Teresa DeBurger, is in the Glendale police station, talking, and just that quickly the police know this killing involves not international but familial politics.

After sending that letter to his father to throw the police off, Arnel had sneaked back to the house from school, climbed through a window, shot Oscar to death with a gun that he had slipped out of a friend's house and then returned to his second-period class. In planning what he believes is a "perfect crime," he forgets to keep it a secret.

How did this quiet, bright boy arrive at such a grotesque moment of violence? The answers reside, once again, in the arena of mens rea, the question of state of mind that is a cornerstone of the Western judicial system—and remains that no matter how much the Philistines may revile it.

To help me get at the poisonous dynamics of a catastrophically warped family, I employ once again the investigator Casey Cohen, the ex-probation officer ("Uncle Casey") who is irrepressibly warm and capable as he interviews people about their lives. But I also do a good deal of this investigation myself. I need to feel what it was like to be a child of that family. Over the course of many interviews I learn about a home operated like a slave camp where the kids serve the father's every whim, where failing to fetch a drink or find his nail clipper is cause for severe punishment, where they have to agree with his every expression or else keep quiet. The mother, Lily, is beaten frequently, especially if she interferes with the father's rulings regarding the children. The grandmother, too, is hit and threatened. The punishment for evoking this man's disapproval has evolved over many years into a routinized rage.

As part of my preparation, I talk to Arnel's sister Chloe, a quiet, serious, pretty sixteen-year-old who makes no bones about hating her father and thinking her brother a hero for killing the tyrant. But Chloe's affect is flat; even when speaking words of anger, there's no emotional edge to her voice. Only a year younger than Arnel, she has experienced many of the very same things that he did and has learned to lock her feelings down tight.

She tells me about the "special belt" that hung in the closet. (For many years Oscar wore that belt and had to remove it from his waist to whip the children; over time he reserved it exclusively for whipping.) The tactic Oscar used was to tell the children to lie down, backsides up, on the floor, sometimes with their clothes on, sometimes with their buttocks bare, and he would pronounce the number of lashes required for an offense. Then the children were ordered to count, so that Oscar might know where he was in the punishment.

"If he didn't hear you," Chloe tells me, "then you'd have to do it over again."

This is a difficult task, counting while being whipped, because you're usually sobbing at the time and can't get the words out, and also the pain and fear tend to make you lose track.

"All the while," Chloe tells me, Oscar is screaming, "yelling, you know, asking us like, are you going to do that again? Like really loud and screaming. 'I didn't hear you! You have to count! How many is that?' "

The beatings are common—at least once a week—starting when the children were about three years old and lasting into their early teens. Often the children are punished for some shared infraction. But Chloe tells me Arnel gets punished more.

Arnel's quandary, during these interminable communal beatings, is that he knows that whoever is farther away from the belt feels its sting more sharply. So when they are ordered to lie down he is caught in the most terrible conflict: should he pick the spot nearest his father's feet or move to the place of greater pain and spare his sister? On those rare occasions when she takes the brunt, the guilt for him is awful.

"There was that one time," Chloe says, "when he got one hundred."

I catch my breath. "You're telling me one hundred belts?"

He was twelve years old and got caught stealing money from an aunt. Arnel was never in trouble with the police—but always deprived of anything he expressly wanted, he early on learned to be deceptive and devious. He received no allowance, except the lunch money he saved. Oscar wanted to control all ordinary expenditures like those on clothes or comics. Lily, the mother, often conspired with the children against her husband by preparing school lunches so that they could squirrel away more of the money Oscar gave them.

Oscar had a penchant for humiliating the children in public. Once when they dropped a bag of popcorn, he made them bend down and eat every one of the kernels, some of them in a puddle, from the ground.

At Filipino community gatherings, which this family often attended, Oscar's associates observed how controlling and restrictive he was. His children were never allowed to play with the others. They had to sit silently by their father's side with their hands clasped in their laps. It struck people as peculiar.

The children could not leave the house without Oscar's permission, Chloe tells me. When it came to Chloe, he was concerned about whether there would be boys or men along. If there were she couldn't go. He wouldn't let her wear dresses, even to family gatherings, saying that he didn't want her legs to show like those of American sluts. (Oscar had perverted sexual tastes, not only showing commercially made pornographic films to friends who visited his home but also showing them those he said he made on his own, evidently with prostitutes.)

Oscar was as obsessive in his control of his wife as he was of his children. Lily had to account for every minute of her day and take his incessant calls at work (he was checking to see that she was working, not socializing with her colleagues). He quizzed her daily about what men she had met or talked to, sometimes hitting her when he didn't like her answers.

Once, in a typical jealous rage at Lily, he threatened divorce. Chloe remembers that as soon as she heard that, "I ran out of there, started banging on Arnel's door. He was in the bathroom taking a shower. He goes what? What? I go they're getting a divorce! I was yelling, I was screaming, I was like jumping for joy."

But the threat was idle (Oscar liked to say that he didn't go through with it "for the sake of the kids"). This family was not going to be released that easily.

"What do you think," I ask Chloe, "drove Arnel to kill him?"

She says, "So that we could be free."

My interviews with Lily, and her later testimony, reveal that Arnel was not acting entirely on his own initiative; he was part of a subtle plot. Inside that house there was a virtually silent but growing conspiracy among the downtrodden to overthrow the common enemy. And Arnel was to be its instrument.

One thing you always want to know—I do, anyway, since I believe in the warrior mommy, the parent who protects her kid—is, Did you ever try to stop Oscar from hitting Arnel?

Lily tells me, "I'd get beat up, too. And he'd beat Arnel worse, to punish me for interfering. My mother-in-law has tried several times. She got hit and the kids got punished worse. So we learned not to do anything. When Oscar would get angry and start a fight in the house, I'd pull my mother-in-law away and the two of us would go into another room and just keep our mouths shut."

Didn't Lily ever try to escape with the children? No. She felt he would find them and kill them; at one point, he told her that if she ran he would chop her up.

Lily details incident after incident that grew out of this nearly perpetual rage. Some of the behaviors that set him off are revoltingly petty. He beat Lily for buying clothes for the children that he had not approved. He terrified the family while they were riding in the van by slamming on the brakes so hard and so often—a sadistic stunt having nothing to do with traffic—that the little table in the van was broken when his own mother, Mercedes, fell on top of it. He bought a shotgun, and a month before he was killed loaded and pointed it at the family, threatening to kill them all for God knows what infraction—even they couldn't remember.

Later these details will contribute to a mosaic depicting in its entirety the stifling and destructive culture of this family.

I ask Lily about the time he began to beat Arnel while the boy, then nine years old, was still asleep.

"Because I interfered," she explains. She had come home from work late and Oscar asked her to check in on Arnel, whom he had punished earlier. In the calm of the moment, he was wondering about the bruises. She asked him why he did that. Arnel had failed to do an assignment for school.

"And I was so tired," Lily says, "I didn't realize I raised my voice. And he said, 'You son of a bitch, what do you mean with a "why"?' He hit me and he said, 'Look at the result of what you're asking.' So he went into the room and Arnel was sleeping and he got his belt and he beat him and beat him and he pulled him to me and I said, 'Okay. Okay. That is okay.' "

By the time Arnel was seventeen—the time of the killing—Oscar found him too big to hit that way anymore but verbally abused him in a continual stream of vituperation. He said the word "Arnel," according to Lily, only with fury in his voice. Meantime, he had started on the youngest kids, Naomi and Joel.

Repeatedly, for one reason or another, Oscar threatened to kill Arnel with the shotgun that he left in plain view. Arnel, obsessed with the first girlfriend of his life to the point of pathology (she was the only one he wanted to be with, to the neglect of all else), figured that Oscar really might kill him when he discovered the boy was flunking out of school.

Added to that somewhat reasonable fear was the most critical factor of all, something Lily said to Arnel in a desperate moment.

They were in the kitchen together, this helpless mother and her son. She was complaining about Oscar, weeping, and she spoke to her son: "I wish he would die."

As I did my homework in preparation for trial, one of my advisers sent me a research paper by a Michigan psychiatrist, Douglas Sargent, on children who kill their parents. Sargent contended that "sometimes the child who kills is acting as the unwitting lethal agent of an adult (usually a parent)." And I thought, Yes, there's something to that. Lily was trapped and afraid, but Arnel, a child in a young man's body, could do it. Arnel could get rid of Oscar for good.

Fortunately, there was no real money in this for Arnel, so the simple-minded among us were deprived of an easy motive. Yet the fact that

Arnel did not kill his father in the midst of some pitched battle but instead had plotted to do it over a considerable period of time was going to make this case more difficult than it might otherwise have been.

Arnel himself is hard to know, difficult to warm to. When I first meet him, he is rigid, almost without emotion. In the simplistic language of the law-and-order crowd, he "shows no remorse." Well, why the hell should he? He lived his entire life under the boot of a cruel and selfish layabout who tormented everyone Arnel loved. Not only is he not sorry, he's quite prepared to take whatever punishment the law imposes. "It's worth it," he says, "so Mom and Chloe and Naomi and Joel can be happy."

I find myself comparing him to a Vietnam War veteran who, having survived a fall into the deepest, darkest pit, cannot talk about it with any feeling at all. It is a particular species of battered kid: some are weepy and hysterical all the time, the others are like robots.

As is typical of my practice I have a string of lengthy capital cases lined up for trial when I accept Arnel's case. It takes me three years to get his case to trial but, intervening workload aside, the delay is also strategic. These battered kids like Arnel have been so thwarted in their development—deprived of autonomy and self-respect—that they are always more childlike than their age and appearance suggest. And I need him on the stand. He has to be able to relate to the jury so they understand how he sees his role in saving himself and his family or he will face a very long time in prison.

This is playing itself out in Juvenile Hall, a rather ugly, underfinanced boot camp for teenagers awaiting trial, where Arnel is so much better off than he ever was at home. He is surrounded by adults who do not torture him. There are rules, but they make a certain amount of sense. The men in charge here even take a liking to him (the first time that has ever happened). He can finish what little is left of high school here and take some college courses. Along the way, he learns about computers and sets about reconfiguring the whole computer system of the Juvenile Hall schools.

The principal of the school tells me that if Arnel had not been available, "we'd have to pay someone about $30,000 to redesign these programs." He says it's unfair that they can't pay Arnel but the rules prohibit hiring an inmate.

I say I think it's fine. (So often in the past, I feared these juvenile institutions did more harm than good, but in this case, it is a godsend.) Arnel gets to spend his days as one year drifts into another working hard, reading computer programs, drafting a curriculum, growing more mature, learning to value himself from the encouragement and support he's getting from the surrogate fathers on the staff. He even starts to trust people a little, something that is never easy for battered kids.

A big threat comes our way, though, shortly after Arnel turns nineteen. Technically, Juvenile Hall is only for kids under eighteen. Those whose cases originate when they are still minors but aren't resolved until after they turn eighteen can also remain at the hall. But by law, when they turn nineteen they're supposed to be transferred to Men's Central Jail, the 8,700-inmate county pretrial detention jail that is considered a tougher place to do time than most of the prisons in the state. I get a hysterical phone call from Arnel and he says they're rolling him up, they're telling him he's being transferred to county jail. I say, "Over my dead body."

I go down to Juvenile Hall to see Judge Jaime Corral, a good guy, an ex–public defender like me, who's the presiding judge, and I show him the notice for transfer. I point out that the Welfare and Institutions Code governing the detention of minors requires that notice be given within thirty days after the inmate turns nineteen of the intention to transfer to the adult facility. All we've gotten is this notice, four months after Arnel's nineteenth birthday.

"Well, where's the previous notice?" he asks.

"I'm not aware of any previous notice, Your Honor."

We have a little hearing after that where the counselors from Juvenile Hall testify to what a great kid Arnel has become and, ultimately, the judge says to the bureaucrats braying for a transfer, "You blew it. You can't throw this kid out of Juvenile. You didn't comply with the terms of the code." So they're not going to be able to transfer Arnel from their budget to the sheriff's budget, the whole mindless point of this exercise.

After the hearing in Judge Corral's court I walk into the back hallway and Arnel is sitting by himself on the bench. I sit down next to him and he bursts into tears, throws his arms around me and hugs me. In two years I had never seen any emotion from this kid.

"I was so scared," he says, "I was so scared." He is sobbing.

"It's okay, honey," I say. "It's over. It's fine. They're not going to move you."

By the time the trial finally starts, we—my associate counsel, Marcia Morrissey, and I—are in a full-blown save-the-child mode. We are going to be the protective mothers he never had. Our affection for this boy is a source of strength for us. In cases such as this it is crucial that lawyers reach the jury on an emotional level. The jurors have to put themselves in the shoes of the defendant to understand how he felt and why he did what he did. If we want the jury to care about Arnel our sincere feelings for him will communicate so much better than mere words. I know that this obvious affection for a client can elicit disdain from some members of the public and media. They're wrong. These same folks are always complaining about how their doctors are too cold and clinical. Well, I don't treat my clients, my patients, that way.

For moods like Marcia's and mine, music helps. By coincidence, we had both just seen *Les Misérables* and were now addicted to its music. She had the American cast tape in her car and I had the British one in mine. Independently we each drove to court singing along with *Les Miz.* There I am, negotiating the hairpin turns on the Pasadena Freeway, trying to hit the high notes of "On My Own"—a soliloquy on loneliness— determined to spare Arnel a tragic life of isolation.

The composition of the jury is as always critical, and in this case we get lucky. The DA actually leaves a juror on the panel who said she had been abused as a child by her alcoholic father. And there's a nurse on this jury, a woman of marvelous compassion, who cries from time to time during the trial. We gamble, too, leaving a Filipino man on the jury, one who might identify with Oscar Salvatierra, but one who complained about the patriarchal nature of some Filipino families when we questioned him during jury selection.

I spend several days with Arnel at Juvenile Hall preparing him; we go over a lot of the incidents. I caution him about losing his temper on the stand. And then, for the moment, he loses his nerve instead.

"I can't do it," he says. "I can't."

I say, "Come again?"

He says, "I can't talk about it. I can't do it."

I say, "Arnel, here are your choices: either you do it and we get you out of here, or you don't do it and you go to prison. Because guess what? I can't do it for you."

I tell him, "I can't testify, Arnel, I can't pretend I'm you. So not only do you have to, goddammit, you're going to. Do you really think I just spent a whole weekend in Juvenile Hall for the fun of it? You're getting on the goddam stand and you're going to tell it—just like it was."

"All right, all right."

And he turns out to be pretty good. A little rigid, still, a bit defensive. But when it comes down to the descriptions, he makes the point.

"You couldn't see the belt but you could hear it coming," he says. "It would whistle through the air. You could tell he was putting everything into it."

"Did it hurt?" I ask.

"Yeah."

"Each one?"

"Every one," he replies.

He testifies that before he killed his father he was terrified of him. But he says that after he shot his father, "I remember the whole day afterward feeling like maybe I had done the wrong thing. I remember actually missing him. I remember thinking that, like, the few times when I was really, really little and I was thinking about him."

You can hear the jurors weeping.

A lot of the trial focused on the testimony of a forensic psychiatrist with graying hair and a glowing tanned, youthful face named William Vicary.

He calls this a "classic case" of family abuse and says on the stand that even though the physical aspects of it are the most dramatic, "The majority of it was domination, intimidation, threats, criticism, humiliation."

Vicary wants to lean over backwards to seem objective, winging it a bit more than an expert I hire ought to, in my view. He concedes to the prosecutor, for instance, that anger might have played a role in Arnel's motivation (a somewhat less compelling reason than terror). And I am really stoked. In the emotion of the moment—when you feel like you're spending a lifetime teetering on a tightrope and any gust might blow you off—I believe he's giving it away because he wants to look so reasonable. I know damned well how strongly he feels about this case and why he is so eager to testify for the defense.

He keeps telling me he's confident in his testimony, though. But I'm having trouble getting over it. "Look, pal," I tell him, "if you think you're going to pull a stunt like this you've got to prepare me in advance." He thinks he actually won the case for me. I feel like I'm going to lose my lunch.

But I needn't have reacted so strongly. We have it sewed up already. The key moment comes when the deputy DA is baiting Arnel about not loving his father. This observation is not going to stun anyone. So I let it go on. No objections. And it keeps going on, pitilessly. She's pulling the wings off a fly. Then, all on his own, Arnel turns to the judge and says, "Judge, do I have to answer that again?"

And the judge, Gil Alston, a professorial-looking man with a maverick streak to him, says, "No, son, you don't. Move on, Counsel." And it's over. The judge has come to Arnel's aid, almost literally putting his sheltering arm around him.

I turn to Marcia and whisper, "We won."

She says, "I know."

Now if we do get the manslaughter conviction I fully expect, I also believe that the judge will go easy on the sentence.

But the job isn't over. I still have to deliver a final argument. I still have to make it good.

I approach this address with the absolute sense that Arnel is innocent. I believe that people who are directly and indisputably maimed by another person's brutality have a moral right to act in reaction to that. I'm not talking about law here. I'm talking about morality. The law may call it manslaughter but I think of it as innocence.

As I talk to the jury, also, I have an extraneous event working on my behalf. In New York, Joel Steinberg has just battered his six-year-old child Lisa to death in a case that has generated revulsion throughout the nation. In that home, too, there was a terrified wife who failed to protect the child. We have a society that claims to care about children. I want to ask the jury, What if Lisa had survived to strike back and Joel Steinberg died instead? Would we be trying Lisa for murder now? Is the only good abused child—the only one who deserves our compassion—the dead one? Arnel chose not to die, that's his crime. He chose not to die.

That part about Lisa Steinberg is my introduction. I have an outline that goes on a long way from that; I intend to go through the evidence, all the abuse all over again. The logical, orderly kind of final argument, with a plea for understanding at the end.

But as I do the twenty-minute introduction, some of the jurors are crying again and I am nearly there, too. So I stop talking. I just say to myself "Stop!" It feels right—why do I have to go through the whole thing one more time? And tactically it's beautiful: if I stop now, the DA will be limited in her rebuttal to the narrow scope of my comments and can't rehash the evidence. She is left with almost nothing to say.

The minute I switch off and walk over to the counsel table, Arnel throws his arms around me and says, "Thank you." And I turn to Marcia and say, "Jesus Christ, what have I done?"

She says, "It was great."

"Are you sure?"

"Yes, yes, it was fine."

And it was. Arnel was convicted of voluntary manslaughter, which carries with it a minimum term of three years—coincidentally exactly what he had already served. The judge released him.

Arnel, these days, works and goes to school and I talk to him every now and then. I don't think the wounds of childhood will ever be truly healed. I really worry about his future as a husband and father, given his role model and the terrible grip abusive behavior has on people, one genera-tion to the next. But who knows? Some people make it. Supportive people can help. The right luck, the right therapist.

One day he surprises me by showing up at the Menendez trial; he wants to lend Erik some support. Of course he couldn't just call me to gain admission—that's too straightforward. He has to come up with some cockamamy ruse. He calls the court and claims he's a messenger from my office. Could he deliver a package? They say yes, and when he arrives the bailiff opens the door. He takes a seat. And then, during a break, he gives me a package.

"What's this?" I ask him.

"Nothing," he says. "It was my way of getting into the courtroom."

"Arnel, all you needed to do was tell me you were going to be here."

"This works better," he says.

As if asking me for something directly was going to bring rejection, humiliation and pain. Or worse yet, be a sign of weakness, of depen-dence. Arnel still can't be entirely straight, still can't really trust. Who says Oscar Salvatierra is dead?

19

The Tough Guy

For one reason or another, in my twenty-seven years in this business I've had very few Jewish clients. There was one guy who got mixed up in shady, dangerous real estate dealings that also happened to involve a triple murder. And then there was Cuban-born Roberto Lopez, who was sort of Jewish—formerly Santeria but now Jewish, by self-proclamation.

Roberto, a drug dealer, is the kind of guy who always tries to keep busy, even in jail. He generally has a gimmick working for him, like arranging to be involved in some legal action (he trained to be a paralegal) so he can be designated to defend himself—and that allows him out of his cell to pay regular visits to the jail law library and frees him to walk around the premises with more liberty than a criminal of his history is usually accorded.

He also figures Judaism is a useful schtick. First of all, kosher food is a big improvement over the mainline junk. And thanks to his faith, Roberto, who is possessed of considerable charm—he's gracious enough to laugh at almost any joke, even if it's on him—also gets to engage in pleasant meetings with the rabbi and with the lady who works at the jail as a liaison to one of the Jewish organizations.

But gregarious and warm as he is, Roberto is impulsive and quick to anger. One day while awaiting trial in the county jail, he calls me at my office, and he is furious, hysterical, completely off the wall.

"Those bastards!" he's shouting into the phone. "Those sons of bitches!" (All of this in his thick Cuban accent.) "Those motherfuckers" —which is by far the most common descriptive in his vocabulary. "Those motherfuckers can't do this to me."

"Roberto, what are you screaming about?"

"You got to do something about this, Leslie. You got to call the Commander."

"Roberto, I still don't know what this is about. Just shut up for a second and then try to tell me the story."

"They wouldn't let me go!" he says, still not exactly tranquil.

I say, "Go where?"

"To services, to services."

"What?"

"You know. Overpass. They wouldn't let me go to Overpass!"

"What's Overpass, Roberto? You're not making any sense. Oh, my God, do you mean Passover?"

"Yeah, that's it. Passover. Overpass, whatever."

"Well," I point out, "maybe when you say Overpass, schmuck, the suspicion dawns that you aren't really Jewish after all."

But the impressive thing is that, according to his own lights anyway, he is still Jewish to this day, even now that he's in a state prison where you get to see a rabbi about once a year, a deprivation that has led him to fight the institution, of course.

I like Roberto. As a client. It's true that he's a professional criminal and so hyperactive he could get on God's nerves. But he's a riot, funny, smart and generous in his way. He is the only criminal I have ever met who, while incarcerated and awaiting final disposition of his case, arranged for embossed stationery.

In red, the letterhead reads "Roberto M. Lopez," followed by his booking number, cell module number and the address of the county jail. He means to be funny with the letterhead, of course, but it also signals something about how seriously he sees himself as a businessman. I mean he's a dope dealer, right? Roberto fits the job's requirements well: he is in fact a violent, ruthless man with an inclination toward commerce. It is a very distinct niche in the criminal world. Roberto is not a serial killer, he is not a drive-by shooter, he is not part of the homicidal-maniac crowd. He's a tough guy but, in his own view, not a bad guy. (As I accommodate myself to that point of view, it occurs to me that this is one more instance where I'm stumbling through a moral swamp, once more immersed in the banality of evil: The best thing to do, always, is not to ruminate too much about it, just do the job.)

Roberto has not managed to make himself wealthy, despite his death-defying business practices. Nevertheless, as I defend him on murder charges, he sends me a mink coat, as if he were a man of means, someone who knows how to show gratitude and has the money to do it. Of course, I can't accept it and don't.

On another occasion, two of us from the defense team show up at his little well-kept house to interview his mother and his beautiful young wife—she looks like Natalie Wood. A few minutes after we get there, a van pulls up and starts unloading a catered meal, for crying out loud, a lavish production Roberto arranged from jail. It's enough food for ten people. There's a mountain of paella and salad and desserts. This is typical Roberto, the Patron taking care of everybody.

The life that led to that embossed stationery began in Cuba, where Roberto was a bicycle racer (his nickname means that: Raquina). After Castro tried to draft him into the army, he swam to U.S. protection at Guantánamo.

From Guantánamo—this is years before Mariel—he catches a boat to Florida. This short, muscular teenager without skills gets into trouble early and decisively there on the streets of Miami. He becomes a dope dealer and uses enough of the product at the same time so that if he hadn't already been jumpy and often irrational, the coke would do the job. Early on, this is a kid whose wiring is crossed. Clever as hell, but mentally not that well put together. He lives in a sea of paranoia. When he gets to prison, it is a frame of mind that probably will serve him well, but for now it just amplifies his hyper behavior.

By the time I get around to actively defending Roberto, he's been charged with murders in two separate incidents and already convicted in the first of them. That was a killing in a motel room in which he appeared to have a good self-defense argument and where the judge made enough serious errors, in my opinion, to justify a new trial, but the appeal failed despite it all. The second case, mine, begins when the police find a car parked on a dangerously seedy stretch of Hollywood's Western Avenue, near a Burger King. The car has two bodies in it, both riddled with 9mm holes, and there are casings all over the street. Clearly, a fully automatic 9mm weapon has been used, an Ingram machine pistol. The patrol officer who comes to the scene writes in his original report that the bodies are those of a man behind the wheel and a passenger who is a cross-dresser, a man dressed as a woman. In fact, the passenger was a bona fide *woman* dressed as a woman. (As if the bullets weren't mortifying enough!)

The cops go from house to house to determine if anybody knows anything. They find nothing. The gun—that efficient, rapid-fire killer of an Ingram—never shows up either. But they know the dead folks are dope dealers and they find a print of Roberto's on the driver's-side window.

Eventually, they come up with their key witness, a guy named Carlos Boroto, also involved in dope and ready to help the police if they'll help him. He tells the cops that he saw Roberto test-firing an Ingram inside an auto body shop. (There are a lot of sleazy auto shops all over L.A., many of them fronts for criminal activity like dope dealing or they perform as chop shops to dismantle stolen cars, and at one time Roberto did own one.) The cops also hear that Roberto owed the now-dead drug dealers money and decided to wipe out the debt by killing them.

I know that Roberto concedes he is the kind of man who will kill under certain circumstances—if someone threatens to kill his kid, for instance. But whether he did this job or not, I'm going to attack the strength of the prosecution case. That's my function. I'm comfortable with it. It is my ethical responsibility to defend a client vigorously, and the code doesn't say "only after first determining that he's innocent."

It looks to me, early on, like the prosecution is going to have a hard time proving that Roberto shot these people. He did know them; he had even socialized with the victims. But beyond that, the cops are leaning real heavily on dope-addled Boroto, a witness of dubious value. (He babbles to the cops in a taped interview that Roberto was dealing "a lotta, lotta, lotta, lotta, lotta, lotta cocaine." We come to call him Lotta-Lotta-Cocaine Boroto.)

As I enter the case, there is a great deal of work to do if I'm going to get up to speed. I'm arriving late on this one, having just finished Salvatierra, and I'm completely stressed out. My buddy Gerry Chaleff, who is co-counsel on Lopez with me, was supposed to have done the preparation already. He just finished representing Roberto on the motel room case. And, given the press of other business, he hasn't been able to get this one ready for trial, which is thirty days away. The case—a capital case no less—is so far from ready that I panic. I had stopped smoking during Salvatierra and now every muscle in my body is crying out for a drag. I feel it in the back of my mouth. I feel it in my brain. I can't concentrate. And then I say, That's it. Either I smoke or this guy dies and, with the flash of a match, I'm back to a pack a day.

Given the little amount of time we have to get ready for the start of the trial, we start picking the jury without having completed the usual defense investigation. Two weeks before the start of the defense side of the case, during a holiday break, my investigator—Cynthia again—and I fly off to Miami for a three-day whirlwind of interviews. All of Roberto's past seems to be back in Miami—members of his family who can tell us more about him, dope dealers and others who know the witnesses, and who can refute the information coming from Boroto.

On the first night of a wild string of eighteen-hour days, I get an extremely late call from Roberto, who like many prisoners uses the phone as his lifeline, his only real connection with the rest of the world. But phone time is always subject to restrictions. I look over at the clock in the hotel room. It's 2:00 A.M. How is he getting to the jail phone at eleven at night L.A. time? And, come to think of it, how the hell does he even know where I'm staying?

"Well, my deah [he has a kind of mock eloquence in his phone manner], you know Roberto is always going to find out where you are."

I say, "Roberto, do you know what time it is? And that I've been out running around all night?"

"Oh, I know, I know," he says, "but what I have to tell you is very important."

It turns out that from his residence at the L.A. county jail he has already spoken to practically everybody we're supposed to meet, cleared the way, even made appointments for interviews. And he provides me with a list of phone numbers and addresses just in case we're missing any (we're not).

One interview we arrange through our own efforts is with the twelve-year-old daughter of the masculine-looking woman killed in the car. This is her child from a previous marriage and the kid is living with the first husband. I am astonished to see how open and willing the girl is to talk to us. She's intelligent, not hostile, and she's adorable. Both she and the victim's ex-husband—living in a ramshackle bungalow in Hialeah—are, in fact, happy to talk to us, helping us with information that documents the drug involvement of the dead woman. It's an unexpected reception. Usually when you approach a victim's family you get the door slammed in your face.

We also talk to one of Roberto's cousins who—according to Boroto —had taken possession of one of Roberto's suitcases, which allegedly contained narcotics. Roberto tells us this is a lie. Any lie we can uncover will discredit Boroto, even if it's not a crucial fact in the prosecution's case. Most times, you can't disprove the big lie, but once a witness's credibility is blown on any significant fact the whole testimony is suspect.

The suitcase didn't have dope in it, and while Roberto's cousin can't prove that, she says her husband can because he opened the bag and it contained only clothing. But there's a complication. Her husband is in a prison in Belle Glade, a little city in south-central Florida on Lake Okeechobee. So Cindy and I and a handsome Cuban detective (to assist with translation) drive up to that godforsaken town, a vibrant center for agriculture but also notorious for the highest concentration of AIDS in the country, primarily among its Haitian workers.

We approach this prison, which has a forbidding reputation. But, as it turns out, isn't so horrible, not to our eyes, anyway. The guards are friendly. We show our ID, and *whoosh!* we're in the gate and on the pastoral grounds of a relatively attractive institution, where you see people busily tending to the plants and otherwise caring for the grounds. The buildings containing the cells are handsome, red brick, just two stories high. (The inmates, of course, fail to see the beauty in the place. Its correctional staff has a reputation for brutality.)

The interview with our potential witness makes my skin crawl. The man we've come to see is there serving a thirty-year sentence for molesting his own child.

We sit outdoors on a bench and talk to this guy to whom I have an immediate visceral negative reaction. He is one of these weepy people, wallowing in his own misery. He wants to know how his daughter is, the one he molested, and I say, "Fine, except she's not too crazy about you." And he breaks into tears and sobs. He says, "I didn't know it was wrong."

I don't need this guy. He didn't know it was wrong! Give me a break. She was nine years old when he started in on her. And anyway, his evidence isn't important enough to drag a child molester in on the side of the defense. We already have enough strange characters to deal with. We'll get at Boroto's lying some other way.

Back in L.A., the trial resumes, and it has its rough spots. A relatively minor one is that my co-counsel Gerry's style and mine are not alike. He's from the aw-shucks Jimmy Stewart school of defense law, where you endear yourself to everyone in earshot. I'm much more aggressive. He likes to keep down the number of objections. I like to object to anything that seems to need it because I do not believe it alienates anyone when you make sure you get your differences into the record. I also think the jury and the client understand that what you're doing is simply fighting as hard as you can.

It gets to a point in the trial where I hop up to object and Gerry tugs on my arm to get me back into my seat. I just look down at him and say, "You've got to stop doing that." And he agrees. He knows that our behavior probably appears worse to the jury than any number of objections will.

A more serious, almost fatal problem is that the Mexican Mafia and their ally in the Aryan Brotherhood, that rising star John Stinson, have decided that Roberto is too loose-lipped to tolerate since he's always shooting his mouth off about their drug dealings. And, with a frightening similarity to the attack on my client Mon, they arrange for Roberto to be ambushed during his trial. Killers jump him while he's on his way back to his cell and stab him repeatedly. All of a sudden I'm representing a defendant who can't show up in court due to what you'd have to say were pretty serious medical reasons, a "no-go med," as we put it.

When I hear he's been attacked, I rush over to the jail ward of the county hospital to see him and there he is sprawled on a gurney. He's evidently been there for hours. He's covered in blood, his face, his hands. Caked in it. I go crazy. I pull one of the nurses over and nearly tear her head off: "This man's been lying here for eight hours and you haven't had a chance to wash his face?"

"Oh, he's all sewn up," she tells me. "It won't do him any harm."

"Fine," I say. "I want a bowl of water and a towel. Now!" They arrive pretty quickly, and I wash him. He looks so pathetic.

Next day, I show up and Roberto is walking around. "What *are* you," I say, "a man of iron?"

"That's me," Roberto tells me, "I'm fine, don't worry."

"What the hell do you mean you're fine? Why aren't you in bed?"

"I don't want to do that," he says.

Four days after he was on the brink of death, Roberto returns to court. He is well buttoned up, because we don't want the jury to see any indication of the wounds. I don't want them to see evidence that he was involved in anything violent—there will be no opportunity to explain that he was in an unprovoked attack. The knife marks are mostly on his back and chest but extend to his forearms so I keep pulling down the sleeves on his shirt. And he walks into court with an almost transcendent naturalness. Nobody in that room ever does realize that his body is a mass of bandages, horribly mutilated. A very tough guy.

On the stand Boroto is easy pickings. He concedes that he lies a lot. He tells us he's been a cocaine dealer and a heroin user and a car thief.

I want to demonstrate that his testimony is even further corrupted because he's also in league with the DA, trying to help the prosecution any way he can—his testimony bought and paid for. To that end, I ask him, "Isn't it a little unusual for a state prison inmate to be running around in civilian clothes down the hallway in the county courthouse, having his lunch bought by the district attorney, not wearing handcuffs?"

The prosecutor objects. "That assumes a fact not in evidence and it's compound, Your Honor"—meaning it has sub-parts requiring individual answers.

The judge sustains.

So I start over. "Have they been bringing you food at lunch while you sit in their office?"

"Yes."

"Have you been moving around during the daytime in this courtroom not wearing handcuffs?"

"No. Just when I go outside to have a cigarette or to the bathroom."

I ask, "And you sit in this courtroom without any handcuffs while we're waiting for things to happen?"

"Yes."

"And you walk down the hallway in the morning and at night, and you're not in handcuffs?"

"Yes, because I asked them for that, if he could do that."

"And he did that for you, didn't he?"

"Yes, because I don't like everybody to be watching me with the handcuffs on."

"And he acceded to your wishes on that?"

"He did that favor for me. That's the one favor that he has done in his life for me."

In the jury's mind, Boroto, so central to the case, was a hard man to believe—about anything.

My client, Roberto, never testifies. The prosecution evidence, once Boroto is discredited, is mostly zilch.

In the end, the jury hangs, nine to three for acquittal. Then, after some complicated calculus involving this case and the one before—which we still hope will be overturned—we accept a plea of manslaughter rather than risk a new trial (which always benefits the prosecution because it has seen the whole defense and can prepare better for it).

But despite a vigorous appeal, that earlier first-degree conviction stands even today. It seems that funny, smart, ruthless Roberto got screwed royally this time around. I do not expect him to get out of prison.

•

As for the behavior of the judge in the second case, I can't complain too much. He smirked a lot, was nasty often, but, surprisingly, most of his barbs were saved for the prosecution. And his rulings, in general, seemed fair—even though the defendant was clearly a member of the criminal class, a fact that often causes judges to lean to the prosecution.

The judge's name was Stanley Weisberg, a dour, uncomfortable man with a dry, wry sense of humor that is always exercised at someone else's expense. He later miscalculated dramatically in full national view, and I believe that rattled him to the core. He was the judge who handled the first Rodney King case. In following the order of the appellate court to move the case out of L.A. County, he settled on white, conservative Simi Valley, where—the legal cynics among us were certain—the cops who beat up King would never be convicted. (Some say his choice of locations was influenced by the fact that Simi Valley was an easy commute to his luxurious Brentwood Park home.) The outcry and rioting after that trial, I believe, just about did Weisberg in, literally. He and his wife, also a judge, were threatened. They needed bodyguards. Psychologically, it's as if the scorn and persecution turned him into a victim. And ever since, in my experience with him, he's been lashing out the way many victims do.

By the time I got him on the Menendez case, I was dealing with somebody who was cold and vindictive. In my view, he had become that scourge of the legal system, the biased judge. When my friend and co-counsel in the second Menendez trial read the court transcript of the first trial, documenting the new Weisberg in action, he shook his head. "I wouldn't have guessed that this was the same man I'd seen before," he said.

20

Outrage

It's the late summer of 1990, and Tim and I have just returned from a house we rent in Ireland, in West Cork. At my office, I learn that Bill Vicary—the same psychiatrist I used in Arnel's case—has been trying to reach me. He's now working with me on Menendez, both as Erik's treating psychiatrist and as an expert consultant for me (a tricky perch since his patient naturally will want some things kept confidential even from me—and has the right to require that). He tells me in his quiet understated way that just in the last couple of weeks while I've been away Erik has begun to open up to him and the great riddle of how this engaging kid could have done what he did seems about to be solved.

"His father's been molesting him for a very long time," Vicary says.

My first thought is a pragmatic, lawyerly one—fine, now we're going to have a defense. But I'm wary.

"Is it true, Bill?"

"Oh, I don't have any doubt about it."

He says he doesn't know nearly enough yet but the molestation goes a long way in explaining the cause of Erik's extreme symptoms of mental illness, the hallucinations, the voices, the uncontrollable crying, the massive depression. He's always known the parents couldn't possibly have been the exemplars they may have seemed to some people at first because, in all the cases of recorded parricide, you don't find benign parents killed by their children. No child ever kills a parent for something so base as pure greed (which, of course, was the prosecution's simplistic theory, when they demonized Erik and Lyle Menendez as part of a script they hoped would end in death). Always something terrible has happened to ensure that this primal bond is not just torn or strained as it is in many families but blasted apart. Now Erik's mental condition matches the family history.

Big cases frequently drag on for a long time, but this was one for the books.

The defense of Erik Menendez will take the better part of six years. I accept the case in March of 1990, two weeks after Erik and his brother, Lyle, were arrested in the shooting deaths of their parents, Jose and Kitty. Just a month later, in April, my co-counsel and I are already deep into a bitter struggle to suppress the tapes of the psychologist Dr. Jerome Oziel in which Erik and Lyle—prodded into fantasy and falsehoods by Oziel —describe the killing of their parents in ways that could damage their defense without shedding any light on their true motivation.

The fight to keep this material out is not resolved until early 1991, after we go from one court to another and finally achieve the right to suppress at least some of it.

Erik and Lyle are indicted in December 1992, and the first of two trials begins in June 1993 (already three years have elapsed, while Erik and Lyle wait in county jail). It runs to mid-January 1994. The televised, tumultuous first trial ends in the two hung juries (Erik and Lyle were allowed separate juries in the first trial but not the second) that so offended and even infuriated pundits and others around the country.

We have to try the case again. This time we spend a year and a half in pretrial disputes as a new prosecution team seeks to limit our defense in every way it can in an effort to ensure the harshest possible verdict. In late August of 1995, we begin selecting a jury for the second trial. Once again, it is a long trial. The patently unjust first-degree murder verdict doesn't come until March 1996.

I do not think that most open-minded Americans ever got a chance to understand this crime for what it was or the true nature of a defense that never sought to excuse what Erik and Lyle did but rather simply attempted, with all the strength and skill it could muster, to achieve a fair verdict.

•

After I hear from Vicary—whose early certainty that the molestation took place as Erik said it did is later buttressed by five other experts—the molestation, clearly, becomes the heart of the case. But in the beginning it's hard to know the precise role it played in the killings. A former juvenile probation officer and lawyer named Paul Mones, who is an authority on parricide, having examined all the known cases of kids who kill their parents, comes aboard as a consultant.

He, like Vicary, proves invaluable to us. But I make a point of telling Mones to confine himself strictly to the other forms of abuse in the family, such as physical and psychological, and not to discuss the molestation with Erik at all. I am the lead attorney here—for Erik's defense, that is, while the incomparable Jill Lansing is Lyle's—and apart from Dr. Vicary's exploration of the area, I want to gradually uncover everything there is to know myself, if possible, on this core issue. Also, I have to be able to gain Erik's confidence and to educate myself so I can run the defense effectively.

Moreover, something tells me that—as honorable and skilled as Mones is when it comes to getting reluctant abuse victims to talk—it's always possible that someone will say the brothers were coached or in some way educated by this expert so that they knew how to say the right things. I want to shut the door on that. No one can accuse me of that kind of coaching, I figure, since at this point I know virtually nothing about the dynamics of child molestation, and never had defended a client who claimed to have been sexually abused as a child.

To educate myself on both the behavior of molesters and the psychological impact of sexual abuse on children I will have to delve into the vast professional literature and core research of the past fifteen years. But I wait until after Erik has revealed all the facts, feelings and pain associated with this ugliest part of his childhood. My temporary ignorance guarantees that I won't inadvertently ask him any suggestive questions. (A recent rash of unproven mass molestation cases demonstrates to me how easily information can be planted in the minds of impressionable youngsters.)

One thing I never read and made sure Erik and Lyle never read was Paul Mones's definitive book on parricide, *When a Child Kills,* published a year after Erik revealed the molestation. (But that fact doesn't stop the prosecution in the first trial from suggesting that the brothers made it all up by reading Mones's accounts of other cases—which, incidentally, I later learned were not at all factually similar to Erik's and Lyle's experiences.)

As I talk to Erik in 1990 and 1991, spending as much as twenty hours a week at the jail with him, our discussions range widely. Like me, he loves history. He wants to talk about ethics. He wants to learn. You say something interesting to him and his face opens with delight.

But he resists talking about sex with his father, even though the subject has finally been broached. He knows he has to talk, but sometimes he can't and actually leaves the moment, in mind if not body; that is, he becomes sleepy, his eyes heavy, his head drooping. Or he suddenly zones out and can't participate anymore. Once, he turned green and had to rush out of the attorney visiting room to throw up. When he returned he said, "I don't want to talk about this anymore."

Of course, I took verbatim notes—on my laptop. Now, as I reread them six years later, my eye falls on an area that begins, "First Oral Sex By Erik—Age Eight."

It's a weekend afternoon. Lyle isn't home, it's unknown if his mother is. Erik is playing in his room with a Hess truck—part of a toy gas station. He recalls the season as springtime. He's wearing white shorts, sneakers, tennis shirt. He hears the doorknob turn—his father.

Father says, "What are you doing?" (Impatient.) "I want a massage."

Erik says, "I'm playing with my truck."

Jose locks the door by propping a slat from the bed under the door-knob and tells Erik to get undressed. Erik does, mostly, but reluctantly. He doesn't take his underwear off right away. Throws the rest of his clothes on the floor.

His father undresses completely. Erik removes his own underwear then, too. Jose lies down on the bed, on his stomach, and requests a massage. Erik is standing on the floor next to the bed, massaging his father's legs. But to massage his buttocks he has to get one leg up on the bed. When that's done, his father directs, "Get on top of me." Erik has to get on the bed kneeling next to his father, who tells him to bring one leg across his much larger body, to straddle him, which causes their naked buttocks to touch and Erik remembers feeling uncomfortable about that.

He massages his father's back for five or ten minutes and Jose sighs, an indication that he is dissatisfied. Jose waves his son off his back. Erik gets off the bed and stands on the floor. His father says, "Go on." Erik massages his father's shins and thighs and skips to his stomach to avoid the erect penis.

"No."

He strokes his father's penis the way his father has been doing to him for some months now.

But that won't do either.

"Massage me with your mouth," his father says.

Erik tentatively puts the penis in his mouth and his father places his hand on top of Erik's head, pushes himself farther into Erik's mouth. Erik gags. His father pulls back and then thrusts again. This goes on for maybe five minutes.

Father is not angry with Erik (which is a relief); he is tolerant. "Okay, that's finished—you'll learn to do better. You can get dressed now."

The sex continues to be relatively gentle and forgiving for about another two years. (This, I later learn, is typical; a molester can't simply rape a child—the child will cry out, complain, know something's terribly wrong. Instead, the molester must gradually seduce the child over a period of time until sex between the two seems routine, habitual, normal, and the child is well trained. Despite this indoctrination, however, the child is inevitably traumatized, often for life.)

According to my notes, the "worst scene," as Erik recalls it, takes place in the winter right after his eleventh birthday. He's pretty sure of the time because the trees in New Jersey—where the family lived before their move to California—are bare.

It's the late afternoon but not fully dark. Lyle is somewhere, but Erik doesn't know where, maybe outside on the tennis court, but definitely not in his room. His mother is home. Erik knows that because he hears his parents fighting, yelling, and then his father pounding up the stairs, steps coming down the hall rapidly.

Father bursts through the door and opens it so forcefully that it slams into the wall; he closes it and doesn't even bother to put up the slat to keep it shut as he usually does. Erik is on the bed. His father tells him to get on his knees. Erik kneels on the bed.

"Not on the bed, on the floor," Jose says, and he is yelling, which is unusual. He swings his arm at Erik, knocking him off the bed, and Erik flies into the wall. Jose has never asked him to kneel on the floor before but now he does. His father unbuckles his pants, takes out his penis, shoves himself into Erik's mouth. Erik is scared. This is much more brutal, more uncaring, than anything before. Erik's teeth keep striking his father's penis but he can't help it because of the force. He feels his father shaking.

"I want you to swallow," his father says, harshly. Erik is gagging. As Jose pulls out, the ejaculate is striking Erik's face, dripping from his nose and chin. Erik is crying.

"Why can't you be a man like your brother?" Jose demands. "You're an embarrassment."

Erik is disgusted by the sex and he is scared. He showers, goes down to dinner but does not raise his eyes to look at anyone. Jose has not joined them, in any event.

Full penetration anal sex will not happen until Erik is twelve. And then it is a rape. He screams during it.

His father tells him, "If you ever cry again or scream I'll make sure I hit you so hard you'll never be able to cry or scream again. Do you understand?" He slaps him.

"Yes."

"Okay, so you'll understand why if I beat you that badly it won't be my fault—and whose fault will it be?"

"Mine."

The sex acts evolve into punishment for the most part. If you lose an important tennis match, it's up to your room, the slat under the door-knob. Disobey instructions on the tennis court and Father will see you in your bedroom. Do badly at school . . . try to run away . . . embarrass the family in any way: you know what will happen.

Sex, or something approximating it, becomes a tool, also, in Jose's mind to toughen his sensitive son. The sex becomes intentionally painful (Erik is cut and punctured with various implements) so that Erik will become inured to it and become stronger. It's for his own good, his father tells him.

Jose Menendez—with a reputation for cruelty and ruthlessness in business that follows him up the corporate ladder, as former colleagues at work readily report, a man who is cruel to his wife, and crueler to his children—is a man of extreme responses. He punches Lyle in the face for protesting his stream of criticism during a tennis practice and the punch splits Lyle's lip so badly that it results in a permanent scar (though no doctor ever sees the wound because the Menendezes do not want to explain it and do not want it reported).

Another trivial infraction leads Jose to tell his sons that they are disinherited, that he has written them out of the will (although he admits to their uncle Carlos, who ultimately testifies to the episode, that he hadn't yet drafted the new will even though he made them believe he had).

•

The sex with Erik continues, with occasional gaps of months or weeks, until Erik is eighteen and ready to go off to college. Throughout these years Erik comforts himself with the belief that his mother doesn't know what's going on. He believes that despite the fact that she never so much as knocks on his bedroom door while her husband is in there and she also regularly "checks him out," inspecting his penis for blisters without telling the child why. When she finds one she pops it.

Kitty Menendez, during a psychotherapy session, once confided to her therapist that she had "sick secrets." According to the therapist's notes he did not press her for an explanation.

But the therapist tells Jill and me in an interview that, in the context in which the comment was made, she was referring to her adult life, not her childhood.

The cruelest moment in Erik's tormented life is arguably not one of these sexual experiences but rather comes on the heels of a major tennis loss on August 7, 1989, during the junior national tennis tournament in Kalamazoo, Michigan. Erik had spent that whole summer training for and competing in the preliminary rounds of that tournament. In spite of exhaustion and unbearable heat, he had performed surprisingly well, far better than his national ranking would have predicted. From the age of eleven on, Erik found that his tennis—despite some awful experiences when he displeased his father—was the one endeavor that brought him some measure of happiness, a feeling of accomplishment and popularity among his tennis-playing peers. By the beginning of the summer, many years of intense training had led him to a ranking of forty-fourth in the country in his age group: a tremendous achievement on the one hand, but not quite good enough for true stardom. By the time he gets to Kalamazoo in August, however, he has risen to eighth place, a mixed blessing because Jose Menendez now has inflated expectations of glory.

He tells Erik he wants him to win it all, more a demand than encouragement (the winner goes on to the U.S. Open—the big time). But Erik does not win; in fact he gets knocked out even earlier than he should, by a markedly inferior player. On the way from the courts, in the car, Jose is explosive, as Erik recalls it later in testimony:

"He told me that all of my training and all of the matches that I had played as a junior came down to this one tournament and that I had failed and I had lost it, and my tennis was meaningless now. And we were driving away from the tennis courts, and he was yelling at the top of his lungs and his veins were bulging in his neck and he eventually just got speechless and he couldn't speak anymore."

They arrive back in Beverly Hills on August 9. On August 10, Jose demands fellatio. It will be the last time.

On August 13, in the study of the Beverly Hills house, the dignified room with the polished wood paneling and the imported Irish Victorian fireplace, the room where serious conversations tend to take place, Jose is laying out Erik's immediate future. He tells Erik that there are specific courses—business courses—that he must enroll in that fall at UCLA. He's considering prohibiting Erik from trying out for the UCLA team, he says, even from playing tennis at all. Erik must maintain good grades, must get into graduate school, that's the important thing.

There's no room for discussion, Father has spoken. Then Jose delivers the final blow: Erik will not be living in the dorm on campus full-time, as he had expected. He will have to stay at home "several nights a week" so that his parents can closely monitor his schoolwork. And, of course, the bedroom will be kept just as it is, ready for him.

For years he had envisioned that the move to college would be the escape route from his father. "I just felt shattered," Erik says. "A lot of my dreams, all of my hopes. I didn't know what to say. I just kept asking, what do you mean? What do you mean? He kept explaining further and I would say, what do you mean? My world was falling away and crumbling.

"It was as though nothing mattered anymore. At times I hated myself. At times I thought I was a coward for letting it continue. But at least I had that dream that it would end, which enabled me to live with it and with myself."

Now he tries to leave home, starts packing his bag, but Kitty comes into the room and furiously pulls his things out of the bag. Jose enters and threatens him, tells him he'd better still be there when Jose comes back from a trip later in the week.

This is just the beginning of that last terrible week in August. And it keeps getting worse. Lyle, who was home on summer break from Princeton, gets into an argument with his mother. It's about the need for the hairpiece Lyle wore glued to his scalp ever since he started to lose his hair at age nineteen. Lyle had never let anyone see him without his hairpiece. It was his secret. Even Erik didn't know about it.

Erik approaches his mother and Lyle as they argue in the foyer and he hears what's going on.

"You don't need it," Kitty is saying.

"I do, you don't understand."

And then, as Erik remembers it, "She reached up and tore off his hair, his hairpiece, and said, 'See, you look fine without it,' and threw it at him.

"I thought that at first she ripped off his hair. I just saw scalp and I was—I was completely stunned. My mother ran up the stairs. My brother was beginning to cry, went out of the living room to the guest house, and I just stayed there in the foyer for a few seconds not knowing what in the world just happened."

His older brother's misery beckons to Erik's own, and he follows Lyle to the guest house, sits on the white couch and, finally, they talk.

"I asked him if he remembered the times when he would ask me if anything was happening between Dad and me; he said no. And I asked him a few more things like that, and then I just felt that he was being stubborn, that he had to have remembered this. I didn't know why he was saying no. So I said, 'It's still happening.' And he said, 'What do you mean? What's still happening?' And I said, 'Just sexual things.'

"He got angry. He asked me how I could let these things happen. He asked me did I enjoy it, did I want it, why I hadn't told anyone. Just a lot of questions that made the situation worse. And I was getting very emotional and I was saying no, no, no, no, I didn't enjoy it. I didn't want it to continue."

Lyle starts pacing, pledges to talk to Jose on Erik's behalf. Erik welcomes the intervention—perhaps Lyle, who had often taken the role of protector and was better at talking with their father, really could rescue him. Erik does not tell Lyle how often Jose has threatened to kill Erik if he ever told anyone, especially Lyle—how he would tie him to a chair and smash his skull just like he had smashed the pet rabbit's skull.

Erik does not tell Lyle about the times his father made him sit naked in a chair facing a mirror:
"Did you tell anyone about the massages?"
"No."
"What am I going to do to you if you tell?"
"Hurt me."
"Wrong." (A wrong answer means Erik has to slap himself in the head.)
Whack.
"What am I going to do?"
"Kill me."
"Right."

•

"I can handle it," Lyle says now.

Erik was hopeful. "I was just falling into that bubble of optimism."

But, of course, Lyle has deluded himself. He can't handle it.

Jose returns from his trip Thursday night, August 17. He and Lyle meet in the study, where Lyle starts out telling Jose that he knows what's been going on between him and Erik and it has to stop. He proposes that the two brothers live together either in Princeton or at UCLA, to which Lyle will transfer. Impassive, Jose warns him not to ruin his own life over something that's none of his business.

Then Lyle loses it. "You're not going to touch Erik again."

And Jose, now enraged, declares, "He's my son, and I'll do what I want with him."

"If you touch him again, I'll tell."

"Well," Jose says, "you've made your decision, Erik's made his and now I'll make mine."

In a little while, Erik learns that something went terribly wrong with the talk. His father comes charging up the stairs and pounds on Erik's door demanding to be let in. Erik unlocks the door and runs to a corner of the room. Jose bellows, "I warned you never to tell Lyle. I told you never to tell Lyle. It's all your fault. Now Lyle's going to tell everyone and I'm not going to let that happen."

Jose moves toward Erik. Erik tries to climb over his desk to get to the door. Jose catches him, throws him onto the bed, but then Jose loses his balance. Erik runs out the door, across a balcony, down the stairs and into the den. Hysterical and crying, he is trying to get to the guest house, where he assumes he'll find Lyle. He runs into his mother, who's in the den, apparently drunk as she often is.

"What's the matter with you?"

"Nothing, nothing. You wouldn't understand."

"Oh, I know. I've always known. What do you think, I'm stupid?"

Erik is stunned. "I always thought," he explained in testimony, "I was helping her by not telling her and protecting her by not telling her; and now she was saying she knew what was going on and I just felt this sense of anguish and rage and shock, hate."

Erik starts to run again, out toward the pool. Kitty is racing after him, yelling, "Get back here, you bastard!" He makes it into the guest house, with Kitty close behind. He tells Lyle, "She knows, she knows everything."

And now Lyle confronts Kitty: "How can you know? Why haven't you done anything?"

And Kitty—so deep in self-pity, alcohol and drugs, especially since she discovered Jose's affair with another woman three years earlier—tells them, "No one ever helped me. Why should I help you? I wish you were never born."

Alone again, Erik and Lyle talk about the precipitating event, the confrontation with Jose. And as Erik hears it—even though he sought the intervention—he is horrified: "I can't believe you threatened Dad like that." Erik is in despair. He's got his head in his hands. "We're going to die. How could you threaten Dad?"

Lyle tries to calm him down. They are vigilant to be sure Jose isn't coming that very minute. Lyle wants to throw some things together and flee. Erik says they won't make it. Jose will hunt them down. Maybe they should go to the relatives for protection. No, the relatives would never take their word over their father's. Maybe to the police. No, Jose is too powerful. Maybe they should get a knife or some weapon to protect themselves.

They seize on the idea of buying handguns. That night, they stay together in the guest house but neither of them sleeps much. Next morning they learn that their decision to buy handguns is impractical because there is a two-week waiting period in California for sidearms. Instead they purchase shotguns, which are relatively easy to obtain.

They are wary, paranoid, scanning for clues of their parents' intentions. When they return home with their newly purchased guns on Friday night, Kitty tells them that a long-planned shark fishing trip on Saturday has been rescheduled from the morning to the late afternoon, which will keep them out on the ocean well into the night. They interpret this as an indication that their parents are going to kill them out there on the boat.

The next day, during the fishing trip, Lyle and Erik keep their distance from Jose and Kitty. For virtually all of the six-and-a-half-hour trip they huddle together, shivering, in the cold-wave-washed bow of the boat. At trip's end they're surprised that they're still alive. Maybe they've been wrong.

After the family returns home, the boys head off to UCLA, where they reassess their situation. Possibly it will all blow over. Erik will stay away from the house the next day, Sunday, and Lyle will remain home looking for an opportunity to reassure his father that he will not expose him.

When they return home from UCLA, Kitty—annoyed that they had to ring at the door to get in because they didn't take a key—is enraged.

Erik tries to calm her down, and she turns on him: "You keep your mouth shut. If it wasn't for you things might have worked out in this family."

That does it. Now Erik is sure again that he and Lyle will be killed. What else could it mean? His parents will never let them leave with the secret. Only Lyle's intention to talk to Jose the next day holds out any hope.

Sunday night when Erik comes home Lyle tells Erik that he failed to find a way to broach the subject of the family crisis with Jose. They decide to leave and go to the movies. Trying to make things seem normal, they inform Jose and Kitty that they're going out. Their parents tell them no, they're not, they can't leave the house that night. Jose orders Erik up to his room, and says he'll be there in a minute.

Lyle calls out to Erik, "Don't go up there. We are leaving." Erik, frightened, keeps climbing the stairs. Now Lyle turns to Jose. "You're not going to touch my little brother."

"He's not *your* little brother, he's *my* son," and again Jose says, "I'll do what I want with him."

Jose returns to the den, leaving Kitty facing Lyle in the foyer. "You've ruined this family," she says. Jose steps back out of the den, grabs Kitty by the arm, pulls her into the room with him and slams the door.

The brothers freak out. Lyle rushes up the stairs, and, his voice constricted with terror, says, "It's happening now. Get your gun."

They both race for their guns, and then to Erik's car for the ammunition. Any second they expect their parents to burst through the den doors to attack them. And Erik believes that when they do come out, he will freeze in terror and be killed. Less than two minutes after the argument, Erik and Lyle enter the darkened den, see Jose standing, apparently moving toward them and, believing he's armed, they start to fire. They both fire and fire until their guns are empty. In the gloom, Lyle sees his mother still moving; he loads another round and shoots her again.

The psychological term is "overkill" and it happens when people are shooting in panic. (It's typically what frightened police officers do when they empty their guns into an assailant, even though one round would suffice.)

In court, my co-counsel, Barry Levin, asks Erik: "Mr. Menendez, do you feel that you were justified in killing your parents?"

"I was not."

"Were you in fear when you killed them?"

"Yes."

"Why did you kill them?"

"Because I thought that they were going to kill me."

"Why, then, don't you think that you were justified in killing them?"

"Because they're my parents. There were no guns in that room, and I realize that now, and it was a horrible mistake."

As so many people familiar with it know, there is much more to this case than I have related here. Some of it I can't go into publicly until everything is finally settled, all the way through the appeal. And in any event I'm too close to it now—feel the pain myself too deeply—to take on every single misunderstanding created in the public about this very sad story. But I've tried to illustrate here the two main thrusts of the defense for anyone willing and able to understand it.

One is that we attempted throughout to establish a classic mens rea argument: the abuse itself never justified the killings, but over twelve years it created a level of torment, hypervigilance, anxiety—an emotional sickness. In one fateful week the wheels came off the cart of the Menendez family as the terrified brothers felt they had to defend themselves against their violent, sadistic father and the mother they saw as his accomplice. Fear took over. It was self-defense, but it was a flawed self-defense, an imperfect one, since the perception of the threat, although genuine, would not have been shared by a reasonable person. Imperfect self-defense has been recognized for many years as justifying a verdict of manslaughter rather than murder.

Fair or not, as a practical matter most jurors are reluctant to decide a case in a defendant's favor by relying solely on his testimony. Corroboration is crucial but often elusive, particularly in cases involving sexual molestation. But incest is almost never perpetrated in public. Although we had ample corroboration from relatives and friends for physical and psychological abuse by both parents, we had no eyewitness to confirm the sexual acts.

Nevertheless, we did have corroboration to offer on the molestation. For one thing, between the ages of six and eight, Lyle, too, was molested by Jose, and a photo shows Jose with his hand on six-year-old Lyle's crotch. More persuasive still are the photographs of Erik and Lyle, taken the day Erik turned six. The pictures are in clear focus and perfectly framed to show each child's naked body—with their genitalia in the center of the shot. The photos are cropped just below the chin. Headless sex objects. The negatives for these photos were saved in a Kodak envelope dated and labeled by Kitty. Another photo was corroborative, too: Erik testified that he was forced to keep Vaseline by his bed for the encounters with his father. In the police photographs of his room, taken the day after the homicides, there it is, a large jar of Vaseline sitting on a shelf just above his bed.

That this family was abusive one way or another was never in doubt. There were the teachers who for years saw a child in trouble but who acknowledge they were too afraid of Kitty and Jose to intervene as they know they should have. There also was all the authoritarian craziness that others could see, and that, too, hinted at the constant cruelty behind closed doors. Some of it was trivial: Jose and Kitty forced the brothers to swallow pills without water, for example. Taken alone that sounds like nothing, but if you begin to understand Jose's need to inure them to pain, it fits in perfectly. If, as a juror or courtroom spectator, you could see it all—with a parade of witnesses testifying to the behavior of this harsh family—you begin to get the context in its entirety. Then everything that the brothers said had happened in private and about their extreme fear becomes more credible. That's why more than half of the jurors from the first trial believed them and voted for manslaughter, resulting in the hung juries.

That's also why, in my view, Stanley Weisberg—the judge who embarrassed himself in the Rodney King trial and who was determined to get a popular verdict this time—gradually crippled and then destroyed the defense: a calculated, brazen betrayal of justice.

The list of antidefense decisions by Weisberg, who was the judge in both trials, began at the beginning and then grew exponentially during the second trial.

Even though the state supreme court had concluded that some of the material obtained from the psychologist, Jerome Oziel, was privileged, Weisberg found a pretext in the first trial to let in the infamous tape in which the brothers describe what led to the killings. (He allows it in the second trial, too, without hesitation—on the legally unsupportable grounds that we waived the privilege the first time so it was waived forever.)

In the first trial he allowed us to present testimony of those relatives, friends, teachers and others who had observed the Menendez clan in public and at home and who helped us create a mosaic of the warped family life that the brothers themselves would then testify about. In the second trial, he eliminated most of those witnesses during the guilt phase and left Erik to tell the horror tale himself without any groundwork laid to buttress its credibility. He did not permit any testimony on psychological—as opposed to physical and sexual—abuse. So no one could take the stand to relate how Kitty publicly and routinely berated and humiliated Erik and how she behaved so coldly toward him that no sensitive person could miss it.

He limited us to one jury this time, so that injurious testimony relevant only to one brother would inevitably damage the other. Even the composition of the jury showed the malevolence of Weisberg's hand. Before the second trial, we had conducted a $45,000 survey. It showed that the people of Van Nuys, California, could not supply an unbiased jury at this stage (overwhelmingly, they believed the verdict the first time should have been first-degree murder). But the people in downtown Los Angeles appeared significantly more open to giving the defense argument a fair hearing. Weisberg kept the trial in Van Nuys anyway, of course. We knew that women were generally more sympathetic to the defense than men, so Weisberg leaned over backwards in the second trial to allow the prosecution to exclude women from the jury (the result: seven men to five women).

In the first trial he permitted us to present three expert witnesses who had studied the family experiences of Erik and Lyle, each expert adding credibility and expanding on the information provided by the others. In the second, he permitted only one, and he forbade that one from expressing his personal opinion that Erik's recounting of the molestation was true, limiting him to saying instead only that Erik's statements were consistent with the scientific literature on molestation, a much weaker assertion.

In the second trial, Weisberg even prevented Erik from testifying about episodes in his own life that helped us show how this family transcended what some might see as normal harshness and was in fact pathological.

If the prosecution doesn't seem alert enough in attacking the defense, Weisberg is certain to give them a hand.

From time to time during the retrial, Weisberg is prodding the prosecution about their intentions concerning our use of imperfect self-defense, the core of our presentation in the second trial as it was in the first. He wants to know whether they are objecting to it. When he first asks them, they say no. By his third inquiry, they've gotten the hint and say, "Yes, Your Honor." Now we will have to argue the issue in court, and this enrages and frightens me. It doesn't make any sense. Earlier, Weisberg seemed to be conceding that imperfect self-defense was a legitimate part of this trial. The very reason we were allowed to introduce our one psychological expert during the course of the trial was that, according to California state law, his testimony was relevant to a claim of imperfect self-defense.

Now—in the last hours of the second trial—Weisberg is wondering whether imperfect self-defense really does apply in this case! It's the same case as it was in the first trial, of course. What the hell is going on here? Is this the final blow? The one component of the defense that the judge focuses on is the requirement that the defendant has to believe the lethal threat to him is "imminent."

My courtroom debate with Weisberg turns out to be an exercise in futility. I'm just hitting my head against a stone wall. He enunciates his understanding this way:

"The defendant must believe that the perceived peril precipitating the need for deadly force is imminent." And then he says, it's not for the defendant to decide what the term "imminent" means; that's an objective term, and the state defines it. Thus, he says, "There is both an objective and a subjective element to this."

I just can't believe he's saying these things. "Your Honor, there is no objective element." Obviously. If the lethal threat the defendant perceived were, in fact, objectively imminent, we'd be talking about justifiable homicide, perfect self-defense leading to an acquittal, not manslaughter. Imperfect self-defense allows for a defendant's unreasonable belief that the danger is imminent.

"The issue," Weisberg says, "is whether or not there is substantial evidence"—this after he has disallowed a hell of a lot of the defense evidence—"of an actual belief by the defendant of imminent peril." And if so, he says, the court is obligated to give the jury the instruction defining imperfect self-defense as manslaughter. "If not, then the court is not obligated to give an instruction."

Soon there is a charade of sorts. Weisberg hands out something he's written for our benefit, his unique definition of imminent peril as it applies to imperfect self-defense. He says he still hasn't made up his mind on what the law requires in this instance. The judge is doing this after our entire defense was built around this particular theory. (At any time earlier, I could have emphasized those elements of the case that support another theory of manslaughter, a heat-of-passion defense—but he waits until now, when the curtain is about to drop.)

I look over the stuff he's written, the law according to Weisberg.

"Your Honor," I say, "I don't understand why we're bothering with this. The court surely knows if it's going to give this instruction or not."

Weisberg says, "If you don't want to look at it, don't look at it. That's up to you. But your opportunity is now, not in the future. It's imminent." (That last, of course, a wiseass joke here in the throes of destroying a defense in a case that could end in the death penalty.)

Then he does it. "I just don't see that there has been presented substantial evidence of imminent danger to justify giving an instruction on imperfect defense." He simply is not going to let the jury even consider our presentation after they heard us build it for four months. He will not let them be confused by the truth as, in his view, the jury in the previous trial was.

And then we start to tumble into Wonderland, a surreal babble where no one is saying anything that the other can follow. Terri Towery—one of Lyle's attorneys this time—says in genuine confusion, "Just so the record is clear, Your Honor, is the court saying there is not substantial evidence of the defendant's belief in imminent danger, or there is not substantial evidence of imminent danger?"

To which Weisberg clarifies, sort of: "That looking at it objectively, that what the defendant said does not constitute imminent danger."

I leap in. "So the court is saying that as a matter of law the belief that at any second people can come out of a room with guns blazing and shoot you is not a fear of imminent danger? That's what the court is saying?"

Weisberg: "For an application of imperfect self-defense, that is not imminent danger."

As my mind swirls in anger and confusion—and hatred—I write the word "OUTRAGE" on a pad in front of me. I write it large enough for Stanley Weisberg to see it.

Weisberg comes out with his final instructions to the jury: the jury can decide on first- or second-degree murder for both Jose and Kitty. Manslaughter will be permitted as an option for the killing of Jose Menendez, but solely based on the theory of heat of passion.

In any event, since the jurors, in Kitty Menendez's case, can only choose between murder and acquittal (acquittal not being an easy option, given the fact that the brothers did kill her with shotguns), I know the tragedy has just about run its course now. The judge has decided that the despised brothers will be convicted of murder. He set us up, protected his own ass, redeemed his public reputation and shielded himself from further criticism.

I feel like I'm back in those early days, a baby lawyer, in the municipal courts, where the ignorant judges were making up their own silly rules. Except this is so much worse. Weisberg is anything but stupid. And a client I care about—a tormented young man who testified bravely—is being railroaded perhaps into the death chamber.

I'm left to deliver a closing argument that surely must have seemed strange to anyone who watched the trial play out. It's as if I'm arguing a different case, closing the show, but somebody else's show. I spent a few days working on it, forging on in spite of my bitterness. The worst misery was in reading through the entire trial record. There they were, all the judge's rulings, now mapped out, their purpose clear: the clever moves of a chess master working toward checkmate.

In the end, the jury decides on first degree across the board.

Some jurors said later they believed much of what we told them, even in this judicially crippled defense, especially about the molestation. (One juror told us he hoped he'd be able to help the brothers in some way in the years to come.) But, evidently, even the more sympathetic jurors couldn't find a legal justification for anything less than first degree. And no wonder.

The Bad Karma Express had come roaring through. Nothing ever went right for Erik and Lyle. So many of the people they trusted—their parents, friends, that psychologist they confided in after the killings—failed or betrayed them. The nation hated these young men whom it mocked for crying on the stand (although that was simply a momentary occurrence in the trial—much repeated by the media). And everything that could go wrong in this trial ultimately did. We saw our clients as cursed. So, whenever some new setback occurred, we on the defense team shrugged our shoulders and repeated our mantra: "Well, this *is* the Menendez case."

A decision of first-degree murder necessitates a penalty trial, in which the jurors will decide on the punishment, either death or life in prison without the possibility of parole. Each side can present new witnesses and evidence in this phase of the case. Here we get the chance to put on the good witnesses we couldn't use earlier in this trial, additional experts (the ones who testified in the original trial but were banned from the first part of this one), as well as the relatives, teachers and coaches whose testimony corroborates Erik and the experts' opinions on the brothers' mal-treatment. (A juror later told Charlie Gessler and Terri Towery, the two outstanding public defenders who were Lyle's lawyers for the retrial, that he wished he'd heard some of this earlier.)

At one point near the end of the penalty phase, there was a distracting blowup. Bill Vicary, one of several psychological witnesses, albeit playing a minor role in the trial, was testifying about the timing of Erik's first report of molestation. Bill had brought to court a rewritten version of his therapy and interview notes. The prosecution had an earlier, uncorrected version of the 101 pages of notes, which I gave them.

Vicary, whom I like and respect and whose input has been invaluable to me throughout the years, has always had the capacity to unnerve me: back in the Arnel Salvatierra trial, I became furious with him for bending over backwards—and distorting his own opinions in the process—to concede a few prosecution points in order to buttress his credibility in the prosecutorial camp. (He sought employment from them, too.)

Now, challenged by the prosecutor's observation of inconsistencies between their two sets of notes, he panicked. He testified that as we prepared for his testimony in the original trial, more than two years earlier, I ordered him to change things or else he'd be thrown off the case. Actually, I told him that he had to edit out material that had already been disallowed by the court's rulings and clarify a few cryptic phrases in his notes so that they reflected what he told me Erik meant. (If he couldn't do that because his memory was no longer clear on what Erik meant, I was under no obligation to call him to testify as a defense witness.) There was never a discussion about removing him from the case —he was Erik's therapist. I expected Bill to edit his notes in the custom-ary way, the obvious crossing out and adding that anyone reading them can see. There was no intention to deceive. He chose, instead, to rewrite entirely the pages that I asked him to edit—without telling me what he did. It turns out he even removed things I didn't discuss with him.

It was, in the end, nothing more than a discovery dispute of the sort familiar to observers of the O. J. Simpson trial. Had we given the prosecution all they were entitled to, or had we improperly held back something on purpose? Whichever it was, it only related to the original trial since the prosecution at this point had the unedited version (the concerns that required editing before were not relevant to the testimony he was about to give now).

Discovery disputes happen every day in court on both sides. What made this a media event is that I found myself in an impossible position when Weisberg asked me to explain in open court—with the prosecution present—what happened to produce two different versions. (I had offered to do it in private.) If I said in open court that Vicary was misrepresenting or misremembering the facts, the prosecution could call me to testify before the jury to impeach my own witness. That would harm my client. I was trapped. On the advice of a lawyer friend, called in to make a horseback decision, I took the Fifth to prevent a public inquiry in the hopes that I could later convince the judge to hear me in private. To my considerable distress (and that of my co-counsel), it only made things look worse.

On the next court day, I withdrew the assertion of the Fifth and relied on protections inherent in the lawyer-client relationship to remain silent.

The media immediately overreacted. To hear them tell it, I was on my way to jail, disbarred and disgraced. It was a ridiculous spectacle, starring all the usual suspects. *Newsweek,* for instance, said I faced charges of evidence tampering, a serious matter. The magazine obviously didn't know the difference between notes created solely to assist a witness's memory and documents intended to be exhibits. At no time were those notes going to be evidence.

But the media—in fact, the information industry in general—has always loved hitching a ride on this Bad Karma Express. And even though my husband is a dedicated journalist, my regard for the press, most of it anyway, is roughly about as high as my regard for the snails that eat the lettuce in my garden.

21

When Worlds Collide

little downward pressure with the heel of your shoe and, just like that, even the most voracious snail is gone forever. It's going to take a lot more effort and a lot more time to sort out the uneasy new relationship between the commercial media and our criminal and civil justice systems.

My personal perspective on this troublesome issue is unique, since I was a participant in one of recent history's most intensely scrutinized cases, the first Menendez trial, and a paid television analyst of another, O. J. Simpson's double-murder trial. I have, in other words, worked both sides of this controversy's street. And, from that vantage point, America's road to justice looks less like a thoroughfare and more like a swamp with each passing month.

To understand why, it's necessary to take a step back and square up the discussion's constitutional and historical corners. First of all, it is essential to recognize that the most difficult questions confronting our society are those that arise out of the exercise of two legitimate but conflicting rights. Resolving such conflicts is *always* a painful proposition. It can be particularly wrenching when the conflict involves the First Amendment's protection of a free press and the Sixth Amendment's guarantee of a fair trial. Several times in this century, for example, extraordinarily rapid technological advances have not only transformed the culture of the American news media, but also thrust it into confrontation with prevailing notions of what the Sixth Amendment requires. In each of those watershed moments, the courts have been forced to intervene to balance the scales of equity between these two indispensable provisions of our Bill of Rights.

One such turning point occurred in 1935, when Bruno Richard Hauptmann was put on trial for the kidnapping and murder of Charles A. Lindbergh's twenty-month-old son. Lucky Lindy's epic solo crossing of the Atlantic by air had made him the darling of a burgeoning popular media, which only recently had discovered the commercial possibilities of celebrity. He was the quintessential blend of traditional American heroism and modern American technology. When Hauptmann's trial began, more than seven hundred print and radio journalists and hundreds of radio and telephonic technicians descended on little Flemington, New Jersey, where the case was tried. To link the reporters to their respective outlets, the local utility installed what was then the largest special-purpose phone system in history, one sufficient by the standards of the time to serve a community of one million people.

The trial that followed was a circus. The courtroom was filled with radio microphones and illuminated by the constant pop of still photographers' flashes; reporters shouted out their own questions to lawyers and witnesses alike. Hauptmann, of course, was convicted and subsequently executed. But judges across the country were horrified by the spectacle and soon adopted stringent regulations governing the use of the relatively new broadcasting and photographic technologies in their courtrooms. Perhaps more important, Hauptmann's conviction remains suspect to this day, as historians uncover additional information on how a large but credulous press corps, hungry for conviction, completely missed repeated instances of blatant official misconduct during the investigation and trial.

Nearly twenty years later, in 1954, something remarkably similar happened in Cleveland, Ohio, where a young osteopath named Sam Sheppard was accused of the savage murder of his pregnant wife. The case almost immediately attracted national attention, partly because of the defendant's wealth, partly because of the whiff of suburban scandal, which prosecutors cultivated by circulating stories of Sheppard's infidelity. In any event, the national media—particularly the newspaper and radio columnists who then were at the apex of their power—descended on the case. The synergy between electronic and print journalists—all feeding off one another's competitive frenzy—produced something qualitatively new, the phenomenon that we now recognize as "pack journalism." The result, as *The New York Times* aptly put it, was a "Roman circus." Sheppard, of course, was convicted and sentenced to life imprisonment.

Ten years later, a brilliant young Boston defense attorney named F. Lee Bailey convinced the United States Supreme Court to reverse the doctor's conviction because, as the majority held, the trial judge "did not fulfill his duty to protect Sheppard from inherently prejudicial publicity which saturated the country." Bailey subsequently retried the case and won his client's acquittal at the hands of a jury that deliberated for less than twelve hours. The reversal he secured for Sheppard helped set new national standards for the regulation of pretrial publicity and the mitigation of its inevitable impact. What usually is overlooked, however, is the other key to Bailey's appeal—that the original trial judge, Edward Blythin, was so prejudiced against Sheppard that he not only harassed his lawyers and gutted their defense, but also expressed his personal opinion that the defendant was "guilty as hell." Somehow none of that made its way into the thousands of newspaper and radio reports filed from the first Sam Sheppard trial. More important, while Lee Bailey restored his client to liberty, there was nothing even he could do to give that grievously wronged man back the ten years he had spent in prison.

Taken together, the Lindbergh and Sheppard cases suggest that, when it comes to press coverage of criminal trials, quantity does not equal quality. In both instances the crush of sensation-seeking journalists managed to deny the men on trial the protection of their Sixth Amendment rights, while failing miserably in their own responsibility to report official misconduct even when its targets are unpopular, as criminal defendants usually are.

Our reigning corps of media sophists can explain all these things away as "aberrations" distant in time. But in his famous study *The Common Law,* Justice Holmes writes that "the life of the law has not been logic, it has been experience." And my experience with the Menendez and Simpson trials has convinced me that we currently are at precisely the sort of juncture those earlier cases posed for the legal systems of their time. Today, when the press somehow decides that your case—among all the hundreds of thousands tried each year—suddenly is newsworthy, you confront not just wire service, newspaper and newsmagazine reporters, but also television in all its varieties, the new generation of opinionated glossy magazine writers, talk show hosts, topical comedians, made-for-television "docudramas" and the print and electronic tabloids. Taken together, their attention creates a kind of critical mass, triggering a vicious and uncontrollable chain reaction throughout our popular culture. Your client's Sixth Amendment right to a fair trial simply implodes.

The first and strongest link in this reactive chain is the camera in the courtroom. Televising trials was a well-meaning—in fact, high-minded—experiment. But we now have more than enough evidence to show that the whole exercise has been a destructive failure; it's time to pull the plug.

The cameras' apologists claim that their right to televise trials is sanctioned not only by the First Amendment's guarantee of a free press and the Sixth Amendment's insistence that trials be public, but also by the public's amorphous "right to know." Let's take those assertions in reverse order:

The Constitution is silent on the "right to know." This notion actually arose during the Progressive era, when reformers rightly argued that conducting the public's business in public made for better, more honest government. The so-called open-meeting statutes adopted by numerous states are products of that era. But none of those laws assert that this right to know is absolute. In California, to take just one example, city councils and school boards are allowed to meet behind closed doors when they consider personnel matters. That's because courts have held that the statutory privacy rights of the individuals involved take precedence over any generalized public right to know. I also would argue that, when it comes to the criminal justice system, this right to know through the medium of television is applied so selectively as to render it virtually meaningless.

The camera boosters' reliance on the Sixth Amendment is similarly unsteady. The Founders insisted on public trials not as an assertion of some broad popular interest, but because they wanted to protect the rights of accused individuals. Their experience at the hands of the British Crown had taught them that secret trials were the tool of oppressive governments. They could not have imagined that public scrutiny might become so exaggerated and intrusive that it would create miscarriages of justice every bit as grotesque as those plotted in the Star Chamber. Moreover, the constitutional requirement that a trial be public is fulfilled simply by having seats available for the public in the courtroom. No one ever has argued before that the court has to accommodate *every* member of the public who wants to watch a particular trial on a particular day. If that were so, O. J. Simpson's trial would have been held in the Los Angeles Coliseum and not in the Criminal Courts Building.

Finally, there's the notion that the First Amendment protects the television news media's right to broadcast from the courtroom. This, too, is specious. Since the Lindbergh kidnapping trial, the principle has been well established that judges may regulate the application of specific newsgathering technologies in their courtrooms. All judges control the presence of still photographers. Even those who permit television cameras set stringent guidelines on what they can and cannot film. Some judges even ban reporters from bringing tape recorders into their courts. If broadcast journalists really want to cover a trial, there is nothing to prevent them from sitting in court, taking notes and then coming out to tell their viewers or listeners what happened. But facts aren't really what they want; they want pictures—and they want them for a reason. Television thrives on the merchandising of spectacles—the current state of professional and college sports and, especially, the Olympic Games is a prime example. Many television executives, constantly in search of the next salable spectacle, believe courtroom trials just might be it. After all, a trial has certain attractive characteristics in common with sports: All the action occurs at a predetermined time, in a predetermined place and according to predictable rules. That makes it relatively cheap and easy to broadcast. The problem is that the loser of the NCAA basketball final goes home to think about next year; if my client loses his capital-murder trial, he goes to the gas chamber. The people at Court TV, the for-profit cable operation most responsible for spawning the current vogue for televised trials, insist that their broadcasts also serve an important educational and public-service function. To borrow a phrase from Lee Bailey's final argument in the Sheppard retrial, that's ten pounds of hogwash in a five-pound bag. If Court TV was out to educate people it would look like C-SPAN. In fact, it most closely resembles ESPN, right down to the expert "color commentators" and breezy wrap-up shows.

The worst mistake a contemporary criminal defense lawyer caught in one of these high-profile cases can make is to believe he or she somehow can manage this onslaught. For example, not long before he became nationally famous for his part in O. J. Simpson's defense, I shared a platform with Bob Shapiro. We'd been invited to address a California State Bar conference concerning media and the courts. Up to that point, Bob was best known for handling Johnny Carson's drunk-driving case and for negotiating a plea bargain on behalf of Marlon Brando's son Christian, who was charged with murder after shooting his sister's boyfriend.

When Bob speaks to our audience, he tells them lawyers can "manage" the press by "spinning" their coverage the way political campaign managers do. I don't agree. When you're defending Johnny Carson on minor charges, you don't have to spin anybody. A press corps that still worships celebrity every bit as much as the press did in the Lindbergh era will spin itself like a top in your direction. It's an entirely different situation when you do what I do: litigate death-penalty homicides for people who are well-known only for their alleged crimes. The day will come, I warn Bob, when he will find himself defending a client in a criminal case so serious that his media friends won't let him close enough to touch them, let alone spin anyone. In fact, when he took on Simpson, the media battered both him and his client. Glamorous Bob Shapiro's spin began to look more like a tap dance, as he slithered as far as he could from the rest of the Dream Team.

During my part of the lecture, I describe the very real harm I've seen Court TV and other broadcasts cause to my clients: Witnesses with useful information but normal senses of privacy shy away from the notoriety the camera confers. In their place you get wannabes, deranged characters with phony stories cooked up to get them a few minutes on the tube. I also talk of how painful it is for defendants brave enough to testify on their own behalf to bare their souls for the titillation of bored housewives and trial junkies, who make no moral distinction between a trial and a soap opera. Finally, I speak of the inevitable and damaging distortions that arise from an aroused media's insatiable need for drama and crisis, whether it exists or not.

I tell them how horrified my journalist husband was when I began expressing admiration for the Canadian and British bans on all pretrial reporting in criminal cases. I recall how he stiffly pointed out to me that such prohibitions flatly contradict our traditional view that the First Amendment precludes prior restraints on publication. But, I tell him, the journalists control the spotlight; they never have to live in its glare.

Few of them, moreover, have any notion of how subversive of your client's Sixth Amendment rights that glare can be—at times, merely because it's such a distraction. Early in the Menendez case, for instance, my secretary is out and I make the mistake of answering my own phone.

"I'd like to speak with Leslie Abramson," says the woman caller.

"You've got her," I say curtly.

The caller turns out to be Shelly Ross, a producer for ABC television's "Prime Time Live." From my message log, I know she's been calling for weeks. I haven't responded. Our investigation and interrogation of potential witnesses has barely begun. We know what our defense is going to be, but there's no way I'm going to share it with the media before our jury hears it. Almost as important is my human obligation to the surviving Menendez family members. The revelation that Jose sexually abused his sons is going to be excruciating for them. I don't want any of them to hear it first on some TV program.

"People usually return my calls," an indignant Shelly Ross tells me.

She then continues with the standard journalist's patter about how crucial it is that I make myself available for interviews so that my "side can get out."

"It's not my side," I tell her. "It's my client's side, and his side happens to be his defense. There's nothing to be gained by giving it away now. The answer is no."

Of course, that doesn't end the matter. Shortly before the first Menendez trial begins, we're fighting in the California Supreme Court to suppress tape recordings made by Erik and Lyle's unscrupulous psychologist, Jerome Oziel. At his prompting, the brothers had confessed the killings to him during a therapy session, which he recorded. He also had secretly dictated what he claimed were notes from other sessions. Oziel passed this information on to his girlfriend, who informed the police. They arrested the brothers and obtained a warrant allowing them to seize Oziel's recordings. Our argument is simple: The tapes contain material that is covered by the therapist-patient privilege, which neither brother has waived. Worse, the so-called confession is utterly misleading, since it contains no notation that Erik and Lyle actually were parroting theories Oziel himself had advanced in previous, unrecorded sessions.

In all my years of practice, I have never argued before the Supreme Court. On the morning of my appearance, I'm a wreck. My husband notices how jumpy I am. "These justices grill you," I explain. "They interrupt your argument, try to trap you into untenable positions."

As I gather my briefcase and files and scramble out the door, I plaintively wonder: "Is it too late to apply to medical school?"

An hour later, I'm standing in the Supreme Court's solemnly theatrical Los Angeles courtroom. The justices are arrayed behind an improbably elevated bench at the front of the room. The court itself is dimly lit, with overhead spotlights trained on the justices' seats and the litigants' podium. As I await my turn to argue, I feel as if my cold and clammy hands may begin to shake.

At precisely that moment, someone shoves a pretty pink envelope into my unsteady grip. It contains a handwritten note from ABC's Diane Sawyer, pleading for an interview with me and, if possible, my client. She promises that her report will be "sensitive." It's a sincere sentiment, for, as I later learn working with her at ABC, Diane is an intelligent and genuinely empathic person.

But at that instant, with my client's very life in the balance, I feel as if I'm being stalked.

If you discipline yourself to keep your client's interests uppermost in your mind, you can find a way to avoid the producers and reporters who descend on a televised trial. What you can't avoid are the so-called expert commentators, who are an entirely new element in the mix of legal journalism. A few are serious professionals, trying to do what they can to illuminate a complex process within our constitutional system. A greater number simply are unqualified, promiscuously offering worthless opinions on cases they couldn't have tried on the best day in their careers. Far worse are the professional legal pundits, usually academics rather than real trial lawyers, who bring their own theoretical—and financial—agendas to bear on their hapless targets. They do real harm.

From our standpoint in the Menendez case, for example, the worst of the lot was the ubiquitous Harvard law professor Alan Dershowitz. Without any real knowledge of the facts in our case, he dismissed our clients' defense and that of Lorena Bobbitt with a sound bite: "the abuse excuse." For a criminal defense attorney, it's appalling to hear someone charged with the responsibility of providing legal education label recognized state-of-mind defenses as excuses. It's like a step back into another era. But for Dershowitz, it was a profitable one—especially when he took the next step and suggested that Erik and Lyle's lawyers had conspired with them to present a knowingly false story. Ultimately, Dershowitz went on to write a book denouncing the "abuse excuse" he'd invented.

My friend Gerry Uelmen, a distinguished law-school dean, had this apt comment about his colleague's conduct in a review for a leading legal journal:

"How sad it is that one who professes pride in the label 'criminal defense lawyer' should be the source of so much of the misinformation and misunderstanding about criminal justice that recent verdicts [Menendez and Bobbitt] have engendered. But that's show business."

For too many of these commentators it's also a kind of intellectual exercise, rather like their schools' moot courts, where you can play out this theory or that without consequence. The real world of criminal trials, by contrast, is fraught with the most serious consequences imaginable. In this instance, the abuse excuse nonsense helped not only to poison the entire pool from which we had to draw our retrial jurors, but also to embolden the judge to gut our legal defense, secure in the belief that an angry public was on his side.

I believe the poisonous public climate created by the academic pundits also had an effect on the way the brothers' retrial was covered by the press. Privately, just about all the reporters who covered the second trial told us they were shocked by Judge Weisberg's obvious bias against our clients. But only two—Martin Berg of the *Los Angeles Daily Journal,* a legal trade paper, and Ken Noble of *The New York Times*—ever noted the judge's conduct in their stories.

When Weisberg severely limited our ability to present evidence of family abuse, one television reporter summed up the press corps's sentiment with the comment, "This judge is really screwing you." None of them, however, ever told their readers or viewers of the blatant unfairness that was a daily feature of the retrial. They all saw it: Weisberg deprived us of most of our witnesses; he limited the scope of our expert testimony; he denied us dual juries; he refused to move the case downtown, where our polling showed that a significantly less biased jury pool existed; he limited Erik's testimony concerning the abuse he had suffered; he allowed the prosecution to use irrelevant and prejudicial evidence to attack the brothers and, ultimately, he refused to give our jury the same manslaughter instruction he had delivered in the first trial. Nearly all these decisions were reversals of rulings Weisberg himself had made in the first trial. If it had been a gymnastics meet instead of a murder trial, Weisberg's spectacular series of flip-flops probably would have earned him a "10." But this wasn't a sporting event. It was a trial, and his reversal of course was a brazen attempt to engineer a verdict.

It worked, and the media shut its eyes. In some ways the press performance in Erik and Lyle's retrial was worse than what occurred in the Sheppard case. There, the media simply missed the judge's bias. In our case, everybody saw it, but only two men had the courage—or common decency—to report truthfully and fully what they had seen.

In part, I believe, those reporters were either intimidated or desensitized by the irresponsible pundits who circled the first trial like jackals. That's why I can't laugh off the Dershowitzes of our new TV world as charming gadflies.

Sometime later, in fact, when both Uelmen and Dershowitz had become members of O. J. Simpson's defense team, I was driving back to my office after visiting Erik in the county jail. When I call in for messages, there's one from Gerry Uelmen. I return his call. For a few minutes, we chat about some legal issues that have come up in Simpson's case.

Then Gerry says, "There's someone here who wants to say hello to you."

"Someone I know?" I inquire suspiciously.

"Someone who wants to be friends again," Gerry responds.

"Gee," I say, "I haven't lost too many friends lately. Who've you got in mind?"

"It's Alan."

"Forget it, Gerry. We never were friends. He's libeled me and, worse, tried to destroy my poor client. When he goes public admitting what a lying jerk he is, I may consider talking to him. Short of that, never."

"Aw, come on, Leslie," Gerry pleads, "he's trying to make up."

"It's not good enough, Gerry. Tell him never!"

Given my animosity toward the TV pundits, how did I end up analyzing O. J. Simpson's trial for ABC News? Well, it wasn't hard to see that the unbelievable Simpson vortex was sucking in everyone with a bar card and even a tenuous claim to some authority on mayhem and murder. But few experienced criminal trial lawyers had yet joined this latest circus-in-the-making. I couldn't claim to be the only specialist in America capable of objective, lucid analysis of a complex trial. But, unlike most of my colleagues, I'd just come through a nasty experience with the media in the first Menendez trial. I wanted to show that it is possible to offer insight without hype, opinion without prejudgment and analysis beyond simpleminded scorekeeping. In other words, I wanted to do it right.

My first move is to call Barbara Walters, with whom I had become friends after she interviewed me for one of her network specials. "Barbara," I ask, "do you think ABC would hire me as an exclusive commentator on the O.J. case?"

"I can't see why they wouldn't," Barbara replies, "but let me check into it."

The next day, she phones back and tells me to "call the bureau chief in Los Angeles. She's expecting to hear from you."

A few days later, when Simpson's preliminary hearing begins, I'm part of the press corps, complete with a stack of plastic-coated passes hanging from a chain around my neck. Every morning, I drive to the ABC studios in east Hollywood and check into the makeup room, where very nice women with very large curling irons do what they can to tame my well-known hair.

"It's a softer look, Leslie. You'll love it."

The first day on the set, I settle into my chair and have my mike hooked up and my earpiece set, so I can hear the questions and comments from the studio in New York. To my dismay, I find that occupying the seat opposite me is former Los Angeles County District Attorney Robert Philibosian, one of the real hardasses to come out of a pretty tough prosecutor's office.

"I'll probably end up fighting with this guy all day," I think to myself.

In fact, Bob and I hit it off from the start. We discover we share a lot of opinions about the way the case is unfolding. We agree that the frantic pretrial publicity has forced the trial to move much too fast for both sides. Bob says he can't understand how the prosecutors possibly could be ready. (In fact, they weren't.) I feel the same about the defense.

As Bob and I talk, it's clear to me that he is not only charming but also —as his comments suggest—someone who was a great trial lawyer before he abandoned criminal litigation for a far more lucrative business practice. What's also clear to both of us is that while our ABC colleagues are smart, hardworking and sincerely concerned about fairness, their attitudes toward this trial are fundamentally different from the ones we bring as fellow trial lawyers. Though we came from different sides of the courtroom, Bob and I quickly notice that most of our colleagues are innocently unaware of the many biases they bring to this case.

Even the very best of them is trying to come to some conclusion about O.J.'s guilt before the prosecution's case has even ended, let alone the defense's. They keep forgetting that on any given day one side may seem to be winning, but on the next day the other side's evidence is more persuasive. The judge admonishes jurors to keep an open mind on a daily basis; there is no one to admonish the media. In a criminal trial, until you hear everything, you don't really know how important or trivial anything really is. But reporters are under tremendous competitive pressure to solve every riddle on deadline. They want every day to be a story with a beginning, middle and end.

So, very early on, most of them decide O.J. is guilty. As one of them said to me on a day that turned out to be one of the trial's most significant turning points:

"See, I told you he did it. Those gloves are a perfect fit."

"Are you out of your mind, girl?" I ask. "They're too small. You're seeing what you want to see."

As it happened, the only fourteen people in America who were protected from my opinion, that of my reporter friend or that of any other media commentator were the twelve jurors and two alternates Judge Lance Ito wisely had sequestered in a downtown L.A. hotel. All they saw was the evidence, and they didn't think the gloves fit. More to the point, their opinions were the only ones that really counted.

In the heady world of broadcast journalism, it's easy to lose sight of that fact. First, there's the experience of being recognized everywhere, from the best restaurant in town to the supermarket. Then there's the daily sensation of being part of what the broadcast world calls "the talent." Everybody, from the network's stars to the men and women on the crew, does everything they can to spoil you rotten.

"Hey, Leslie, you need anything? You looked great last night."

At first, all these comments about my appearance are flattering. Gradually, unease sets in.

"Thanks," I say, "but how did I sound?"

"Oh," comes the somewhat hesitant reply, "that was good, too."

Beyond an overriding preoccupation with appearances and impossibly quick judgments, there is another problem with this new brand of courtroom journalism that is most obvious in the print press. Everything changes, but not always for the better—and a prime example is the way the influence of the opinionated glossy magazine writers is supplanting the traditional journalistic ethic of objective, balanced reporting of criminal trials.

Take, for example, *Vanity Fair* magazine's trial correspondent, Dominick Dunne. Before he began attaching himself like a lamprey to other people's trials, he was a failed movie producer who had made a second career for himself as a sort of jumped-up romance novelist. Then he suffered a terrible tragedy. His young daughter, a promising young actress, was strangled to death by her boyfriend during a quarrel. There's nothing worse than the loss of a child, and those who suffer it are entitled to grieve as they must. Dunne's feelings were compounded when the trial of his daughter's killer resulted in a conviction for manslaughter rather than murder. He did what I suppose many writers would do under the circumstances: He turned his dead daughter into material.

I happen to believe that there is a necessary distinction between journalism and therapy. But in a society consumed with victimization and the confessional style, Dunne's combination of the two looked like a winning formula to his magazine's editors. They've since let him apply it to a number of trials, including Menendez and Simpson. The fact that he brings to his work a virulent predisposition to assume the guilt of anyone accused of a crime, especially homicide, apparently is beside the point. You don't have to be Sigmund Freud to figure out what's going on here. His tragic life experience would disqualify him from sitting on the jury in any murder case, but in his editors' eyes it seems to supply, if not a kind of special authority, at least a titillating twist. Unfortunately, their successful promotion of his reports has led other magazines to enlist Dunne clones. Most try to match not only his reflexively pro-prosecution attitude, but also his gossip-column style, which blends celebrity name-dropping with anonymous—and, therefore, uncheckable—"sources."

My favorite example of this method is a scene Dunne imagined and subsequently has repeated over and over. In it, he has Jose and Kitty Menendez eating strawberries and ice cream on their den couch moments before they are gunned down. To add an element of further pathos, Kitty is in the process of filling out Erik's college application. It's a moving scene; the problem is, none of it is true.

The strawberries-and-ice-cream myth was created by someone in the L.A. County Coroner's office, who told it to the press in the week following the shootings. It was contradicted at trial. Dozens of reporters and magazine writers, including Dunne, as well as Court TV's viewers, heard the testimony of the investigating officer, Leslie Zoellar:

There was one empty glass on the coffee table. It bore traces of what looked like a dessert, but the contents never were analyzed to determine what it contained or how long it had been there or who ate whatever was in it. In my cross-examination of Zoellar, I made it clear that there was no food of any kind in the room when Jose and Kitty were shot. Moreover, forensic analysis showed that there was no way either victim could have been holding a glass when the shooting occurred.

Similarly, there was no college application. The shootings occurred in August, months after Erik had been accepted at UCLA for the fall 1989 semester. What the police did find scattered on the floor next to the den coffee table were some brochures describing a UCLA summer school program that concluded before August 20. There was no application. Nothing was written on the brochures. The police didn't even bother to collect them as evidence.

Still, the strawberries-and-ice-cream fable made its way from Dunne's magazine piece into the stories of the inept *Los Angeles Times* reporter who covered the case, and from there to everywhere under the electronic sun.

What made the destructive inadequacies of this sort of journalism so apparent to all of us on the defense team was the presence in our court of a superb "traditional" journalist, Linda Deutsch of the Associated Press. Linda, who is considered America's premier trial reporter, has covered all the "trials of the century" for the past twenty-five years. Her reports on both Menendez trials and on Simpson always were straight-on, completely factual accounts of the day's events and the significance of the witnesses' testimony. During the first Menendez trial, she frequently expressed to me her distaste for the inaccuracy and lack of balance in the *Times'* reports, which she clearly understood had the potential to prejudice our unsequestered jury. As it happened, they helped create the climate of public animosity toward the Menendez brothers that made it impossible for us to pick an unbiased jury for the retrial.

I still recall the day the habitually circumspect Deutsch asked me, "Did you see that piece in the *Times* this morning? It's really weird. I keep asking myself, Was I in the same courtroom that he was in yesterday? Are we watching the same trial?"

Given their origins and techniques, it's not surprising that opinionated print journalists of this new kind have their biggest impact in popular culture. Their work provides most of the fodder for the nightly Leno and Letterman jokes that demonize and dehumanize people accused of crimes until not even the most skillful advocate can rehabilitate them.

Worst of all are the so-called docudramas the television networks now rush into production before a case is even submitted to the jury. At one point, for example, I went to court to try to stop the broadcast of a scheduled Menendez TV movie. I failed, as I knew I would. But sometimes you have to do things simply to fight your own debilitating sense of powerlessness. Actually, there were two of these television films, both predictably hostile and mean-spirited, particularly in their irresponsible fictionalization of the Erik and Lyle characters. Both movies were based on the press corps's favorite premise: The brothers were spoiled brats who killed their parents for money. None of the jurors, even those who ultimately convicted them, believed that after hearing all the evidence. But here were these false, ugly portrayals, utterly heedless of their impact on the first and second trials. One of the films—a two-part CBS adaptation of Dunne's magazine articles—naturally repeated the infamous fables of the strawberries and the college application. In fact, scene after scene in both movies was contradicted by the actual evidence admitted at trial. But when a smooth screenplay is at stake, truth is an inconvenience easily overcome.

Considered together, these intrusive new technologies and the new media culture they seem to have spawned pose a serious new challenge to the due-process and fair-trial guarantees we all enjoy under the Sixth Amendment. We Americans entrust the most serious imaginable decision —life or death—to our criminal trial courts. As a consequence, all the participants—judges, lawyers, defendants, witnesses, jurors—are held strictly accountable for their conduct by the law. All the participants, that is, but one: the media. Despite its increasingly influential role in this critical process, it remains for all practical purposes unaccountable to anybody but its stockholders and their desire for profit.

Unaccountable power inevitably corrupts all who wield it. For the sake of our free press no less than for that of our criminal justice system, it once again is time to reexamine the balance between the First and Sixth Amendments.

22

Grief
_____

I'm waiting in the attorney visiting room at Men's Central for Erik to come down. He's on the other side of the building up one flight in a cell, seven by eight feet, where he lives by himself. (It's a luxurious place compared to the four-by-eight cell you get in state prison and usually share with a roommate.) It takes him a long time to get down to the visiting area and my eyes roam around: the red "No Physical Contact at Any Time" sign means not even any handshaking when you greet your client.

The booth I'm in is enclosed in Plexiglas, and there is a narrow Formica table running the width of the cubicle. The table is divided by a Plexiglas partition that goes only halfway up toward the top of the booth so you can talk face-to-face even though you're physically separated. This booth is next to the one O. J. Simpson spent most of his days in talking to lawyers (there's no restriction on time for attorney-client conversations). Voices carry easily through the ventilation system; I can hear a young attorney down the aisle trashing his client's defense because he wants him to go for a plea. I can't let that continue, for the lawyer's sake: I go down there, explain to the attorney that this whole conversation is being heard, and he says, "Oh, my God, I didn't realize."

Just outside the booths is another type of meeting area: long counters like those at a luncheonette, attorneys on one side, shackled clients on the other. This place hasn't changed much in a long time. A few cubicles down from where I am now is the one where an assailant was waiting to attack Mon back in 1992. He burst out of the booth and leaped over three of the counters to stab him.

Finally I see Erik come through the door to the left with an officer. He's wearing his blue county jail uniform. He sits down and, with the familiarity of six years in this one jail, he reaches to his left with his right hand and cuffs his left wrist to the shackle on the table. We can talk now.

It's only my second time here since we learned he was going to prison for life. I am still, in my own way, grieving and incredulous. "We knew we were screwed," I say, right from the start of the second trial when we couldn't change the venue, couldn't get out of Van Nuys.

He says, "I don't want to talk about it." And my sadness concerns him. He tells me it hurts to see others grieve, "like watching your own funeral."

He's been spending a lot of time, he tells me, trying to figure out how to make his dismal life useful. He's looking forward to college: we've already arranged with an Indiana University professor to design correspondence courses for Erik and Lyle.

As we talk, Erik's eyes are wide and intense, his voice low and rich (he is much more manly at this stage than he has ever been portrayed). He says what he hopes to do is study psychology, "probably child psychology and work with teenagers." He's developing a scheme where maybe he'll be able to write to abused kids residing in detention centers and maybe in fifteen or twenty years the system will allow him to meet one or two of them, and he'll be doing some kind of therapy that he hasn't figured out yet.

This is not reasonable. I do not believe they will let him ever have that kind of interaction.

"Look," I say, "you know the therapy for abused kids these days isn't so effective; maybe what you ought to be thinking about is coming up with new treatment modalities, doing the research and then publishing. We can see to it that you get all the material you need."

He thinks about it. His elbows are on the table and his hands are clasped. He's resting his chin on his hands. "That's a very good idea," he says, "really good."

"We could get you all kinds of stuff, what's working in treatment programs, what isn't." He's listening closely.

When he talks about the prison days to come (as soon as he's formally sentenced in a few weeks), he says very slowly so that the individual words sink in, "Life . . . without . . . the . . . possibility . . . of . . . parole."

He looks for a metaphor, an image. "It's like you're a beam of light in a box and there are no cracks in the box."

He can't get over the fact that this sentence is meant to be permanent. "That's not punishment," he says, "that's torture." His idea of punishment is that it is what parents ordinarily do, something meant to change you, not merely to exact pain. I tell him he's naïve. No one believes in rehabilitation or treatment anymore. No one expects prison to change him in any positive way and no one cares if he suffers. Exasperated, he says, "That doesn't make sense. After all, it is called the Department of *Corrections.*"

Erik is trying not to rely on the coming appeal (even though Weisberg's incredible decisions throughout the trial have the appellate lawyers licking their chops in anticipation). He's seen too many people fool themselves into thinking they'll be getting out in a few years, "lying to themselves," he says. Instead, he's talking himself into believing that he will do so much good as a professional that people will want him freed and that maybe the times will change, the government will change. And when he has somehow proven his extraordinary worth some good governor will commute his sentence to life with the possibility of parole. At least then, he'll get the chance to make his case to a parole board the way most lifers can. (What he doesn't know is that no life-sentenced prisoners are in fact being granted parole in California under the current regime.)

We discuss, as we often do, suicide. For a while, he was in the habit of looking up at the ceiling light in his cell and imagining himself dangling. "When it's a reality in your mind," he says, "then you can do it." But ultimately he couldn't. He says that Lyle needs him and he can't leave Lyle. Even though it's very unlikely they will be living together in prison, they hope to be able to see each other there.

Erik has been attempting to will himself into feeling happier, even now. He read somewhere that if you smile and behave happy it makes you feel happy and he's been trying that, fully aware that to some people he seems to be smiling inappropriately. But even in our conversation now he is cycling between hope and despair. He is trying to find out if he can live as a permanent prisoner. "I've never felt so alone. Nothing anyone tells you can help you now. You're helpless. You've hit bottom."

As I leave that jail where he has already spent six years, I am wondering about our country, our people, the folks who think the right thing to do is to lock this young man up at a cost of $30,000 a year for maybe fifty or sixty years, without any hope that his case will be assessed again one day. I wonder about the moral fiber of a people who know damn well that he poses no peril at all to society. The terrible inequity of it hits me, how this sweet, dear young man is being punished the same as some of the most hardened criminals who ever lived in California. It is so painful for me to realize that I was able to open the doors for so many of my other clients and help them to be free again but for this one, the best one, I have failed.

This one has fallen prey to a nation wallowing in hate.

Awhile back, a friend sent me a copy of an editorial from a paper across the country, in south Florida, written just after the guilty verdict but before the jury had decided on whether the punishment would be life in prison or death. And the editorialist, fairly leaping up and down in anger over a "charade of lies and phony excuses and crocodile tears" in the defense, applauded the jury for a verdict that "fits the crime." And the editorial went on to say, "Pray that now the jurors have the right stuff to recommend . . . a sentence that does the same."

Over there in Florida, three thousand miles away in some air-conditioned office overlooking the Atlantic, they were praying that the state of California would kill Erik Menendez, a young man they never met and about whom they knew almost nothing true. They were praying for it! Bloodthirsty bastards.

23

...and Laughter

In my business, you can't always have the victory you want. But if you want to stay sane, you learn to take the wins you can get. The courts deprived Erik and Lyle Menendez of the lives they deserved, but there still were things we could do to make sure they would experience at least some happiness.

A few weeks before formal sentencing on July 2 and the grim trip to prison, Lyle tells me that he wants to marry Anna Eriksson, the striking young woman who has been visiting, calling, and writing him for more than two years. I had seen her in attendance throughout the second trial. Erik had told me she was Lyle's girlfriend, but she was so quiet and unobtrusive that I had never spoken with her. At first I dismissed the idea. My experience of these marriages is that few of them last very long and that in most of them the woman is exploited. But when I spoke with Lyle it became clear to me not only that he and Anna had considered what they were up against, but also that they loved each other.

After the verdicts, we all were searching for some ray of hope, and Lyle and Anna's marriage suddenly seemed to offer just that. It was a way of looking past the tragic present by giving both Lyle and Erik—the prospective best man—a chance to participate in at least one normal joyful human activity.

For anyone else, this would have been a snap. County jail inmates marry their sweethearts all the time. The bride simply obtains a license and the inmate's lawyer arranges transportation to an agreeable judge's court, where the ceremony is performed. But, of course, *this is the Menendez case.* Nothing is easy; malice is everywhere.

The one judge I have no intention of asking is Stanley Weisberg, whose presence would make the entire ceremony perverse. Moreover, who would want to be married by a judge who clearly bore you such ill will? These ceremonies are almost always performed by the trial judge, but with Weisberg off our list, I need to find a judge who is not only agreeable, but also gutsy enough not to care if Weisberg takes offense. I run through the alphabetical listing of Superior Court judges and bingo—there, in the *B*'s, is Judge Nancy Brown. I had known her since I began practicing law and found her to be not only an amiable, intelligent and fair-minded jurist but that rarest of judges, a courageously independent one concerned with justice in its broadest sense. She had, for example, recently refused to allow the district attorney in her court to seek a life sentence, under California's three-strikes law, against a man accused of stealing a swallow of vodka from a supermarket. "I am not," she told the prosecutor, "a judge in Nazi Germany."

Even so, I telephone her with some trepidation—it's hard to know who these days will be willing to board the Bad Karma Express. It's risky to show the Menendez brothers even the smallest kindness.

"Now, you can say no—I'll understand," I tell her, then ask if she'd consider performing a marriage for Lyle Menendez.

"I'd be happy to do it," she says. "I can't see any reason not to do something routine like this. I don't have any problem with it." Except one. She doesn't want a media circus, and, God knows, neither do I. The ceremony is planned for July 1, the day before sentencing. All the parties agree to keep the plan a secret until it's accomplished.

That agreement holds for about six weeks. Then, Erik and Lyle, breaking their six-year silence, grant their one and only televised interview. It's with Barbara Walters on ABC's "20/20" and it airs on June 21. As Erik and Lyle are nearing the end of the conversation, which Barbara conducts in her trademark style, understanding but probing and direct, she asks if there's anybody special in their lives. Lyle, the incurable romantic, can't resist telling the world about Anna. He says yes, there is, and he names her, and he says they're going to get married, though he doesn't say when.

Predictably, the media begins pursuing the "story" and Anna like a pack of baying hounds. The phone calls start: "Is it true that Lyle's getting married today?" Sillier yet, "I hear Erik is getting married tonight at the county jail." Luckily, these inquiries are easy to evade or deny: "Don't be ridiculous. If there's a wedding today, I haven't been invited," or "First I've heard of it." But my heart is sinking. What will Judge Brown say when she hears that the media is snooping around?

In any event, the media is not the worst problem we face by a long shot. Others are doing everything they can to prevent Lyle from getting married.

In early June, as she is getting ready to leave on a three-week vacation, Judge Brown instructs her bailiff to prepare the "removal order" that directs the sheriff's office to transport Erik and Lyle on July 1 from the jail, six blocks away, to her court. Days before the scheduled ceremony, while she is still out of town, her order is countermanded. Judge John Reid, an abrasive ex–district attorney who is filling in for a week as the supervising judge of the downtown criminal courts, issues his own order instructing the sheriff in charge of the jail to disregard Judge Brown's removal order. I learn about this from a late-night television news report.

The next morning I telephone Reid's office. Neither he nor his superior, whom I also call, responds. I am outraged at Reid's interference and at his discourtesy—he did not even bother to notify us of his secret action. I fax him a letter expressing my objection to his unprecedented intervention. He ignores it.

Meanwhile, I can't find out where Judge Brown is vacationing, and the wedding, as scheduled, is only a weekend away. So I write a letter to her, too, telling her that she's been overruled by Reid (who, in any other week, would not rank as high as Nancy Brown does in the hierarchy of judicial seniority). I include a copy of my letter to Reid and write that I'll understand if she decides to pull out of this thing now that it's getting ugly. Rather than mail the letter, I do the simpler thing, just drive it over to her house, which is not far from mine, and drop it through the mail slot in her door.

Judge Brown gets back on Saturday night. She opens my letter and goes nuclear. She's offended. No one has ever overruled her like this before. She's performed many inmate weddings in her twenty-eight years, without any interference. She calls Sheriff Block and learns that under the terms of Reid's order Erik and Lyle cannot be transported to any court besides the trial court except with Weisberg's permission. I'm not surprised. On Sunday, she calls Reid and then Weisberg. Neither returns her call. So she forges on. She tells me to notify the nonincarcerated

participants in the wedding to be in her court Monday morning as
planned because she's still hoping she can talk Reid out of this. She also
has me tell the press to be there.

She finally reaches Judge Reid early on Monday and he refuses to
budge. He claims he's trying to protect her from an investigation that
could follow if she spends taxpayer money for a frivolous transportation
expense. I can't help wondering where he was when the Menendez brothers were bused all over the county for years, often to the wrong court or
on the wrong date, without anyone being blamed, let alone investigated.
Nancy Brown knows something phony is going on. The cost for the trip
from the men's central jail to the courthouse, six blocks away, is negligi-
ble, probably zero, since vans and buses are ferrying people back and
forth all day long.

Despite Reid's intransigence, we're asked to remain in Judge Brown's
court. And we do, waiting to find out how the drama will unfold, like
players stranded outside the doors of a locked theater. There's Anna over
there, anxious and bewildered, in her white satin suit with rhinestone
buttons, her beautiful long blond hair falling to her waist, and there are
the lawyers who have represented Lyle in his trials, as well as his aunt
Terry and the brothers' priest, Father Ken Deasy. Also present are a
dozen reporters, and television and still cameras, invited not to record a
wedding but to capture for the public Nancy Brown's response to her
colleagues' machinations.

At the designated hour, there is no groom, but there is an unusual
press conference. From the bench, Judge Brown declares how angry she
is, denouncing the meddling by Reid and his pretense of saving her from
trouble with the Commission on Judicial Performance. (Reid makes no
public statement in response.) She is supremely calm, never raising her
voice and devoting most of her talk to an explanation of the routine
nature of inmate marriages and her own extensive experience in performing them. She also throws in some kind words about the defense
lawyers and, amazingly, says she feels honored to have been asked to
perform a wedding for Lyle Menendez, a participant in what she calls "an
American tragedy."

After freely answering questions from the press, she retires to her
chambers with the lawyers, where she calls Sheriff Block to see if the
wedding can be held at the jail (as Reid had disingenuously suggested).
Block tells her that's impossible—no weddings are performed at the
jail. (I know they happen virtually every day in the attorney room with
mail-order minister/notary publics performing the rites.) Undaunted, she
then tells the sheriff that if cost is the problem in transporting the broth-

ers to her courtroom, I've agreed to pay for it—I figure it can't run more than three hundred dollars, since that's the daily cost for transporting them from the jail to the trial court in Van Nuys, which is twenty miles away. The sheriff insists that the cost to travel those six blocks is in the thousands of dollars. What a crock.

"Sherman's in on it," I say.

Judge Brown says, "Looks that way."

All right, then, if cost is the problem, why not do it in Van Nuys the next day? Erik and Lyle will already be there for sentencing. She'll offer to drive over and perform the ceremony during lunch in any of the twenty-five empty courtrooms in that courthouse.

Judge Brown calls Weisberg, who expresses his irritation.

"Why didn't you call me first?" he snaps. His court is out of the question. And as to any other, "they're not going anywhere." Not even down the hall.

So it's just as I imagined: Weisberg's malice toward these defendants is so extreme that he is willing to wage this sort of petty campaign against anyone who attempts any small kindness toward the Menendez brothers. A friend suggests that perhaps he just wants to avoid public censure for allowing the wedding of a convicted killer to take place. People will find out about it. They'll want to know: What kind of punishment is this? You're supposed to torment these people, not help them out. I don't buy it. But for his and Reid's interference, Judge Brown, who cared not at all about a public outcry, would have taken the hit alone.

Next day, we're all assembled in Weisberg's court waiting for the sentencing hearing to begin and I'm still obsessing about how to get Lyle, Anna and Judge Brown in the same room. Then, whammo, the mist lifts from my brain and it dawns on me that they don't have to be in the same room at all—proxy marriages are performed all the time, so why not for them? Since the bride signed the license at the marriage license bureau, all we need is Lyle's notarized signature on the document. Then, all we have to do is get the additional signature of someone authorized to officiate over marriages and bingo, they'll be married. We don't really need a ceremony at all. I run this past Judge Brown, who agrees. But she doesn't want to deprive them of a ceremony. I have another thought: Could she perform the ceremony over the telephone in a conference call?

"I'll research it, but I can't see why not," she says.

"Can you do it tonight in my office? I don't want to give them any more time to think of other ways to stop us."

"Fine," she says. "What time and what's the address?"

At 7:30 that evening, Anna arrives at my office on Wilshire looking like she's just come from a workout. It's a ploy to throw the lurking media off the scent. No satin suit this time. She is dressed in gray workout pants, T-shirt and sneakers, with all that hair braided up under a base-ball cap.

With us are the judge—gravelly voiced from the respiratory infection she picked up on vacation—my assistant Jill Rosenberg (who's been doing the legwork for the wedding for weeks now), and Aunt Terry. The judge sits at the chair behind my desk. Anna stands in front of her, backed up against my computer, in order to be close to the phone. The rest of us arrange ourselves around the desk.

From their separate locations in the jail, first Lyle and then Erik call in.

"Lyle, are you ready?" whispers Judge Brown, voice fading fast.

"I'm ready," says Lyle, out of the speakerphone.

"Erik, you're there?"

"I'm here," says the best man.

"Okay. Here we go."

Judge Brown begins as if all are present: "We're gathered here to-day . . ." Despite the hoarseness, her voice seems to grow in power as she pronounces the familiar words with clarity and emphasis all the way to the part, directed to Lyle, in which she says, "With this ring I thee wed."

Always quick on her feet, Judge Brown improvises, "Now, since you are not here in person in Leslie's office right now, I'm going to say that at some future date you are going to place the wedding band on Anna's ring finger and you, Anna, will place the band on the ring finger of Lyle."

The judge has chosen a reading for the occasion, but first she gives Lyle and Anna a chance to speak to each other.

Lyle begins. "Okay. I'm very nervous, but I gave it a lot of thought." His nervousness is audible as he draws a deep breath, and the whoosh of it fills my office miles west of the jail. Addressing Anna, he says, "The thing I thought about most is the struggle and the incredible sacrifices you made with such dignity and without complaint, and I thought about the obstacles and your determination and I thought it all remarkable." He talks about how much fun they've had together, despite everything. He says, "I think the people who know us see us as so much happier since we came into each other's lives. . . . I adore you."

And she says, "Lyle, I want you to know that you are my guardian angel and I'll never leave your side and I love you." She's crying. I'm crying. Aunt Terry's crying.

Judge Brown reads the passage, which seems particularly apt: "Sing and dance together and be joyous, but let each one of you be alone, even as the strings of a lute are alone though they quiver with the same music."

She pronounces Lyle and Anna husband and wife; they make loud lip-smacking sounds to represent kisses and she tells them to "embrace each other in your mind's eye." She signs the license.

Aunt Terry leans in the direction of the speakerphone and says, "Lyle? Hi, sweetie, how are you?"

Lyle declares, "It's the best day of my life."

Aunt Terry, barely able to get the words out through her tears, says that she'll visit him in prison, but her words are inadvertently chilling: "I'll see you in the next place," she says.

And then, "Erik?"

"Hi, Aunt Terry."

Erik tells her how glad he is that she was there for the wedding, then, choking up, whispers simply, "Adios."

For my part, I tell everyone to keep this event secret for six months, by which time Erik and Lyle will have been assigned a permanent prison and Anna will have been granted visiting privileges with Lyle. I don't want any malicious reverberations against any of them.

I intend to visit the brothers in jail the next day, but for now I have to rush home for a meeting with Dr. Michael Baden, the renowned pathologist, who's working with me on a new murder case. But in the morning, before I leave for the jail, Jill Rosenberg calls.

She's learned from one of the men on Lyle's cell block that in the middle of the night Erik and Lyle were spirited off to North Kern State Prison, the classification center north of Bakersfield. In the history of the L.A. County Sheriff's office no inmate had ever been transported to prison that quickly after sentencing. I later learned that other prisoners who were on line, waiting to leave that night, were sent back to their cells to make room for Erik and Lyle. Whose order was that?

But we had beaten them to the punch. I started to laugh.

I called Judge Brown, who was home in bed, and gave her the news.

We laughed together.

Acknowledgments

If nothing else, writing this book has made me mindful of the debt of gratitude I owe my many clients and their families who have honored me with their trust and respect. I am particularly grateful to the men and women whose stories are recounted in these pages.

To anyone who knows something of contemporary American letters, praise for my editor, Alice Mayhew, may seem superfluous. I would be worse than remiss, however, if I did not thank both Alice and her associate at Simon & Schuster, Elizabeth Stein, for their wise, patient, and professional direction. Similarly, my agent, Kathy Robbins, not only paid me the matchless compliment of believing that my story was worth sharing, but also did me the great favor of introducing me to Rick Flaste, whose skill made its telling possible. Rick and I began as collaborators and will continue as lifelong friends.

Many colleagues, friends, and family members generously shared their memories and written records with us. Two of them—the inimitable Paul Fitzgerald and my old friend Gerry Chaleff—are due special thanks. So, too, is Rick's wife, Dale Flaste, who put her own work aside to lend her considerable organizational skills and personal warmth and encouragement to this arduous task.

As they have so often been, my dear friends Joan Didion and John Gregory Dunne were a source of sustaining friendship and good counsel throughout this process. My gratitude and admiration for them require no elaboration.

Index

About the Authors

Leslie Abramson has twice been named Trial Lawyer of the Year by the Los Angeles Criminal Courts Bar Association, most recently in 1995 for her work on the first trial of Erik and Lyle Menendez, and she was the first woman president of the California Attorneys for Criminal Justice. She was a regularly featured commentator during the O. J. Simpson trial for "Nightline." She lives in Los Angeles.

Richard Flaste was a reporter and editor for *The New York Times* for twenty-six years. He lives in Fort Lauderdale, Florida.